RUGBY WORLD CUP

A HISTORY IN 50 GREATEST GAMES

RUGBY WORLD CUP

A HISTORY IN 50 GREATEST GAMES

ROB CLARK

DEDICATIONS

To the memory of my dad, whose love of rugby has become my own.

To those who had the foresight and determination to set up a Rugby World Cup and to turn it into the incredible sporting event it is today.

First published by Pitch Publishing, 2015

Pitch Publishing
A2 Yeoman Gate
Yeoman Way
Durrington
BN13 3QZ
www.pitchpublishing.co.uk

© Rob Clark, 2015

A CIP catalogue record is available for this book from the British Library.

ISBN 978 178531-053-9

Typesetting and origination by Pitch Publishing

Printed by TJ International Ltd, Cornwall, UK

CONTENTS

ACKNOWLEDGEMENTS

When I started researching the history of the Rugby World Cup, I found there weren't nearly as many books on the subject as one would expect. However, those that there are proved to be an excellent and invaluable source and I am indebted to the following: *In Pursuit of Bill: A Comprehensive History of the Rugby World Cup* by Lance Peatey; *Story of the Rugby World Cup* by Nick Farr-Jones; *World Cup: Rugby's Battle of the Giants* by Gerald Davies; *Rugby Disunion: The Making of Three World Cups* by Derek Wyatt; *The Little Book of the Rugby World Cup* by Paul Morgan; *101 Moments of World Cup Rugby* by Wynne Gray; *The History of the Rugby World Cup* by Gerald Davies; *Union – World Cup Winners* by Peter Murray; *White Gold: England's Journey to World Cup Glory* by Peter Burns; and particularly *Thirty Bullies: A History of the Rugby World Cup* by Alison Kervin.

A special nod to the ESPN website, which is undoubtedly the best source of statistical information relating to the Rugby World Cup that there is, and the ideal place to double-check information on team line-ups and scorers and other facts and figures.

I am indebted to the BBC and to a whole host of our national newspapers and their journalists, including Mick Cleary, Robert Kitson and John Mason, whose reports I have sometimes quoted from, and to the National Newspaper Library in Colindale.

A personal thanks to Nick Axford, Kevin Peters, James Baker, Martin Peters and everyone else with whom I have been to rugby matches over the years.

Thanks to my wife, Sarah, who has managed to put up with not only my passion for the game, but also the fact that I have passed it on to my children, Matt and Ellie.

And finally I appreciate the support, and patience, of Paul and Jane Camillin at Pitch Publishing. Apologies to anyone I have inadvertently missed out from the above list.

Rob Clark

INTRODUCTION

When the Rugby World Cup was first mooted, in the mid-1980s, it was very much a Southern Hemisphere-driven initiative, not least to stave off the growing influence of rugby league which, in Australia at least, was threatening the very existence of the amateur code – as it then was. The Five Nations teams were lukewarm about the prospect, and tales which came out of the English, Scottish and Welsh camps in particular indicated that they weren't approaching the first competition, in 1987, with perhaps total dedication to the cause.

In the 28 years since the first Rugby World Cup, the tournament has grown spectacularly, beyond the wildest dreams of even its most ardent proponents. According to World Rugby, attendance figures have grown from 604,500 in 1987 to almost 1.5m in 2011, while income from gate receipts, broadcasting rights and sponsorship have also grown exponentially between 1995 (the first World Cup from which there are accurate figures) and 2011. The 2003 final between Australia and England remains the most-watched rugby match in the history of Australian television.

It is now, arguably, the third biggest global sporting event, behind only the summer Olympic Games and the FIFA World Cup and, like them, its four-yearly cycle is well established, giving just the right amount of time for the increasingly popular, and populated, qualifying competition to take place, and for the excitement and anticipation to build. If there is one lesson rugby could learn from football it would be not to seed the tournament too long in advance of it starting – the 2015 edition has thrown up the ludicrous situation of host nation England, two-time winners Australia and fifth-ranked Wales (who reached the semi-finals in 2011) all featuring in Pool A, with only two of the three able to qualify for the knockout stages. It seems unfortunate that the tournament will lose a potential winner before even reaching the quarter-final stage.

That apart, the growth of the Rugby World Cup can justifiably be called a phenomenon. From its beginnings in 1987 when the places were filled by the seven International Rugby Board (now in its new guise as World Rugby) members plus nine invited nations, it now boasts a qualifying tournament which in 2015 involved 80 teams as far flung as Guam and Finland, and St Lucia and Vanuatu. The 2015 qualifying competition began less than six months after the 2011 World Cup Final had taken place, and the first match, between Mexico and Jamaica, was refereed by Craig Joubert, one of the world's top referees and the man who had taken charge of that 2011 final between New Zealand and France.

The Rugby World Cup has had to cope with the advent of professionalism and the reintroduction into the sporting arena of South Africa. It has had to appreciate that a sport which grows ever more physical by the year requires sufficient rest and recovery time between matches, and a sensible amendment to the increasingly rigorous concussion protocols – which allows for temporary replacements along the same lines as blood injury replacements – will be in force at this year's competition. It has had to address the issue that the big rugby-playing nations, the so-called Tier 1 countries, tend to dominate when it comes to the latter stages of the sport's most coveted prize, and organisers have tried hard to level some aspects of the playing field, including persuading the Tier 1 nations to play midweek games to allow the smaller nations similar rest periods, which, again, will happen in 2015.

In among the ongoing issues, however, the Rugby World Cup has thrown up the most incredible matches, some of the greatest tries we could ever hope to see, and brought to the attention of the wider sporting public the names of the biggest stars in the game. This year's RWC will see games spread throughout England (and occasionally in Wales), and many steps have been taken to spread the gospel.

As for the on-field action, who can ever forget the performances of France? Upsetting the Australians in the first Rugby World Cup with the late drama of that Serge Blanco try? Doing the same to New Zealand in the course of scoring 31 unanswered points on the way to their 1999 semi-final victory, and so nearly repeating that feat four years ago when they could, and probably should, have beaten the All Blacks in their own Auckland backyard. Not to mention the 2007 quarter-final when the whole New Zealand nation was outraged that they could possibly be victims of a forward pass...

Who can fail to be thrilled by the sight of the Pacific nations playing their own particular brand of off-the-cuff rugby? Not just Samoa's two wins over Wales, but Fiji and Tonga's performances as well. We delight too at the occasional presence of Portugal and the Ivory Coast, alongside the likes of Georgia and Romania who continue to confound the odds – and lack of resources in those countries – and qualify on a regular basis.

And always, of course, there are the players. The scything runs of John Kirwan and Serge Blanco, the brilliance of Rupeni Caucaunibuca, the speed and strength of Jonah Lomu, the startling pace of Takudze Ngwenya, the drop kicks of Joel Stranksy, Jannie de Beer and Jonny Wilkinson. And that's without mentioning the likes of Zinzan Brooke, David Campese, George Gregan, Peter Fatialofa, Sean Fitzpatrick, Grant Fox, Bryan Habana, Gavin Hastings, Christopher Lamaison, Jason Leonard, Brian Lima, Victor Matfield, Gareth Rees, Jason Robinson, Joost van der Westhuizen, Shane Williams and Keith Wood. Not to mention the leadership of World Cup-winning captains David Kirk, Nick Farr-Jones, Francois Pienaar, John Eales, Martin Johnson, John Smit and Richie McCaw. I could continue, but instead why not read on and enjoy reliving some of those great moments for yourselves.

So far and so fast has the Rugby World Cup developed that it is easy to forget 2015 will be only the eighth time it has been held. And yet already it is a sporting occasion to rank with the biggest and the best. Long may it continue.

22nd May 1987
Venue: Eden Park, Auckland
Attendance: 20,000

New Zealand 70 Italy 6

New Zealand	Italy
John Gallagher	Serafino Ghizzoni
John Kirwan	Massimo Mascioletti
Joe Stanley	Oscar Collodo
Warwick Taylor	Fabio Gaetaniello
Craig Green	Marcello Cuttitta
Grant Fox	Rodolfo Ambrosio
David Kirk (capt)	Fulvio Lorigiola
Richard Loe	Guido Rossi
Sean Fitzpatrick	Giorgio Morelli
Steve McDowall	Tito Lupini
Murray Pierce	Franco Berni
Gary Whetton	Mauro Gardin
Alan Whetton	Piergianni Farina
Michael Jones	Marzio Innocenti (capt)
Wayne Shelford	Giuseppe Artuso

Half an hour had gone in the first Rugby World Cup (RWC) and hosts and favourites New Zealand were leading 9-0 when debutant flanker Michael Jones scored the first try. Benefiting from a strike against the head at a scrum by Sean Fitzpatrick (the young hooker was playing in place of captain Andy Dalton and played so well that a fit-again Dalton was unable to reclaim his place in the final), Jones scored from a neat pass back inside from Grant Fox when it appeared as if the fly half was going to go wide.

There could scarcely be a more fitting scorer of the first World Cup try as Jones is undoubtedly one of the best back-row forwards ever to have played the game, possibly *the* best.

Interestingly Jones had in fact played a game for Western Samoa (as they then were) in 1986, a match against a Wales touring side which Western Samoa lost 14-32. Jones was born in Auckland and went to both school and university in New Zealand, but qualified as his mother was Samoan. Although he was to coach Samoa from 2004–07, Jones switched allegiance in his playing days in order to compete at the first World Cup since Western Samoa were not invited to take part (of which more later). Jones's combination of pace, fitness, physicality and handling ability were to become legendary and he virtually redefined the role the openside flanker through his series of top-class performances at the 1987 RWC.

Jones would go on to play 55 matches for New Zealand, and missed many more for which he would have been chosen through a combination of injury (an inevitable by-product of the way he played) and his religious beliefs, which meant he wouldn't play on a Sunday. By comparison the great Fitzpatrick, whose career spanned a similar period, acquired 92 caps. Jones suffered two serious knee injuries, in 1989 and 1997, and numerous other knocks. Most notably Jones was to miss the 1991 RWC semi-final against Australia, which New Zealand lost, because it was on a Sunday, and with it their crown. That New Zealand were prepared to accommodate Jones's refusal to play on Sundays tells you all you need to know about how highly he was valued. Jones himself was slightly embarrassed that he would always be first choice, however well his cover played when he was unavailable. But at the same time he wasn't prepared to compromise his principles. 'I made up my mind on the subject when I was 16 or 17 and I'm so grateful to the coaches and players I was involved with who accepted it,' he once told the *New Zealand Herald*. 'But you don't put God in a box in deciding what you do and don't do on Sundays.'

But on this day in May 1987 in Auckland all that was still some way off. What was right here, right now was the explosive nature of a back-row forward who combined the traditional strength of that position in terms of being first to the loose ball and supporting his pack, with the speed and handling skills of a back. The sheer stats of 16 tries in 55 appearances does not begin the tell the tale of a man who was so ubiquitous that spectators occasionally wondered if there were two of him on the park simultaneously. Indeed there might as well have been for when injuries robbed Jones of his prodigious pace he simply switched from openside to blindside and concentrated on tackling and defensive duties, at which he proved equally adept.

Jones's opening try at the 1987 Rugby World Cup has been immortalised in a sculpture which is on display at Eden Park, where it all began. Created by a local artist Natalie Stamilla, it is based on a photograph taken by Stamilla's father, Geoff Dale, a press photographer at the time. It is a fitting, and lasting, tribute to both the moment and the man, a player former New Zealand coach John Hart called 'almost the perfect rugby player'.

Michael Jones rightly takes the plaudits for being the first man to score a World Cup try, but it wasn't, of course, the first try of that first match. After 14 minutes Australian referee Bob Fordham was left with little option but to award a penalty try after Italian captain Marzio Innocenti had dived into a scrum to prevent the All Blacks going for the pushover try which appeared to be there for the taking. Maybe it was a simple rush of blood to the head from Innocenti – as a doctor he could no doubt tell us – but there certainly wasn't much doubt about his guilt. Italian protests were notable for their absence.

Thereafter Italy fought hard throughout the first half to keep the score respectable. They somehow held out a succession of scrums on their line until finally Kirk spotted a small gap on the blindside and scooted over for New Zealand's third try, to put them 17-0 ahead. An Oscar Collodo drop goal, calm as you like from fully 40 metres, shortly before half-time and penalty straight after the resumption from a similar distance saw Italy trail only 17-6. But New Zealand began to apply relentless pressure and slowly that told on the Italians, who in those days were not part of the Northern Hemisphere's Five Nations Championship and had had little exposure to the level of play which was routine for the All Blacks.

First, centre Warwick Taylor (who won 24 caps for the All Blacks) went over and then Craig Green added a quickfire double (he was to score four more in the later pool game against Fiji), and by the halfway point in the second half the score was up to 36-6. Immediately after Collodo's penalty, Serafino Ghizzoni dropped Fox's kick-off behind his own line, leading to a five-metre scrum. New Zealand moved the ball quickly from left to right; Taylor shipped the ball on to Kirwan and to John Gallagher and then looped round to retake the ball and go over in the corner. Green, who had looked a threat throughout with his pace, then got in on the act. An explosive break from Kirk took the play from one 22 to the other and after a couple of phases of play they ran a tap penalty which resulted in a scrum virtually on the Italians' line and all it took was quick ball, a swift pass from right to left by Kirk and Green ran in unopposed.

Green's second try was a result of quick accurate passing down the line, and Fox's conversion took the score up to 33. Still the tries kept flowing, with prop Steve McDowall the next to go over, then in the 68th minute captain and scrum half David Kirk combined with fly half Grant Fox to put the powerful winger John Kirwan over in the corner. Fox nailed the conversion, his fifth successful kick out of eight, a relatively low return from one of the most metronomic kickers in the game.

Then from the Italian kick-off came the moment which seared the Rugby World Cup into the public consciousness. Kirk caught the ball deep in his own 22, passed to Fox who, deciding against the kick to safety given that his side were by now leading 48-6 and the game was well won, shipped it quickly on to Kirwan. Kirwan took off down the centre of the pitch and just continued his run. There was the odd feint, the hint of a swerve, but once Kirwan had got away from initial Italian attempts to tackle him, he mostly ran straight and found himself in space so kept running.

'I remember thinking I'd just go for it,' Kirwan later recalled, 'and thankfully all my mates just stepped aside and left me to it. I kept on going and before I knew it I'd made it all the way through.' It's a fairly modest description of one of the great solo tries, and one which captured the imagination worldwide.

Kirwan added that the All Blacks were 'failing to click as a team' in that first match, but captain David Kirk disagrees, 'Many say it was not until John's wonder try that we came to life, but I don't remember it like that. I thought we played pretty well from the beginning and we were always in command.'

It's often forgotten that Kirwan was within a hair's breadth of one of the most memorable hat-tricks of all time. The Italian restart from his second try went straight into touch, Kirk took a quick throw-in and the big winger was off and running again. He possibly could have made it to the line himself but with just one cover tackler he took the more sensible option and turned the ball back inside for Kirk to claim his second try of the afternoon. And it was thoroughly deserved after Kirk had done incredibly well to get up in support of the flying Kirwan.

A disheartened Italy were to concede two further tries in the dying minutes, the first to Stanley who finished off a scintillating running move from Gallagher and Green, and the last of the day to Alan Whetton, who was on the shoulder of Green to take a short pass from Green and plunge over.

In spite of the score, the All Blacks did make quite a few handling errors, but these were put down to a combination of the wet weather and the new ball, a

Mitre brand with which the players were not familiar. And there was also plenty of evidence that their traditional running and handling skills, support play and all-round knowledge of the game was going to make them the team to beat.

Off the pitch it had been a low-key start for the World Cup in many ways. Auckland, known as the City of Sails, is a rugby hotbed and Eden Park a fabulous stadium, but the kick-off time for this first match – 3pm on a Friday – was a strange choice. Rugby had never been played on a Friday in New Zealand before, and as it was a normal working day it wasn't that surprising that the ground was only half-full.

Looking at the pictures, both still and video, it's remarkable how accessible the players and pitch were – cameramen and indeed fans were gathered only just beyond the white lines and there is very little sense of it being a major sporting occasion. And the less said about the rather bizarre BBC Rugby World Cup theme tune, the better, though for the true fans among you, it can still be found on YouTube. In any case, fans in Europe weren't able to see any of the games live on TV, not even the final, because the satellite links of the day simply weren't up to the task.

For all the slightly amateurish aspects of the start of the tournament – TV coverage missed Fox's conversion of the penalty try because it was showing repeated replays of the Innocenti offence which had led to referee Fordham's decision – it's easy to forget that rugby union was indeed an amateur sport in those days. Many of those involved, players and officials, on and off the pitch, were not getting paid. Nevertheless, the action was sufficiently compelling to get the tournament off to a solid start, and a new era in world rugby had begun.

23 May 1987
Venue: Lancaster Park, Christchurch
Attendance: 17,000

France 20 Scotland 20

France	Scotland
Serge Blanco	Gavin Hastings
Patrice Lagisquet	Matt Duncan
Philippe Sella	Keith Robertson
Denis Charvet	Douglas Wyllie
Patrick Esteve	Iwan Tukalo
Franck Mesnel	John Rutherford
Pierre Berbizier	Roy Laidlaw
Pascal Ondarts	David Sole
Daniel Dubroca (capt)	Colin Deans (capt)
Jean-Pierre Garuet-Lempirou	Iain Milne
Alain Lorieux	Derek White
Jean Condom	Alan Tomes
Eric Champ	John Jeffrey
Dominique Erbani	Finlay Calder
Laurent Rodriguez	Iain Paxton

What must France and Scotland have been thinking when they lined up for their Pool 4 match on the second day of the 1987 Rugby World Cup? Each had travelled to the other side of the world only to face one of their most traditional rivals from opposite sides of the English Channel, players with whom they were already very familiar. In fact the two sides had produced a cracker of a game in that year's Five Nations Championship, with France just edging it 28-22 thanks in large part to a hat-trick from the mesmeric winger Eric Bonneval.

That match had taken place in front of over 49,000 fanatical Frenchmen at the Parc des Princes in Paris, so it must have seemed a little surreal to be facing the same opponents in front of a little over a third of that many fans – only 17,000 were in the ground for the 1pm kick-off on the first Saturday of the World Cup.

To further add to the sense of familiarity, 25 of the 30 players who had started the Five Nations match also started this World Cup game. Somewhat surprisingly France had changed both their wingers, Bonneval and Philippe Berot, who between them had scored all four of their country's tries in the Five Nations clash, and also second rower Francis Haget. In their place came Patrice Lagisquet, Patrick Esteve and Alain Lorieux respectively. Scotland meanwhile switched only two, and in a little quirk of fate, they were also the two try-scorers from the Five Nations meeting: Keith Robertson was called into the centres in place of Scott Hastings and Derek White took over from John Beattie (though White played in the second row and the versatile Iain Paxton switched to number eight).

France, who had won the grand slam earlier that year, went into the match as favourites and duly outscored the Scots on the try count – three to two – as they had earlier in the year but the reliable kicking of Gavin Hastings kept the game tight throughout.

The first score of the match came from an electrifying break by the effervescent Finlay Calder less than two minutes into the match. Juggling a ball he had won at the tail of a line-out, Calder just retained control and then seared through the French defence before putting the supporting White over. Unfortunately Hastings missed a relatively straightforward conversion; perhaps given that the match was only just over a minute old, he just hadn't warmed up. Even worse for Scotland, the exceptional fly half John Rutherford suffered a serious knee injury shortly afterwards and was out of not just this match but the entire tournament.

The French hit back, also off a line-out, in traditional French mode with quick hands through the backs and a loop round from the great Philippe Sella gave them an overlap which Sella finished comfortably in the right-hand corner. France made it look easy again a few minutes later when scrum half Pierre Berbizier sold a dummy and waltzed through. And France looked to have scored again when the two wingers combined; first Esteve blazed infield, then Lagisquet went wide and looked to have scored in the same corner as Sella earlier only to have the 'try' ruled out by New Zealand touch judge Tom Doocey. Doocey indicated that Lagisquet had hit the corner flag before he had got the ball down, and it was therefore touch in goal. Under the rules then in force, that meant a 22 drop-out, which enabled Scotland to clear their lines. The replay showed it to be a reasonable, if hairline, decision.

More drama followed as Serge Blanco took a quick tap penalty while both Berbizier and Matt Duncan were receiving treatment for injuries. Blanco ran 60 metres for a cheeky score which the cameras failed to properly pick up, but although there were some boos from the crowd, the Scots seemed to accept that it was a perfectly fair play and there was little sign of complaint from them, either at the time or after the game.

At that point Scotland, who had long led but in the second half had been fighting an increasingly desperate and energy-sapping defensive action, looked a spent force. The smart money would have been on France scoring more rather than Scotland fighting back. The smart money would have been wrong. This was a good Scotland side, combining the experience of the likes of John Rutherford and Roy Laidlaw in the backs, and Colin Deans and Iain Paxton in the forwards with a number of players who would become all-time greats of Scottish rugby during the course of their careers – Gavin Hastings, John Jeffrey, Finlay Calder and David Sole among them.

Scotland had given as good as they got in the scrums and line-outs throughout and had competed ferociously at the breakdowns. They somehow found one last effort and put together a series in French territory which ended with a try for Matt Duncan in the right-hand corner. Quick hands from Laidlaw and White gave the powerfully built Duncan just enough room to get over, holding off Sella.

Duncan's score came almost five minutes into injury time and Hastings's failed attempt at a conversion was the last kick of the match and left it tied at 20-20.

'Scotland played very well,' said the great Sella. 'It was good for our team too because it woke them up for the bigger matches later in the tournament.'

With Romania and Zimbabwe making up the rest of Pool 4 it always looked likely that both countries would progress to the quarter-finals, and so it proved. Scotland scored 11 tries in their 60-21 win over Zimbabwe then rounded off their group matches with another nine – including a hat-trick for John Jeffrey – in their 55-28 win over Romania. Even those 20 tries did not prove sufficient to snatch top place in the group from France, however. In expansive mood the French matched those 55 points against Romania but went two better against Zimbabwe in a 13-try, 70-12 win.

It's worth remembering that Romania were a handy side in the 1980s. They had recorded wins over France (twice), Wales and Scotland in their own country, and drawn 13-13 with Ireland at Lansdowne Road. The year after the 1987 World Cup they travelled to Wales and won 15-9 in Cardiff. Sadly, the revolution in 1989 – which saw the overthrow and later execution of their country's long-standing Communist leader Nicolae Ceausescu – also led to a decline in the nation's rugby fortunes. Leading clubs Dinamo Bucharest and Steaua Bucharest were police and army sides respectively and they lost both funding and personnel as a result of the coup.

Florica Murariu, the tough-as-teak back-row forward who had scored a try against Wales in Bucharest in 1983 and led his country in the Cardiff victory, was an army officer who was shot dead at a roadblock.

But in 1987 the political upheavals were still in the future and Romania were a force to be reckoned with. For Scotland to put 55 points on them was impressive, even if they did concede 28 in reply (two of the three Romania tries that day were scored by Murariu).

What that meant for Scotland was a return to Christchurch for a quarter-final against an increasingly menacing All Black side, a fate which Scotland captain Colin Deans later said he had felt was always on the cards. 'We went with the intention of winning it,' he said. 'That was the plan. We had world-class players in key positions and we played what was in front of us. We knew we had to top the group, but lost out on try difference.' Deans was at least happy with the venue for that quarter-final, describing the Lancaster Park pitch as 'like a bowling green' such good condition was it in.

In the first quarter-final Scotland put in what is often described as a 'brave' performance; meaning, essentially, that they were run off their feet but never gave up. Scotland had little answer to the power of the All Blacks and though they tackled their hearts out, they could never break the shackles; New Zealand scored tries by Alan Whetton and John Gallagher, both converted by Grant Fox who added two penalties to one from Hastings. New Zealand just kept possession and stifled the life out of the battling Scots. 'They play at a higher level,' admitted Deans, ruefully. His New Zealand counterpart David Kirk was more damning. 'We beat Scotland comprehensively. They offered nothing,' was his pithy comment.

The contrast between the way the two sides viewed the contest: New Zealand approached the quarter-final in the same vein as their coach had expressed before the match. 'When the death or glory time arrives, you don't mess around,' declared Brian Lochore. And they didn't. Scotland were more intent on partying. 'Being Scotsmen, we liked to have a good time,' said Deans. 'We were disappointed to lose to New Zealand but we had the best parties ever out there.'

And after the World Cup parties, there were more on the way home as the Scottish squad stopped off at Disney World where, according to Deans, they 'took the place over, singing and dancing all day.'

Ian McGeechan, the legendary Scotland and British & Irish Lions coach who at the time shared the coaching duties with Derrick Grant, had said before the tournament, 'We were all quite excited by it, but it was not over-serious. No one was quite sure what to make of it all and in Scotland before we left there was a reluctance about it.'

This was a good Scotland team, with the potential to be a great one, but like all the Northern Hemisphere sides their approach to the World Cup was much less 'professional' than that of the Southern Hemisphere sides at that time.

24 May 1987
Venue: Rugby Park, Hamilton
Attendance: 12,000

Argentina 9 Fiji 28

Argentina	Fiji
Sebastian Salvat	Severo Koroduadua Waqanibau
Marcelo Campo	Serupepeli Tuvula
Diego Cuesta Silva	Epineri Naituku
Fabian Turnes	Tomasi Cama
Juan Lanza	Kavekini Nalaga
Hugo Porta (capt)	Willie Rokowailoa
Fabio Gomez	Pauliasi Tabulutu
Fernando Morel	Sairusi Naituku
Diego Cash	Salacieli Naivilawasa
Luis Molina	Rusiate Namoro
Eliseo Branca	Koli Rokoroi (capt)
Gustavo Milano	Ilaitia Savai
Jorge Allen	Peceli Gale
Jose Mostany	Manasa Qoro
Gabriel Travaglini	John Sanday

I f the European teams had had a long journey to the World Cup in New Zealand and Australia, it was nothing compared to that undertaken by Fiji. The Fijians were one of the nine invited countries and were delighted to be involved, but on 14 May – barely a week before the big kick-off – a group of armed men, led by army colonel Sitiveni Rabuka, broke into the Fijian House of Representatives, based in Suva, and ordered the country's MPs out of the building.

The source of friction was the election of Timoci Bavadra as Prime Minister – Bavadra had come to power through the support of the Indo-Fijian community and Rabuka claimed he was acting to prevent discrimination against the indigenous Fijians. Whatever the merits or otherwise of his arguments, Rabuka's coup was met with little resistance inside the country and no intervention from outside it. Australia, New Zealand, the UK and the USA did, however, suspend foreign aid and refused to recognise the new government. Australia additionally instituted a trade embargo.

Fiji was, briefly, isolated and the Rugby World Cup organisers grew increasingly concerned that Fiji would be in no fit state to take part in the tournament. In fact, coach George Simpkin had already received assurances from Rabuka that a plane would be available to take the team to New Zealand. 'We will be there,' Simpkin unequivocally told the *Fiji Times*, and they were.

Anybody who loves rugby, whatever their personal affiliations, will always have a soft spot for Fiji. Wonderful to watch, they still play rugby with the abandon that you can witness on the Fijian beaches but which tends to find greater expression in the wide open spaces of Sevens more readily than in the tighter structures of the 15-man game. That notwithstanding, the sheer enjoyment Fijians evidently get from their rugby – the running, handling and off-the-cuff play is so spontaneous it's impossible not to get drawn in by it – made them hugely welcome participants in the first World Cup.

'We had Western Samoa ready to fill in if Fiji players couldn't get out of their country,' recalled Sir Nicholas Shehadie, a former captain of Australia in his playing days, later president of the Australian Rugby Union and one of the guiding lights behind the inaugural World Cup. 'It was good that it didn't come to that though because Fiji turned out to be a very popular team at the tournament.'

Not only popular, but worthy invitees as they became the only country from outside the seven International Rugby Board members to progress to the quarter-final stages. And the platform for that progress was their opening match against Argentina.

Although everyone was delighted to see Fiji turn up, their lack of preparation and their understandable concerns about what was taking place back at home, where the coup lingered on, made it seem unlikely they would be able to do themselves justice. In her excellent book on the Rugby World Cup entitled *Thirty Bullies*, Alison Kervin recalls Simpkin explaining the difficulty of any sort of training for the Fijians, 'Getting the players together was difficult enough, given that they were all out working on different islands, but the next task after that was trying to persuade them to work on any kind of forward play. They hated it. All their strength lay in their lower body, so while they could run well and had strong muscle definition in their legs, they had nowhere near enough upper body strength for the international game.'

As they took the field for their first match, the eyes of the rugby world were on them…

Ominously, Fiji gave away penalties from each of the first two line-outs, and lost the first scrum against the head, but the great Hugo Porta missed an attempted drop goal, and his first kick at goal by some considerable margin, while his second attempt was the worst penalty kick at this or any other World Cup. Another who was no fan of the new Mitre ball. Fiji's first penalty was an ambitious 59-metre kick by Severo Koroduadua Waqanibau which was a full ten metres short and several metres wide of the posts. Scrappy play without much in the way of a pattern developing was the order of the day in the first quarter with the Argentinians kicking less than expected and the Fijians more. Few passes stuck, though, and much of the kicking from hand was aimless at best, terrible at worst.

In keeping with the general tone of the match, the first try came from a succession of errors. The worst of these was committed by, of all people, Porta. Trying to clear the ball from inside his own 22 following yet another messy line-out, Porta succeeded only in kicking the ball straight at hooker Salacieli Naivilawasa, and flanker Peceli Gale was on hand to take the ball and canter in from a few metres out. Koroduadua added the conversion and Fiji led 6-0 having had virtually none of the ball.

Five minutes later Fiji benefited from a reversed penalty decision when what was to have been an Argentinian penalty was instead given to Fiji for a stupid and unnecessary push long after the whistle had gone. Koroduadua knocked it over to increase Fiji's lead. Suddenly Argentina started to look a bit worried as

Fiji grew in confidence and the Pacific Islanders began to be awarded the bulk of the penalties by Scottish referee Jim Fleming. The Argentinians continued to try to keep the ball tight and use their forward power, but the Fijians coped well around the fringes and the Pumas' passing and kicking was not accurate enough to break through.

Shortly before half-time, the Fijian back row combined beautifully as John Sanday started a move which was taken on by Manasa Qoro and finished off by Salacieli Naivilawasa. Although Koroduadua missed the conversion, Fiji were 13-0 ahead at half-time.

Just three minutes into the second half Fiji increased their lead still further when quick ball after a high kick had caused confusion set and winger Kavekini Nalaga away down the right. Nalaga had 30 metres to the try line and it looked like he had taken it too close to the touchline and could be forced out by the covering defence but he switched on the after-burners and got round the outside of full back Sebastian Salvat. Willie Rokowailoa took over the place-kicking duties, in only his second appearance for Fiji, and promptly slotted a left-footed kick to put his team 19-0 ahead.

Argentina finally got on the board with a simple penalty and steadied the ship, but their lightweight backs were largely manhandled out of the game by the huge Fijians. A Koroduadua penalty just as the game entered the final quarter restored Fiji's 19-point lead and Argentina's efforts to run the ball from deep rarely came to anything. The Fijians, by contrast, were running and handling as a team and their support play was superb, a fine piece of open play resulting in a line-out close to the Argentinian line.

From there it was a simple jump and catch from second-row forward Ilaitia Savai and a plunge over the line for Fiji's fourth try of the game. Savai was a popular scorer having played much of his club rugby the previous season at Eden Park for Waikato. Koroduadua added the conversion to take his record to four successful kicks from seven attempts and the lead was increased to 28-3. The game was done and dusted, with Argentina's solitary try – a pushover from their powerful scrum – far too little, too late to make any difference other than to the scoreline, which finished 28-9.

Fiji took a gamble in their next match, fielding a severely under-strength side against New Zealand (and duly being thrashed 74-13) in order to save their first-choice players for the final group game against Italy. It almost backfired when the Fijians lost 18-15, but the four tries they scored in the game against Argentina ensured their progress to the quarter-finals, and the knockout stages.

Their opponents were France, and it was this match which deservedly brought the Fijian style to a wider audience. Abandoning any semblance of a 'classic' rugby structure, Fiji exalted in playing a form of Sevens rugby with 15 men on the pitch.

After an early penalty from Guy Laporte had put them ahead, France were given a taster of what Fiji had in store for them on 14 minutes. A decent up-and-under from Serge Blanco went loose and scrum half Paula Nawalu was on it in a flash, breaking upfield and passing out to Tom Mitchell. Mitchell had a searing turn of pace and left most of the French for dead. 'Mitchell's going all the way,' said commentator Bill McLaren. Not quite, Pierre Berbizier got across for a great cover tackle. But flanker Manasa Qoro was on hand to take the scoring pass.

Koroduadua would have had another try but for a moment of carelessness. A big hit on Franck Mesnel around the halfway line led to the massive fly half breaking away and down the touchline, but carrying the ball in one hand as he liked to do Koroduadua looked up and momentarily lost control, letting the ball squirt out of his hand. 'People in Fiji still mention that today,' says Koroduadua. 'No one has forgotten.'

Duly warned about what Fiji could do, France, wisely from their perspective, shut up shop and decided they would rely on the superiority of their set-pieces. Two close-quarter tries from scrummages and a further one from a line-out gave France control of the match and they rammed home their advantage with a fourth from Patrice Lagisquet. Fiji closed the game with the best try of the six scored in the match, however, and the abiding memory was of Fijian brilliance rather than French efficiency. Refusing to learn from Koroduadua's earlier mistake, Jone Kubu strode forward from full back clutching the ball in one hand and setting up a try for Jimi Damu.

Australia and New Zealand had been aware of what Fijian rugby had to offer long before the inaugural World Cup, but now the rest of the rugby world knew it too. And they liked what they saw. From this moment on, there has always been a buzz whenever Fiji play; it's impossible not to be wowed by their irrepressible, off-the-cuff style of play and their sheer love of the game.

8 June 1987
Venue: Ballymore, Brisbane
Attendance: 15,000

Wales 16 England 3

England	Wales
Jon Webb	Paul Thorburn
Mike Harrison (capt)	Ieuan Evans
Kevin Simms	John Devereux
Jamie Salmon	Bleddyn Bowen
Rory Underwood	Adrian Hadley
Peter Williams	Jonathan Davies
Richard Harding	Robert Jones
Paul Rendall	Anthony Buchanan
Brian Moore	Allan Phillips
Gary Pearce	Dai Young
Wade Dooley	Richard Moriarty (capt)
Nigel Redman	Bob Norster
Peter Winterbottom	Gareth Roberts
Gary Rees	Richie Collins
Dean Richards	Paul Moriarty

Having being drawn in the same group as co-hosts (and favourites) Australia, England found themselves playing out their entire tournament in that country rather than in New Zealand. Their three group matches were all at the Concord Oval in Sydney, but for this quarter-final they switched to Brisbane; that was because defeat in their opening match by Australia left them in the runners-up spot and having to move cities.

England's opening match had surprised everyone, including probably themselves, as they played a more exciting brand of rugby than had been anticipated.

They gave Australia a real scare and ten minutes into the second half they were level at 6-6 after a try by Mike Harrison, converted by Jon Webb. The lightning fast Rory Underwood had brought the ball out of defence before linking with his centres, Kevin Simms and Jamie Salmon. Salmon sent a long pass out to Webb who put Harrison in at the corner.

Then the New Zealand referee Keith Lawrence committed a howler. He allowed a David Campese 'try' to stand when it looked for all the world like the Aussie winger had knocked on; Campese's own expression was a surefire confirmation of what had happened. It seemed to knock the stuffing out of England and they conceded another try soon after to Simon Poidevin. With the penalty count against them also very high, England just didn't have the wherewithal to recover.

They did play solidly enough in their other two group games, a 60-7 win over a game but outgunned Japan and a 34-6 win over the USA, with captain Harrison getting on the scoresheet both times, giving him the enviable record of scoring in all three group games.

And so it was to the quarter-final match against Wales, and knockout rugby.

The 1987 Five Nations campaign had not been a good one for either side, with each recording only a solitary victory and England finishing the competition propping up the table. But the Wales versus England match was famous more for the physical nature of the game than any great rugby being played. There was argy-bargy from the start and an early line-out resulted in punches being thrown – these days yellow if not red cards would have been brandished within ten minutes – and the match simmered throughout.

Although Scottish referee Ray Megson took little action at the time, Richard Hill, Graham Dawe, Wade Dooley and Gareth Chilcott were all given international bans after the match. Hill was stripped of the captaincy and didn't feature in another Five Nations match for three years.

As a result, both sides were much changed when they took the field for their World Cup quarter-final, although the great Dai Young was the only debutant on either side. Young played 51 times for his country either side of a six-year stint in rugby league with Leeds and Salford (he won 14 more Wales caps as a league player). He also went on three Lions tours, winning three caps, and since finishing playing has been a highly acclaimed coach of Cardiff Blues, London Wasps and the Barbarians.

In the event the game, played in wet conditions, was a damp squib. The notion that England were starting to put their moves together proved unfounded, and Wales offered little more, but were quick to seize on English mistakes and score three tries, through back-row forward Gareth Roberts, scrum half Robert Jones and centre John Devereux. The reliable boot of Paul Thorburn converted two of them. All England had in response was a penalty from Jon Webb. Despite profiting from a penalty count massively in their favour, England seemed unable to put any coherent moves into action, much less an overall gameplan.

Gerald Davies, himself a Welsh legend, had little hesitation in describing it as a game 'of depressingly low standards' and said only those Welshmen who could see no further than victory over 'the old enemy' could have taken much pleasure from it. It was largely a spoiling performance, won, for the most part, without the ball.

England captain Mike Harrison seemed at a loss to know what had gone wrong. 'I have no idea why England performed so badly,' he said frankly, if a little worryingly given that he was responsible for the on-field leadership and direction of the team. 'We were very buoyant and confident beforehand yet we didn't produce it on the field. All the Welsh points were given them: they didn't create, they seized on our mistakes and that was the most disappointing feature.'

Dean Richards and Brian Moore had little doubt where the blame lay: an r&r break on Hamilton Island between the pool games and the quarter-final. 'It was just a great big jolly,' recalled Moore. 'Everyone just pissed around.'

'We were preparing for an important match against Wales by going paragliding, water-skiing, sunbathing and relaxing on the Great Barrier Reef,' said Richards. Even Harrison admitted that, looking back, 'Some of it was a bit daft.'

England were not to be spared after their shockingly bad performance against Wales. The *Daily Telegraph*'s doyen of rugby reporters, John Mason, gave a damning appraisal of English efforts, describing them as 'dreadful. Shorn of ideas [and] tactical appreciation.' The sole saving grace was that the violence of the Five Nations encounter a few months earlier was not reproduced.

If Wales won the battle, England arguably won the war. It wasn't until 2011 that Wales surpassed their quarter-final place in 1987; by the time they managed that, England had reached three World Cup finals and won one of them.

But for now it was Wales who marched on to the daunting task of attempting to halt the All Black juggernaut, a task that proved way, way beyond them. Wales took a heavy beating in their semi-final, losing 49-6 – they were outthought, overpowered and run ragged at every turn. However, they bounced back to produce their best performance of the tournament in the third place play-off where they beat Australia 22-21.

The third place play-off is the match no team wants to play. It's superfluous to the main event and keeps the players who lost in the semi-finals a few days earlier around to no real purpose. It is to the immense credit of Wales and Australia, therefore, that they produced a scintillating match which almost succeeded in turning the game in Rotorua into something relevant.

Before the game Australia were red-hot favourites, but within four minutes of kick-off that had all changed. Australian flanker David Codey had already received a warning from English referee Fred Howard when he piled into a ruck with complete disregard for where – or on who – he was landing. Howard had no hesitation in sending Codey from the field. He was the first Australian ever to be sent off in a Test match and although he did appear the following month in the one-off game against New Zealand (which Australia lost 30-16 in Sydney), and captained the side, that was the last of Codey's 13 caps for his country.

To add insult to injury, Paul Thorburn kicked the resulting penalty to put Wales in front. Not long after, a superb break by Jonathan Davies, in a move taken on by John Devereux and finished off at blistering pace by Ieuan Evans, was recalled for a forward pass which was a marginal call at best. Michael Lynagh levelled the scores after 12 minutes, but Wales got the first try with a rolling maul. Again the Aussies came back, Matt Burke taking a great line through the Wales defence from a pass by his captain Andrew Slack.

Wales were trying to maintain a running game, at pace, but the plan misfired later in the half when they lost the ball deep in their own 22 and presented winger Peter Grigg with a simple run in to put Australia 15-7 up. Then a great steal by debutant Richard Webster in midfield gave Wales the opportunity to score through Paul Moriarty. Thorburn's conversion meant that Wales went into the break only two points adrift at 15-13. A penalty apiece came in the second half before a calm drop goal from the always-cool Lynagh extended the Australian lead to 21-16.

It looked like that was the way it would stay, but an always entertaining match had a sting in its tail. A Wales scrum on the Australian 22 saw Davies put up a bomb, re-gather and quick ball through the hands enabled Thorburn to put Adrian Hadley over in the corner. That still left Wales trailing by a point, though, and Thorburn's kick from wide on the left was as difficult as could be. He nailed it.

'The conversion was right on the touchline,' recalled Thorburn, 'but there were no particular nerves. When you are a kicker you just try to focus on the job in hand and go through the basics. I had missed a couple during the game but I was striking the ball well, as I had been all through the tournament. As soon as I struck it I knew it was over.'

Australia mounted one last attack and briefly it looked like they might have men over, but they lost control of the ball and it was Thorburn, fittingly, who booted it into touch to end the game.

Was it a good thing for Wales to win that match, against the odds? That might seem a strange question to ask, but it's a pertinent one because it arguably gave Wales a mistaken view of exactly where they were in world rugby terms. Victory over what was, essentially, a 14-man team sent them home happy but their view of the World Cup was perhaps summed up by their team manager Keith Rowlands saying, 'Ah well, the sooner we can get home and continue beating England, the better.' But the rugby world had moved on; winning internecine battles was no longer where it was at.

13 June 1987
Venue: Concord Oval, Sydney
Attendance: 18,000

Australia 24 France 30

Australia	**France**
David Campese	Serge Blanco
Peter Grigg	Didier Camberabero
Andrew Slack (capt)	Philippe Sella
Brett Papworth	Denis Charvet
Matt Burke	Patrice Lagisquet
Michael Lynagh	Franck Mesnel
Nick Farr-Jones	Pierre Berbizier
Cameron Lillicrap	Jean-Pierre Garuet-Lempirou
Tom Lawton	Daniel Dubroca (capt)
Andy McIntyre	Pascal Ondarts
Bill Campbell	Alain Lorieux
Steve Cutler	Jean Condom
Jeff Miller	Eric Champ
Troy Coker	Laurent Rodriguez
Simon Poidevin	Dominique Erbani

The inaugural Rugby World Cup had seen some wonderful performances, from Fiji in particular, some spectacular solo and team tries and some exciting finishes. All it needed to cement its standing was one truly great match. And in the semi-final between Australia and France, it got one.

Australia had started the tournament as the favourites, at least in their own minds, and in coach Alan Jones they had a (very) vocal exponent of their merits. And why not?

His touring team had won a rare grand slam of victories over the Home Nations in 1984 (England, Ireland, Scotland and Wales were all beaten, as were the Barbarians), and had recaptured the Bledisloe Cup in 1986 by beating the All Blacks in New Zealand. In the same year they had beaten France in Sydney, so having faced, and conquered, all their main rivals within the previous 24 months, they had good grounds for optimism. Jones's record of 16 wins from 20 matches in charge was impressive, although all four of those defeats were by New Zealand, generally thought to be Australia's only serious rivals for the crown.

'Australia had become the team to beat,' said Jones. 'We started doing the unexpected and as soon as we did that, we started winning.'

At the World Cup, Australia had had a lucky break to beat England and had otherwise not looked half as impressive as the All Blacks, beating the USA 47-12 and Japan 42-23 after a couple of shocks along the way. The quarter-final was comfortable enough – 33-15 over Ireland, four tries to two – but their brilliant fly half, Michael Lynagh (now an equally brilliant commentator and pundit) recalled, 'The team just didn't feel the same [as in the previous year]. The writing was probably on the wall after unconvincing performances in all of our pool games. Japan turned out to be a particularly tough match – they played well and we played very poorly, particularly in the first half.'

For all Lynagh's reservations, Australia still went into the semi-final as hot favourites, and few were betting against them. Lynagh himself was quick to punish French indiscipline, kicking the Wallabies into a 9-0 lead with a drop goal followed by a couple of penalties, though he missed another drop attempt. Didier Camberabero put his first penalty well wide, then hooked his second to the left of the posts.

Australia were unlucky to lose both centre Brett Papworth and second row Bill Campbell in the first quarter of the match, with Anthony Herbert and David Codey replacing them. It looked briefly, and much more worryingly, that Lynagh might also have picked up an injury, but a change of shorts appeared to address the problem! Shortly after, he nailed a huge penalty from inside his own half but then missed what looked a much simpler kick when the ball refused to curl in but held its line out wide of the far post. The Wallabies were never able to shake the French off.

Australia just about survived a superb move with good cover defence in the right-hand corner, but having taken solid line-out ball, Codey was somehow stripped of possession by Alain Lorieux who peeled off and sneaked round the blindside before the Australians were aware of quite what had happened. Lorieux had the strength, and reach, to get the ball down in the corner and Camberabero then struck a sweet kick to add the conversion and haul the French right back into the match. And that was it for the first half; 9-6 to Australia, with little indication of the fireworks still to come.

Lynagh got the second half under way, but it was soon France on the attack; a sniping run around the fringes from Berbizier followed by a more direct charge from Lorieux and suddenly there was some space. Quick ball and Philippe Sella was over between the posts. The conversion gave France a three-point lead, but Australia hit back with a David Campese try. A searing break through the middle from Lynagh whose long pass was tapped down by Peter Grigg into the arms of one of the deadliest finishers in world rugby; 15-12.

Lynagh then hit the post with what should have been a simple penalty, and Campese almost snaffled a half-chance when the French passing inside their own 22 was a little risky. Fortunately for them Campese just knocked on while juggling with the ball and trying to bring it under control.

In typically Gallic fashion, however, the French broke out of defence at speed – Denis Charvet made the initial break and it was taken on by Blanco. He weaved in and then out to split the Australian defence before putting Lagisquet in the clear. The flying winger made no mistake and Camberabero once again kicked the conversion to restore the France lead, 18-15. A simple Camberabero penalty for an Australia offside stretched the lead to six points.

France continued to incur the displeasure of Scottish referee Brian Hamilton, however, especially at the line-out, and from one virtually on the French line, Codey pounced on a loose ball and charged over. Lynagh's conversion tied the scores once more, at 21-21.

When the French backs tried to run the ball out of defence and got caught in possession another Lynagh penalty gave Australia a narrow lead. However,

Camberabero held his nerve to capitalise on a rash shoulder charge on him when he was breaking down the right to kick his second penalty and tie things up with a just a couple of minutes remaining.

The game looked destined to go into extra time, but France had other ideas. They stole Australian ball midway between their 22 and ten-metre line and Lagisquet kicked to almost the same spot in the Australian half. But a fatal moment of indecision enabled Dominique Erbani to seize the loose ball and keep the French going forward. They moved it right, then back left, Lagisquet made ground and the ball found its way to Blanco on the left wing via a simple little pass from Rodriguez. A burst of pace from a virtual standing start gave Blanco just enough room to beat the cover and dive over right in the corner. Camberabero kicked a fantastic conversion from the touchline to provide the icing on the cake and give him a personal return of four successful conversions from four attempts to go with his two penalties.

'Formidable!' repeated the French commentators over and over. 'I've watched a few great games in my time but I'm not sure there have been many, if any, that have come close to matching this one,' said the great Philippe Sella. 'It's a bit of a blur, but I remember our lock forward Alain Lorieux arriving [at the up and under] first. From there the first players on the scene were Pascal Ondarts and Jean-Pierre Garuet-Lempirou, our two props. They passed the ball between themselves like they were centres and played the ball out to the right. The ball got near the touchline then came back to the left side. Serge sprinted into the corner, some of the tacklers came close but he managed to dodge them all and dive full stretch at the line.'

Blanco himself recalls, 'We were waiting and waiting for the referee to blow for full time, but play went on and on. And then came a sequence of play which was something else. There were so many of us involved, one after another. I was inspired by this great rolling wave of play to make a supreme effort.'

In the wake of that seemingly endless piece of play, bodies were strewn all over the pitch – Australians in despair, Frenchmen in delight and players from both nations in sheer exhaustion.

Blanco has also spoken of how, by the time he and his team-mates had showered and changed, the stadium was deserted, and in darkness. 'We went out on to the pitch, did a lap of honour and then we sat and sang songs for half an hour,' he recalls. Only the French…

The ramifications for Australia, however, ran far deeper. Devastation was writ large on their faces as they trudged off the park and it didn't take long for stories to start emanating from the Wallabies camp. Rumbles about ructions, primarily centred on their flamboyant coach, Alan Jones. 'Instead of training in the mornings, as we used to,' said scrum half Nick Farr-Jones, 'we would only train in the afternoons. The reason was that Alan said he had an "unbreakable" commitment to broadcasting a morning show on Radio 2UE.'

Farr-Jones later described his World Cup experience in 1987 – the semi-final defeat followed by the third place play-off loss to Wales – as so bad that it almost led to his retirement from the game. 'We really had gone from the heights of world rugby to its absolute depths,' he wrote in his 2003 book *Story of the Rugby World Cup*. 'At 25 I was contemplating early retirement. Quite simply [the game] was no longer pleasurable.' Fortunately for rugby fans, it was not the last we would see of Farr-Jones.

Such matters were dismissed out of hand when Australia were winning, but became a consideration the moment they weren't. Then Jones's insistence of maintaining his broadcasting commitments became an indication that his mind wasn't fully on the team. After their tournament was over, the Australians seemed to lose all interest in the proceedings, failing to turn up to the presentation of their fourth-place award. On one level this is understandable; the team had, after all, been favourites so fourth place was bound to be a disappointment. But on another level a wider appreciation of the game and the role of a first World Cup in broadening its scope would have been welcome.

The New Zealanders, meanwhile, were delighted to see that they would be facing France rather than Australia in the final. 'It was very interesting when France scored that final try,' said All Blacks coach Brian Lochore, quoted in Philip Derriman's book *The Rise & Rise of Australian Rugby*. 'It was very obvious who our players wanted to play in the final – and it wasn't Australia...They saw Australia as very strong opponents while the French side is always very fickle and we reckoned that they had had their big game. It would have been a tougher game in the final if we had played Australia.'

Blanco said it was the sort of game where 'anything and everything might happen. No one in France or Australia will ever forget it.'

6

20 June 1987
Venue: Eden Park, Auckland
Attendance: 48,000

New Zealand 29 France 9

New Zealand	France
John Gallagher	Serge Blanco
John Kirwan	Didier Camberabero
Warwick Taylor	Philippe Sella
Joe Stanley	Denis Charvet
Craig Green	Patrice Lagisquet
Grant Fox	Franck Mesnel
David Kirk (capt)	Pierre Berbizier
John Drake	Jean-Pierre Garuet-Lempirou
Sean Fitzpatrick	Daniel Dubroca (capt)
Steven McDowall	Pascal Ondarts
Murray Pierce	Alain Lorieux
Gary Whetton	Jean Condom
Michael Jones	Eric Champ
Alan Whetton	Laurent Rodriguez
Wayne Shelford	Dominique Erbani

The question on everybody's lips was whether France had another big game in them. Could they reproduce the sparkling form of the semi-final and cause another upset?

The answer, in short, was 'no'. Whether this was due to their exertions of a week earlier or to the performance of the All Blacks in the first Rugby World Cup Final is a moot point. Serge Blanco has gone on record as saying that France's aim was always to prevent a New Zealand-Australia final, to prove that the Northern Hemisphere could have a say, and that having achieved this they just couldn't quite rediscover the degree of desire and motivation that they had found in the dying seconds of their epic semi-final victory. 'We were in a rather relaxed state of mind,' he said. 'We were almost happy just to be in the final and perhaps we didn't prepare as well as we should have done.'

Captain Daniel Dubroca – by all accounts an inspirational figure – had declared that the home advantage which the All Blacks enjoyed tipped the scales firmly in their favour, 'We have only a 25 per cent chance of winning,' he said. 'The All Blacks have the normal 50 per cent plus 25 per cent because they are playing at home.'

Despite their reservations, France were well in the game at half-time. They trailed 9-0 at the break, to a Grant Fox drop goal and a Michael Jones try (Fox converting) inside the first quarter, but had steadied the ship and when Didier Camberabero got them on the board with the first score of the second half, France trailed 9-3. Blanco felt that his team deserved even more than that having had three successive scrums virtually on the New Zealand line right at the end of the first half, without getting a penalty for their efforts. Looking back at this sequence now, it does appear that New Zealand were fortunate not to be penalised, but whether it would have given France the initiative to go on and win the match must be open to doubt. Overall it appeared that the All Blacks had the edge in pace, power and desire throughout.

Instead of finding succour in their first score of the final, France were pushed on to the back foot by the superb tactical kicking of Fox. A rolling maul resulted in a scrum on the French 22 with the All Blacks put-in, and the next phase of play saw a penalty awarded for offside. It was a tight decision, but Fox made no mistake in extending New Zealand's lead to nine points again at 12-3.

In relentless rain, New Zealand played clever possession football and the conditions mitigated against France getting their running game going with any consistency.

There had been an element of luck about the first try which came when Fox missed an attempted drop goal but Patrice Lagisquet just failed to gather the loose ball and instead the poacher supreme in Michael Jones, snaffled it. But no such fortune was needed for the second: Warwick Taylor and Joe Stanley combined well in midfield and with front-foot ball, Kirk fed Fox who turned it back inside to Michael Jones, who in turn fed Kirk – following up as all good scrum halves do – and he burst through the despairing French tackles and went over for the second try of the game.

This time, Fox missed the conversion but it scarcely mattered. Mere minutes later Kirk made a lightning break from deep inside his own half; having dummied to kick he found acres of space down the right and when the cover came in he went to ground where the ball was picked up and immediately slipped to John Kirwan on the outside. Kirwan had already shown throughout the tournament that he was both quick and strong and he made the run-in from about 35 metres look simple.

Again Fox missed the conversion but at 23-9 New Zealand shut up shop and played safe, taking the penalties when they came and adding six more points to their tally from French indiscipline.

With virtually the last play of the game, Pierre Berbizier got over right at the posts and Camberabero added the extras to make the final score 29-9.

'Deep down, I had no doubt we'd beat either France or Australia,' said Kirk. 'France had very strong forwards and their backs read like a who's who of legends of French rugby – Sella, Blanco, Berbizier…We had lost a Test to them the year before and they had won the previous two Five Nations Championships and they asked a lot of us, but once I scored [the second try] I had a gut feeling we would be champions.'

'We beat the French by playing precisely and relentlessly,' said full back John Gallagher. 'Our job was to impose our own rhythm and style on the match.'

'The final was a wonderful occasion,' said Sean Fitzpatrick, initially only in the team owing to an injury to Andy Dalton but showing such supreme form that he kept his place even after Dalton was restored to fitness. 'To play at your home ground, in your home town, in front of a capacity stadium on an awesome spring afternoon – it doesn't get a lot better than that!

'Did I enjoy the final itself? Probably not. I enjoyed it a lot more once the whistle had gone and it was over! The celebrations were actually pretty tame, though. We went back to our hotel, had a couple of drinks in the bar and went to bed. You have to remember that we were amateurs so most of us were back at work on the Monday.'

It's a theme also picked up by Gallagher, 'The Monday after the Saturday final I was back at work as a policeman. It was difficult to do my job because I was recognised all the time. Being a World Cup winner had some good spin-offs, but I never did any undercover work again!' On a more serious note he adds, 'There was no money in rugby union then, no money in being an All Black. That's why four of us went to rugby league before the next World Cup.'

Players from all the countries had similar difficulties, with England full back Jon Webb being allowed to sit his medical finals three weeks early so that they didn't clash with the World Cup, while captain Mike Harrison had to use up his holiday allowance and pointed out, 'You need an understanding wife!' Scotland captain Colin Deans, a salesman, made a point of praising his 'supportive boss', while roofer Alan Tait said he was lucky that his employer was a rugby fan and happy to give him the six weeks' leave, albeit unpaid.

To this day Brian Moore, who was just finishing his legal training, believes that it was not a level playing field, 'It didn't keep you awake at night, but it did niggle. It wasn't that we minded not receiving money, it was just that we minded not being on the same conditions as the teams we were competing against. It was frustrating that nothing was ever done about it.'

Deans says, 'I remember seeing some adverts on the sports channel – Andy Dalton was advertising machinery on his farm, Andy Haden was advertising oil…' The Scottish Rugby Football Union actually lodged a complaint, while Wales full back Paul Thorburn recalls the players being reminded of their amateur status only to turn on the TV and see All Blacks advertising various goods. 'They said they weren't being paid,' says Thorburn, 'but there was a lot of scepticism among the players and a feeling that we weren't competing on equal terms.'

The All Blacks denied the rules were applied differently in New Zealand, with Fitzpatrick, now a highly respected TV pundit, saying, 'Being a builder, I was back on site bright and early Monday morning.'

However, the notion of amateurism and how it appeared to be applied in different countries was an ongoing debate among unions, players and fans and was set to rumble on for several more years until the game would go fully professional. The players certainly began to feel increasingly like second-class citizens in comparison to the union officials; in her superb book *Thirty Bullies* Alison Kervin quotes Harrison as saying, 'We were [not] made to feel all that "special" – the players flew economy and the committee were in first class.'

But that is an argument for another time. On one question, everyone was agreed. New Zealand were not just worthy, but rightful winners of the first World Cup."

'We were disappointed to have lost,' said Serge Blanco, 'but we were happy for the All Blacks. It would have been a great injustice if they hadn't won.'

In truth New Zealand were rarely challenged. Deprived of a game against their Southern Hemisphere rivals in Australia – the only team most gave any chance of victory over the All Blacks – they simply progressed calmly towards their stated goal. 'Planning was central to our success,' said Kirk. '[The management team] worked out what style was needed to win, picked players who could play that style and – boom – we won. Much of our victory was down to the clear thinking in advance.'

The seeds of victory were almost certainly sown the previous year after New Zealand's ill-fated 'rebel' tour to South Africa, a sporting pariah at the time on account of the country's apartheid policies. The Cavaliers, as they were known, certainly lived up to their name in their attitude to rugby in South Africa, and in trying to claim that sport and politics could be kept entirely separate.

For almost the first time in their history, New Zealanders were looking at the sport a little askance. Players were deemed to have more mercenary considerations and that tarnished their hero status. In a stroke of genius coach Brian Lochore restored that faith by insisting during the RWC that the All Blacks stayed in small towns rather than the big cities, that they trained at schools and local clubs, and that they intermingled with the fans.

Media coverage was extensive throughout New Zealand – television, radio and newspapers. Which was just as well because in the UK and Ireland it was virtually non-existent. 'The Northern Hemisphere sides didn't really want a World Cup in the first place,' points out Fitzpatrick. 'It was very much a Southern Hemisphere initiative. Even at home the fans struggled to buy into the idea, but our World Cup was very much like a PR campaign.'

Former England player Derek Wyatt, in his 1995 book *Rugby Disunion*, says, 'The New Zealand nation became caught up in the event and was, it is no exaggeration to say, in love with the tournament. The enthusiasm generated a rugby bonhomie the like of which had never been seen before and in some towns the crowds seemed bigger than the populations.'

'We didn't really know how big the World Cup would be,' admits Fitzpatrick. 'Even after the final we were sort of like "Ah well that's done, what now?"'

But if the players weren't entirely certain about 'what next', the administrators and the fans certainly were. The concept of a Rugby World Cup had been warmly embraced, it had proved immensely popular and the best team had won. From this moment on, rugby was going to be considered in four-yearly cycles and while the Five (later Six) Nations Championships, the Tri Nations (later Rugby Championship) and tours would all remain an important part of the rugby calendar, the landscape had changed forever.

The last word should go to a player, and an All Black, in the shape of Zinzan Brooke, 'The difference between rugby before there were World Cups and after is massive. I was lucky enough to play in both eras and the whole of international sport has changed. Now it's save yourself for the big one – the Rugby World Cup. Every other match is a stepping stone on the way and the World Cups have become everything and winning them means everything.'

7

3 October 1991
Venue: Twickenham, London
Attendance: 70,000

England 12 New Zealand 18

England	New Zealand
Jon Webb	Terry Wright
Rory Underwood	John Kirwan
Will Carling (capt)	Craig Innes
Jerry Guscott	Bernie McCahill
Chris Oti	John Timu
Rob Andrew	Grant Fox
Richard Hill	Graeme Bachop
Jason Leonard	Steve McDowall
Brian Moore	Sean Fitzpatrick
Jeff Probyn	Richard Loe
Wade Dooley	Ian Jones
Paul Ackford	Gary Whetton (capt)
Mike Teague	Alan Whetton
Peter Winterbottom	Michael Jones
Dean Richards	Zinzan Brooke

As in 1987, so in 1991. The four intervening years might as well not have happened as a New Zealand team featuring seven of the side which had lifted the trophy in 1987 took the field at Twickenham against the co-hosts of the second Rugby World Cup. And it was like we had never been away as the first try was scored by... Michael Jones.

Five of the eight All Black forwards from four years earlier were still there, with Richard Loe taking over from John Drake in the front row, Ian Jones from Murray Pierce in the second row and Zinzan Brooke from Buck Shelford in the back row. None of these changes could be construed as weakening the side, which started the tournament as the favourites to retain their crown. The backline had maybe lost a little of its lustre, with the likes of John Gallagher and centres Joe Stanley and Warwick Taylor gone, replaced by Terry Wright, Craig Innes and Bernie McCahill respectively. But Grant Fox was still there to kick the goals, John Kirwan remained one of the world's best wingers and if Graeme Bachop didn't have the captaincy credentials of David Kirk, he lost little by comparison as a scrum half.

England, meanwhile, had added some more steel to their pack with Jason Leonard coming in to the front row – where he would remain for over a decade. Paul Ackford was to prove the perfect partner for Wade Dooley in the engine room and Mike Teague had joined Dean Richards and Peter Winterbottom in a back row which looked big and nasty, in the nicest possible way. An accomplished half back pairing of Richard Hill and Rob Andrew were on the same wavelength, while the centre partnership of Will Carling and Jerry Guscott was on its way to becoming one of England's very best. The solidity of Jon Webb at full back and the searing pace of Rory Underwood on the wing (where he was joined by

Chris Oti) all combined to make England look a tougher proposition than in 1987.

But before assessing the state of the game on the pitch, it's necessary to have a look at what had been happening in the rugby world off it, between the first and second World Cups.

The instigation of a Rugby World Cup had been a Southern Hemisphere initiative, but by 1991 the Northern Hemisphere had begun to catch up with the concept. The venue of the second Rugby World Cup was a hodge-podge, with all the Five Nations teams hosting matches in the group stages and an attempt to divide the knockout games between the nations on a reasonably even basis making for a disparate and occasionally confusing tournament. However, it was probably a necessary compromise in order to get total buy-in from the senior nations in the Northern Hemisphere.

With the RWC's higher profile, and expressions of interest from 33 countries, it proved necessary to hold a qualifying competition. The eight quarter-finalists from 1987 were excused the need to take part in this, and in the event little changed from the first World Cup, with Canada, Argentina and the USA qualifying as the Americas representatives (qualifying served only to establish the 'seeding' of the three countries, which finished in that order); Zimbabwe once more representing Africa; and Italy and Romania joining the Five Nations teams as Europe's qualifiers. The one change – and a significant one it was to prove to be – was that Western Samoa topped the Asia and Oceania qualifiers, ahead of Japan (who once more qualified), Tonga and South Korea. Western Samoa, then, effectively took Tonga's place in the finals.

The 1991 Rugby World Cup was to be treated like a major sporting event this time around, with massively increased coverage on TV and in the press. In part, of course, this was due to the matches being shown at viewer-friendly times in the Northern Hemisphere, unlike four years earlier. There were still issues, one being that only France and Wales had floodlights so the opening match at Twickenham had to be played in daylight hours, though why on a Thursday afternoon is a good question. It was also true that the Northern Hemisphere players and officials alike had decided to embrace the event fully, and to prepare their teams for serious competition rather than the extended party of 1987.

With commercialism, however, came huge demands on the players. There was an obvious anomaly that the game of rugby could no longer be said to be amateur, but the individual players most certainly were. So on the one hand the players were expected to act more 'professionally' than in 1987 with regard to their training and preparation, but on the other they were not allowed to be paid money for playing. More controversially, nor were they allowed to make money on the side from any 'rugby-related' activities. It was a story which was set to run and run until it was properly addressed.

The great Australian coach Bob Dwyer accurately summed up the situation in Lance Peatey's excellent book *In Pursuit Of Bill*. 'The Home Unions warned that creating a Rugby World Cup would push the game towards professionalism,' recalled Dwyer. 'I thought that was a load of rubbish at the time, but they were absolutely right. Suddenly there was this prize every team desperately wanted to win, and in order to win it they had to spend a lot more money and ask a lot more of their players. Inevitably those players had to sacrifice more work time and they needed to be compensated for it somehow.'

In the meantime there was the question of whether New Zealand were still the team to beat. England certainly seemed to think so, and had been holding the All Blacks model up as the one to emulate for nigh on four years. There was more than a bit of logic in that, of course, given how superior they had been in 1987, but was there a danger that England were playing the last World Cup rather than the current one? It's easy to forget that in the days before autumn internationals and summer tours, the major nations from the two hemispheres rarely met: England had not faced New Zealand in the four years between the first and second World Cups; they had not, in fact, played each other since the 1985 England tour. The mystique, the aura, surrounding the All Blacks had therefore had little opportunity to diminish.

'We had their greatness rammed into us,' recalled England captain Will Carling. 'Over and over again. We had countless videos of their training and it did condition us to thinking that we were going to come up against this mighty machine, which was unbeatable.'

England had, however, developed into a good side in the intervening years. The famous, or infamous from an England point of view, defeat by Scotland in the 1990 grand slam decider had, probably, done England a favour. Hindsight is always 20-20, but England had looked imperious in 1990 until their grand slam juggernaut had come to a juddering halt at Murrayfield as a rampaging Scottish team, hyped up with nationalistic fervour, won the decisive game 13-7. England, while not exactly going back to the drawing board, had learnt the lessons of that defeat and tightened up their play and would claim back-to-back grand slams in the 1991 and 1992 Five Nations Championships. This meant they were, indisputably, the best team in the Northern Hemisphere at the time of the 1991 World Cup; what they were not, however, was a team with a huge variety of styles or the ability to play off-the-cuff rugby. Carling had tried to introduce a more flowing form of rugby in 1990 and it had backfired on him and his team in that grand slam decider. For the 1991 Five Nations Championship, they returned to basics and seeing that it served them well, they stuck to it.

Carling admitted, 'Murrayfield was the big turning point for me as a captain. I realised we had to be more ruthless and professional in our approach to these games.'

Not that you would have known it from the hesitant, fumbling and generally incoherent performance which opened the tournament.

Three Webb penalties and a Rob Andrew drop goal to three Grant Fox penalties saw England lead 12-9 at half-time, but they seemed uncertain in their gameplan. Ten minutes into the second half Michael Jones scored what proved to be the only try of the game, after a swift back move involving Bachop, Kirwan and Innes which was worthy of a better match. It was a set move, but one launched expertly by Graeme Bachop's sprint down the blindside following a scrum. A loop move and an accurate pass from Innes enabled Bachop to give Kirwan a little space out wide and when Kirwan was tackled he had the presence of mind to to roll the ball back inside. Jones, following up as all good flankers do, was first to the ball. Fox converted and later added another penalty to put New Zealand ahead by a converted try which England rarely looked like scoring.

The scrum count was 19-5 in New Zealand's favour, which may well be an accurate reflection of England inaccuracies, but it mitigated against the possibility of the home team getting any sort of rhythm into their game, let alone momentum.

New Zealand, even more surprisingly, were scarcely any better. As the watching Australia captain Nick Farr-Jones said, 'Players were not composed and didn't look to have too definite a gameplan. We know we have to show more composure.' New Zealand coach Alex Wyllie perhaps put it best when he described the match as resembling the first game of a tour – which for the All Blacks it was, in effect. 'It was just about getting a win under the belt,' said Wyllie.

A measure of how disappointing the opening match was can be found in the fact that none of the excellent Rugby World Cup histories give much more than a few lines over to detailing it. For England it meant a longer, harder route to the later stages of the tournament, on the road and away from the security of Twickenham. For New Zealand, it looked like business as usual, but in fact there was clearly some nervousness there of a kind rarely displayed in their 1987 triumph.

New Zealand were to progress comfortably as Group A winners following a 46-6 win over the USA and a tighter 31-21 victory over the Italians. Admittedly the Italians had discovered a world-class kicker in the years since their devastating defeat in the opening match of the 1987 World Cup – Argentinian-born Diego Dominguez would go on to win 74 caps for Italy and to this day remains one of only five players to have scored more than 1,000 points for his country (the list is headed by Dan Carter, with Jonny Wilkinson, Neil Jenkins and Ronan O'Gara the others to figure in the 1,000 club). Nevertheless, the fact that the 64-point margin of 1987 had come down to ten points in 1991 was an indication that not all was well in the All Black camp, at least in terms of their points-scoring.

England also progressed to the knockout stages with relative ease following their opening-day disappointment, beating Italy 36-6 in their second game and the USA 37-9 in their third.

6 October 1991
Venue: Cardiff Arms Park
Attendance: 45,000

Wales 13 Western Samoa 16

Wales	Western Samoa
Tony Clement	Andrew Aiolupo
Ieuan Evans (capt)	Brian Lima
Scott Gibbs	To'o Vaega
Mike Hall	Frank Bunce
Arthur Jones	Timo Tagaloa
Mark Ring	Stephen Bachop
Robert Jones	Mathew Vaea
Mike Griffiths	Peter Fatialofa (capt)
Ken Waters	Stan To'omalatai
Laurance Delaney	Vili Alalatoa
Phil May	Mark Birtwistle
Kevin Moseley	Mat Keenan
Emyr Lewis	Sila Vaifale
Richie Collins	Apollo Perelini
Phil Davies	Pat Lam

Western Samoa were more than a little put out not to be invited to the first Rugby World Cup and they entered the qualifying stages for its second incarnation feeling they had a point to prove. Having edged out Tonga from the qualifying competition, they found themselves drawn in a tough Pool 3 alongside Australia, Argentina and Wales. Although they were deemed a tough team to play, no one really expected them to chalk up a win.

How wrong we were.

First up for the Pacific Islanders was a trip to the national stadium of Cardiff Arms Park to take on hosts Wales. Wales were not a great team at the time: rock bottom of that year's Five Nations Championship with only a 21-21 home draw against Ireland to their name, set against heavy defeats in Scotland (32-12) and France (36-3) and a 25-6 loss to England in Cardiff. They had some decent players, particularly among the backs where captain Ieuan Evans had the solid pairing of Mike Hall and Scott Gibbs in the centres, the more maverick talent of Tony Clement at full back and the genius of Robert Jones at scrum half.

When they took the field against the Western Samoans, only hooker Ken Waters was making his debut whereas the Islanders were blooding four players for the first time. Two of these were the second-row players Mark Birtwistle and Mat Keenan, who each went on to win a handful of caps, but the others were to become global stars. Frank Bunce played in all four games for Western Samoa at the 1991 World Cup before switching allegiance to New Zealand and winning 55 caps for them as a strong-running, and even stronger tackling, centre. Pat Lam debuted at number eight and would go on to win 34 caps for his country, while also becoming a popular figure in the English Premiership with Newcastle Falcons and Northampton Saints. Lam is now head coach at the Irish province of Connacht and an occasional TV pundit who remains a mightily impressive figure on and off the pitch.

In 1991, rugby in Wales was already in a parlous state. Defections to the paid ranks of rugby league had undoubtedly hurt them and they had won only a handful of matches between the first and second World Cups. Respected journalists such as Gerald Davies were even beginning to question whether the decline might be terminal, while the management team, headed by Bob Norster – a highly respected former player – was unable to decide on the best XV. Since suffering a catastrophic 12-try, 63-6 rout on the summer tour to Australia, Wales had changed two-thirds of the team, but had not given themselves enough time, or sufficient matches, to bed in the new combinations.

From the outset, the Samoans tore into Wales, their forceful approach and very physical, confrontational style of play rocking the Welsh players. With their ferocious tackling – often high but usually just about on the right side of the law – the Samoans smashed into the Welsh time and time again, with Phil May, back-rower Ritchie Collins and Clement all forced off the pitch by injury, further disrupting the Wales team.

'This game is all about physical confrontation,' explained captain Peter Fatialofa afterwards. 'Tackling hard is second nature to us. Our tackling is legitimate and has always been a crucial factor in our game. We commit ourselves immensely hard to tackling but there is no cheating about it.'

Fatialofa was always a larger than life character who won 34 caps for Samoa between 1988 and 1996 – a large number for a country which was not often afforded the opportunity to take on the 'big guns' of established International Board nations in that era. 'Fats', as he was universally known, sadly died in November 2013 at the age of just 54, and Pat Lam said of his former captain, 'It's impossible to exaggerate how central Peter was to what we achieved in 1991. His job description might have been "captain", but he was much more than that to everyone in the squad.

'It was Peter who did the player recruitment before the tournament and he was the heart and soul of the side during the competition. He brought people together, he could relate to young and old alike and he always had an enormous smile on his face. He put Samoan rugby on the map but he did it with real modesty and a sense of humour.' Prop Fatialofa actually was a piano shifter by day – he worked for the family removal firm.

The game reached half-time with the score at 3-3, a simple exchange of penalties. But Wales were rocking, and they rocked even harder when Samoa opened the second half with a try. In the first minute, centre To'o Vaega made a searing break, kicked ahead and chased his own kick alongside Robert Jones. It appeared at the time that Jones had just got to the ball first, and viewing the incident again now, it is absolutely clear that he did, but referee Patrick Robin of France raised his arm to signal a try. It was a terrible decision, even if Samoa deserved to be ahead, and the conversion added insult to injury, putting Samoa 9-3 up.

There was no dispute over the legitimacy of the second Samoan try in the 52nd minute, however, which stemmed from a beautiful running and handling move finished by back-rower Sila Vaifale. Vaifale was by far the least celebrated of the back-row trio which also featured Lam and Apollo Perelini, but he took his moment of glory with aplomb to extend the Samoan lead to 13-3.

Inevitably, the Samoans began to tire in the fourth quarter and at last Wales began to make inroads. The fightback really started to take shape when Arthur Emyr crashed over for a try which Mark Ring converted to close the gap to 13-9. A crucial penalty from Mathew Vaea established a two-score lead for Samoa, which was needed when an injury-time try from Wales captain Ieuan Evans brought them back to 16-13 with just a couple of minutes left on the clock. The conversion was missed, but was of little consequence as it was the final play of a momentous game.

'We had become far too parochial and insular,' said Evans, 'and this was the result. We probably got what we deserved after years of going through umpteen coaches and having a revolving door policy with players. As usual we had sacked another coach just before the World Cup and I had just been handed the captaincy. That said, we had enough ball to have won and we felt we had let a lot of people down. The players were crestfallen.'

Fly half Ring added, 'I never once thought during the game that we weren't going to win. Our scrum dominated them and you should never lose a game where you've destroyed an opponents' scrum. But I was really disappointed in our three-quarters play – I was putting the ball out to our centres with time to spread it wide but they had limited vision and they just kept getting smashed by the likes of Frank Bunce.'

It was the first World Cup upset of one of the established nations and though Wales will take little consolation from the fact, it was exactly what the Rugby World Cup needed.

Ring admits, 'The rest of the world saw it as the start of the expansion of the game globally, and I suppose it was an important part of history, though there was no way we could appreciate that.'

It is a theme which was picked up by Bryan Williams, the Western Samoa team manager, 'It is a great milestone for our rugby and we hope more International Board nations will visit our country after the World Cup is over.'

As for this game, Williams said, 'We have found our place in the sun.' He continued, 'The guys were confident because they had worked hard, but on the other hand they were unsure what to expect. The noise and the traffic really bothered some of them and on the pitch there were times when they couldn't hear line-out calls because of the noise the crowd was making, but they were always confident.'

Another of the team's star players, Brian Lima, said, 'It was crazy at home. Rugby is the number one sport in Samoa so loads of people gathered to watch it, particularly at the ground in Apia.' Lima was the youngest player to feature in the 1991 World Cup, being still a teenager at the time, but he was to go on to win 64 caps, scoring 140 points, and earned himself a nickname of 'The Chiropractor' thanks to his shuddering tackling which was deemed to rearrange his victim's bones.

Those who felt this upset victory might be a one-off for the Pacific Islanders were quickly disabused of the notion when Samoa held favourites Australia to just 9-3 in their second match – three Michael Lynagh penalties to one from

Vaea. And it could have been even tighter if English referee Ed Morrison had sent off Wallaby flanker Brendon Nasser for a horrible high tackle. Even the Australian commentators at the time queried whether it would lead to a sending off, and it would certainly be a red card offence in the modern era. Interestingly it was to be Nasser's last Test for his country.

'Everyone really stood up to take notice of Western Samoa after they beat Wales,' recalls Lynagh, 'and it was good that we had something to gauge them by. We played in atrocious conditions and it was a big test for our pack. There were some really big hits coming in and we lost Nick Farr-Jones early on. We made it through in the end but we were all pretty sore for a while after that match.'

Ultimately it was a combination of the poor weather in Pontypool and an inability to win clean line-out ball which cost Western Samoa dear, but they re-grouped for their final group match against Argentina. This was an initially brutal game, with sendings-off on both sides – Keenan for Western Samoa and Pedro Sporleder for Argentina – for fighting. Even the ref had to be replaced, Jim Fleming coming on for injured compatriot Brian Anderson. But after trailing early on, the Samoans got on top and eventually ran out comfortable winners by 35-12, with six tries including two each from Lima and winger Timo Tagaloa.

Tagaloa in particular caused havoc when running with the ball, setting up Lima's first try with a powerful run down the left wing before shipping the ball on to Fatialofa until it found its way to Lima, making the extra man on the wide right. Lima's second try came from a move which began deep in Samoan territory with full back Andrew Aiolupo. Aiolupo's lightning break split the Argentine defence and while his chip ahead was probably meant for himself it was collected by Lima at top speed to go over in the right-hand corner. Tagaloa benefited from quick ball from a scrum and a gain-line break by the powerful Bunce; Tagaloa picked the right line to glide through the gap, and in the second half he cut a nice line, simply bounced off a couple of fairly feeble attempts at a tackle and was over again.

The result confirmed Western Samoa's progress to the quarter-finals, and Wales's exit. As one wag put it, 'Thank goodness we weren't playing the whole of Samoa.'

5 October 1991
Venue: Stade Jean Dauger, Bayonne, France
Attendance: 5,000

Canada 13 Fiji 3

Canada	Fiji
Scott Stewart	Severo Koroduadua Waqanibau
Pat Palmer	Fili Seru
Christian Stewart	Noa Nadruku
John Lecky	Savenaca Aria
Steve Gray	Tomasi Lovo
Gareth Rees	Waisale Serevi
Chris Tynan	Pauliasi Tabulutu
Eddie Evans	Epeli Naituivau
David Speirs	Salacieli Naivilawasa
Dan Jackart	Mosese Taga (capt)
John Robertson	Sam Domoni
Norm Hadley	Ilaitia Savai
Alan Charron	Alifereti Dere Ratu
Gord MacKinnon	Laisenia Katonawale
Glen Ennis (capt)	Ifereimi Tawake

At the first World Cup, Fiji were everyone's 'second team'. The joyful abandon with which they played their rugby and the enjoyment they seemed to get out of it were infectious, and brought a smile to the faces of everyone who saw them.

When Fiji took the field for their first match at the second World Cup, led by the magician that was Waisale Serevi (the actual captain was prop forward Mosese Taga, but it was Serevi who was the spiritual leader of Fijian rugby at the time), we all expected more of the same.

First up for Fiji were Canada, who had actually recorded their first World Cup victory on the opening weekend in 1987 when they had easily beaten Tonga, 37-4. Canada had, however, not been able to make too much impression on the more established nations in their group, losing 46-19 to Ireland and a similar 40-9 to Wales, with the two Five Nations teams progressing to the knockout stages. But in 1991 Canada had a handful of players who had already experienced a World Cup, including Scott Stewart and Pat Palmer in the backs, and, of course, Gareth Rees.

This was Rees's second Rugby World Cup and he would go on to play two more, gaining 55 caps in total, 24 of which would be as captain; stints at Wasps and Harlequins in later years were to make him a firm favourite with English fans and in 2011 he was inducted into the IRB (now World Rugby) Hall of Fame. Along with Samoa's Brian Lima, Rees was the first player from outside the so-called 'big' nations to be so inducted.

But in 1981 all that was still some way into the future, and Rees had a match to win. He was helped in that aim by the presence of some world-class forwards. The massive Norm Hadley had come into the second row, making his debut

41

shortly after the 1987 Rugby World Cup and in the back row captain Glen Ennis (another who had played in the 1987 campaign), now had alongside him Al Charron and Gord MacKinnon. MacKinnon had made his debut back in 1985 but had missed out on the 1987 RWC and was desperate to make up for the fact. Charron had debuted in March 1990 in the 15-6 win against Argentina at the wonderfully named Burnaby Lake Rugby Club in Vancouver (a match refereed by Australian Kerry Fitzgerald, who was also in charge of Canada's opening World Cup game).

With Canada not given too many opportunities against top tier nations in those days, Charron had played only four more matches for his country between making his debut and the start of the 1991 RWC. By the end of his playing career a dozen years later, however, Charron had become the most capped Canadian player of all time, with 76 appearances – a record which will stand for at least a couple more years yet. He's also equal seventh on the list of all-time Canadian try-scorers, with current number eight Aaron Carpenter the only forward who has scored more points than Charron.

Canada were clearly building a good team, but until the World Cup no one really knew quite how good.

Charron and his back-row colleagues had a vital part to play against Fiji in closing down Serevi. Of course Serevi's reputation had been built on his Sevens skills, but many of them – his hitch kick, his startling pace off the mark, his steps off either foot to change direction, his little chips through to create space – were eminently transferable to the 15-man game, and you couldn't take your eyes off him for a second. Serevi is undoubtedly one of the greatest Sevens players of all time, and his list of achievements in the shorter form of the game includes winning the Rugby World Cup Sevens in 1997 and 2005 and the Hong Kong Sevens on seven separate occasions. But the 1991 RWC was not a happy campaign for the Fijians.

Rees kicked superbly to keep the Fijians on the back foot throughout, and also notched three penalties to keep the scoreboard ticking over, albeit slowly. The decisive score was Scott Stewart's try which started from an overthrown line-out on the Canadian left which was superbly picked up by Rees. He moved it swiftly on and the move was continued down the right by Christian Stewart at pace and then by the supporting MacKinnon. Play was switched back from right to left and hooker David Speirs played a crucial role in flipping the ball on to Steve Gray, the left winger. Gray cut back in and found his full back up in support with just enough room to dot the ball down despite the close attentions of Serevi.

Losing this first game to Canada seemed to knock the fight out of the Fijians, and they were well beaten by France three days later, losing 33-9. A hat-trick from Jean-Baptiste Lafond, plus two from Philippe Sella and a sixth from Didier Camberabero was a shattering defeat for the Fijians. So demoralised were they that they even managed to lose their third and final group game to Romania. This meant that once again Romania had notched up a victory at the World Cup finals; and a more significant one than their one-point win over Zimbabwe in 1987. Romania as a country had experienced a revolution between the first and second World Cups, and could easily have been forgiven for neglecting its rugby for more important matters – it was an astonishing feat for the team even to qualify for the 1991 competition. Not only did they beat Fiji, but they ran Canada close, matching their two tries with two of their own and only losing by eight points, 11-19. With France winning all three of their games and Fiji surprisingly losing all theirs, the Canada v Romania fixture was, ultimately, the one which decided second place in the group, and it was all credit to Romania that they came so close to progressing.

Instead it was Canada who had that honour, a narrow 19-13 defeat by France costing them the chance of top spot. After an early penalty, Lafond scored France's opening try with a sharp turn of pace, but a line-out steal from John Robertson enabled Mark Wyatt to put Canada on the scoreboard in the 27th minute. And then in the dying moments of the first half, Wyatt went over for the try which brought Canada back within two points of France at half-time. In a match which simmered throughout, Pascal Ondarts was extremely fortunate to remain on the pitch after landing a flurry of punches on scrum half Chris Tynan. However, a glorious chip and re-gather from Lafond saw Philippe Saint-Andre put clear for France's second try to stretch the lead to 13-7. A mammoth drop goal from Rees closed the gap once more, but France played safe rugby to notch two further penalties and ensure that they always stayed just out of reach.

It meant Canada faced the 'pleasure' of taking on the All Blacks in the quarter-finals. 'We had come to the tournament to show what we could do,' recalled Rees. 'But we'd been on the road for so long that by the time the quarter-finals came round the guys were completely exhausted.'

At least Canada got to stay in France for the quarter-final. Having played their group games in Bayonne, Toulouse and then Agen, they were obliged to travel to Lille while the All Blacks crossed the Channel from their England base. The match, on 20 October, took place on an absolutely sodden pitch, which made the quality of the game even more remarkable. Rees says he remembers the rain as being torrential, 'I went out before the game to practise drop-outs and Grant Fox was doing the same thing. There was a layer of water on the pitch and the ball simply wouldn't come up for the kick. We looked at each other as if to say, "How are we supposed to play on this?"'

The Canadians played well, and showed enough to give the All Blacks a real fright, scoring good tries through Charron and Tynan, with Rees's kicking as solid as ever. It was only the greater attacking ability of New Zealand which enabled them ultimately to run the Canadians off their feet. The first All Blacks try came from an up and under which Grant Fox would be unlikely to rate as one of his best, but which somehow found its way to full back John Timu appearing on the right wing. Timu lost his footing, but the slip actually benefited him as it enabled him to evade the cover defence and he had the presence of mind to hold on to the ball and dive over.

A scrum close to the Canadian line provided a simple first-phase chance for Bernie McCahill to score his first try for his country, and Zinzan Brooke was the beneficiary of another scrum deep in the Canadian 22, when a set move put him in acres of space and he cantered over unopposed. A more messy scrum produced the fourth New Zealand try, in the second half, when scrum half Graeme Bachop was the quickest to sense an opening down the blindside and John Kirwan took the pass at pace, his speed and strength from short range being too much for the Canadian defence.

Canada hit back, driving over from a line-out and Tynan getting the ball down. Two years later Tynan, then at Cambridge, faced his half back partner Rees in the Varsity match at Twickenham. Tynan, who had a BA in political science from the University of British Columbia, had come to Cambridge to study land economy, but ended up on the losing side against Rees's Oxford. Canada were still playing some good rugby, but when they got stripped of the ball from a maul deep inside the New Zealand half, the All Blacks did what they do so well from turnover ball and their pacy backs took it the length of the field in a blink of an eye for Timu to go over for his second of the game.

Still Canada weren't finished and Charron barged his way over for the Canucks' second try to leave the final score 29-13 in favour of the defending champions. 'We felt we had something to prove,' said Charron, 'and we did that.' Canada had certainly made their mark, and shown that even the major nations had to take them seriously.

'We would like to think that one of the reasons the All Blacks did not beat Australia [in the semi-final] was because we had taken quite a lot out of them,' said Rees.

10

20 October 1991
Venue: Lansdowne Road, Dublin
Attendance: 54,500

Ireland 18 Australia 19

Ireland	Australia
Jim Staples	Marty Roebuck
Simon Geoghegan	David Campese
David Curtis	Jason Little
Brendan Mullin	Tim Horan
Jack Clarke	Bob Egerton
Ralph Keyes	Michael Lynagh
Rob Saunders	Nick Farr-Jones (capt)
Nick Popplewell	Tony Daly
Steve Smith	Phil Kearns
Des Fitzgerald	Ewen McKenzie
Donal Lenihan	Rod McCall
Neil Francis	John Eales
Philip Matthews (capt)	Simon Poidevin
Gordon Hamilton	Jeff Miller
Brian Robinson	Willie Ofahengaue

The pick of the quarter-finals at the 1991 Rugby World Cup turned out to be the Ireland v Australia match at Lansdowne Road. At the group stages, Ireland had recorded 55-11 and 32-16 wins over Zimbabwe and Japan respectively, but when Scotland repeated that season's Five Nations victory at Murrayfield, beating Ireland 24-15 in the decisive group game, it gave the Irish the tougher quarter-final match.

Australia, while not imperious in their group games were nevertheless undefeated and everyone assumed they would have too much firepower for the Irish. But that reckoned without the passion of both the Irish players and their supporters, their objective being, as one commentator described it, 'the creation of chaos'.

Straight from the kick-off, punches were thrown and if few connected there was still a level of intent there which would have seen yellow cards – at least – shown to Ireland captain Philip Matthews and Australia number eight Willie Ofahengaue in the present era.

In conditions markedly better than those Canada and New Zealand were experiencing in Lille, Lansdowne Road witnessed a clash of styles as the Wallabies attempted to keep the ball in hand while the Irish were content to kick it up in the air and see what happened.

Australia had the first opportunity after six minutes, but Michael Lynagh missed a simple kick from about 30 metres after Neil Francis had been penalised for a line-out infringement. Then Ralph Keyes dropped a straightforward pass in his own 22 and Ireland were lucky they were able to scramble the ball away without conceding anything. Keyes, who was 30 at the time of the World Cup, was never able to tie down the fly half position and make it his own but played pretty well throughout the tournament and certainly wasn't the weak link in the Irish team.

On 16 minutes Keyes cleared well from an awkward position, but from the resulting line-out around 30 metres out, quick ball from Farr-Jones, Lynagh and centre Tim Horan gave Campese the space to cut back on the angle and he burst past the Irish defence. A little step off his right foot, a burst of extreme pace and he was away. Lynagh converted to make it 6-0. However, Farr-Jones was struggling with a knee injury which forced him off soon after the opening score, to be replaced by Peter Slattery.

The scrum half change made little difference to the shape of the match, with most of the play continuing to take place inside the Irish half, though Keyes at least notched a penalty after 24 minutes when the ball hit the inside of the post and went over. Ireland briefly built up a head of steam and chucked the ball around a bit without ever really threatening the Australian line. However, Keyes did slot an equalising penalty when some Australian backchat saw them marched back a further ten metres, bringing it within Keyes's kicking range.

Keyes had a long-range effort with about five minutes left of the first half, from just inside Irish territory, but the kick never had the legs and the teams went into the break still tied at 6-6.

Australia re-took the lead just four minutes into the second half when Lynagh slotted a penalty, and Keyes's immediate response from wide on the right was pulled horribly wide of the left post. However, Keyes's up-and-unders continued to create havoc in the Australian ranks and ten minutes into the second half a spell of Irish pressure ended with a simple drop goal by Keyes to tie the match up once again.

Australia raised their game to score their second try of the match. From a scrum on their left, quick ball, fast passing and the appearance of full back Marty Roebuck in the backline to create an overlap gave Campese a simple run in. A Lynagh conversion took the score out to 15-9, but there was still almost half-an-hour to play and while the Wallabies had the edge in territory, Ireland actually had slightly more possession.

Ireland increasingly tried to get Simon Geoghegan into the game, and the 22-year-old winger, who had made his Ireland debut in that season's Five Nations Championship to dramatic effect, scoring tries against Wales, England and Scotland, looked dangerous in attack whenever he was given any space in which to work. Geoghegan was a fantastic player to watch, a broken-field runner par excellence with pace to burn and a devastating sidestep. Former Ireland coach Eddie O'Sullivan described him as 'one of that rare group of players who could electrify the crowd'. Geoghegan won 37 caps, and it would have been a lot more but for persistent injury, in particular problems with a toe which forced his early retirement. Geoghegan scored 11 tries for his country, which sounds scant reward for such a talent but in truth he rarely got the ball in an era when Ireland were not all that strong and played a largely one-dimensional, ten-man game.

In this quarter-final he looked menacing whenever he got an opportunity, but that wasn't as often as he would have liked. His Australian counterpart was much the busier man: twice Campese was called on to force opposing winger Jack Clarke into touch when a missed tackle would have led to an Irish try, and on another occasion had to scramble back and kick out from behind his own line. That passage of play led to a penalty for offside, and Keyes kicked an easy three points to bring Ireland back within range again. Jason Little thought he had scored Australia's third try but was penalised for not releasing after a Geoghegan tackle – a decision which looked marginal at best since Little didn't appear to be held.

Ireland spent much of the next 15 minutes deep inside their own 22 but for the most part defended their line without too may alarms. And then they raised the siege in spectacular fashion. From an Irish scrum they moved the ball quickly for once and a clever Jim Staples kick through saw Clarke put pressure on Campese then hold the ball up for just long enough for the charging flanker Gordon Hamilton to arrive. Hamilton still had some 30 metres to go, but spurred on by the crowd and the adrenaline he had just enough to hold off the covering Bob Egerton who had had to come from the other wing. A jubilant Hamilton just sat there with an arm raised and a big grin on his face as Lansdowne Road erupted. Keyes's excellent kick from wide on the Irish left extended the lead to three points with less than five minutes to play.

A major shock was on the cards, but Australia stunned the whole of Ireland by not settling for a penalty or drop goal, which would have tied the match and brought extra time, instead looking for the try. Another simple but swift passing move from the back of a scrum, called by Lynagh, saw Campese hold off Clarke and while Brendan Mullin got across to stop the flying winger, Lynagh was on hand to seize the loose ball and just get over in the corner despite the attentions of Clarke. Lynagh couldn't add the extras, but Ireland had run out of time to respond.

'We came together [after Ireland had scored] and I tried to calm everyone down,' recalls Lynagh. 'I set out a straightforward plan which was to kick long from the restart, Ireland would kick it out and we would have a line-out. From there we would run the same move that had worked for us earlier in the match. Thankfully it all fell into place.'

A heartbreaking moment for Ireland. 'The lads gave everything that was asked of them,' said captain Philip Matthews. 'The gameplan that we wanted to play we more or less stuck to, considering the conditions. The support was tremendous and god I'm proud of each and every one of them, you know.'

'Ireland just didn't give up,' said Campese immediately after the game. 'That was 80 minutes of rugby! We knew what sort of team they are, every time they got in our half they put the pressure on.'

Geoghegan himself said, 'It was an incredible game. Campese scored that great early try when he came between the centres to touch down under the posts, but after that we played very well. We competed very well up front but in terms of moving the ball they were streets ahead of us. We could have won the game, and probably should have. When Gordon [Hamilton] scored with only six minutes to go, I think we would have beaten any other side in the world, but to be fair to the Australians they deserved to win because of their willingness to throw the ball around when they were under the cosh.'

'Cometh the hour, cometh the man,' was Australian coach Bob Dwyer's verdict. 'Interestingly the reserves, who were sitting in front of me, turned around and said, "We have enough time, we just have to do it right" That try put into perspective the philosophy that the team had developed – if you focus on performance and doing the small things well, the results will follow.'

For a young Irish team it meant an end to their World Cup adventure. A 24-15 defeat by Scotland at Murrayfield in their Pool 2 encounter had condemned them to second place despite comfortable enough wins over Zimbabwe (55-11) and Japan (32-16), and was probably an accurate reflection of where they stood at the time. Scotland were undoubtedly a stronger, more experienced team at that time and had beaten Ireland in that season's Five Nations Championships, also at Murrayfield, while Ireland had also lost at home to both England and France. However, Ireland had showed a marked improvement from the previous World Cup – which was the last time these two countries had met – when they had been beaten 33-15 in Sydney.

For Australia, it was onwards and upwards, though not without the mightiest of shocks. 'We were lulled into a false sense of security,' said Dwyer. 'We thought it would be an easy victory and we nearly paid for that thinking.'

26 October 1991
Venue: Murrayfield, Edinburgh
Attendance: 60,000

Scotland 6 England 9

Scotland	England
Gavin Hastings	Jon Webb
Tony Stanger	Simon Halliday
Scott Hastings	Will Carling (capt)
Sean Lineen	Jerry Guscott
Iwan Tukalo	Rory Underwood
Craig Chalmers	Rob Andrew
Gary Armstrong	Richard Hill
David Sole (capt)	Jason Leonard
John Allan	Brian Moore
Paul Burnell	Jeff Probyn
Chris Gray	Paul Ackford
Doddie Weir	Wade Dooley
John Jeffrey	Mickey Skinner
Finlay Calder	Peter Winterbottom
Derek White	Mike Teague

Scotland had looked mighty impressive in despatching the surprise package of the tournament, Western Samoa, in the quarter-finals. Winning Pool 2 had afforded them the privilege of remaining at Murrayfield for all their matches right up to the final, if they got that far, and also kept them away from the big guns of the Southern Hemisphere with Australia and New Zealand both on the other side of the draw.

With their fanatical support behind them and the growing belief that they had the ability to go all the way, Scotland had become a very difficult team to beat and proved that in the way they showed no fear against the rampaging Western Samoans in the first quarter-final. Having watched Wales lose to the Pacific Islanders and Australia be pushed all the way, Scotland were taking no chances. They varied their game beautifully, with half backs Gary Armstrong and Craig Chalmers orchestrating a mixture of kicks, passing and running moves to keep the Samoans off balance.

Even so it took until almost the half-hour mark before Scotland registered their first score, a try which came courtesy of a neat chip from Chalmers. There appeared to be little danger initially, with plenty of Samoans back covering but some indecision as to who would take control of the ball, combined with the effects of the wind, led to hesitation. Tony Stanger didn't hesitate and dived on the loose ball; Chalmers added the conversion.

The second try came from quick thinking by Armstrong, taking a free kick inside the Samoan 22 with a quick tap and letting his forwards drive on for John Jeffrey to score. It was a killer blow for Western Samoa, coming on the stroke of half-time, although Samoa did have the chance to strike back right at the start of the second half but instead of going for the try they really needed, they settled

49

for a drop goal from Steven Bachop which did little to bring them fully back into the game.

Scotland controlled the second half, affording Western Samoa few opportunities in attack, and then with seven minutes left to play, they put the result beyond all doubt. From a shortened line-out on the Scottish right, hooker John Allan drove at the heart of the Samoan midfield, quickly supported by the rest of the pack. A superb offload from captain David Sole kept the move going at pace and eventually Jeffrey went over for his second of the afternoon.

It was something of an anti-climax for Western Samoa after their heroics in their earlier games, but from the start there was a slight sense that they had already achieved what they set out to achieve. Scotland, for their part, had clearly come into the game prepared – no surprise for a team coached by the great Ian McGeechan who had said beforehand, 'We have done our homework on them.'

So to the semi-final and a visit from the Auld Enemy south of the border with the ultimate prize at stake: a place in the Rugby World Cup Final.

The Scottish team was led out by John Jeffrey, who had announced his intention to retire at the end of the tournament and hence was making his final appearance at Murrayfield, win or lose (the final was at Twickenham, the third place play-off in Cardiff). After the preliminaries were over, Rob Andrew kicked off and the game which would see a Northern Hemisphere team reach the World Cup Final again got under way.

It was a cagey affair, with neither side attempting too much in the way of creative play, but the occasion, and the reward, lent it an air of intensity throughout, as did the uncertainty as to who would be the victors. England won an early penalty through the driving play of their forwards, but full back Jonathan Webb missed from wide on the left from just fractionally outside the 22. England continued to apply most of the early pressure with Scotland rarely far outside their own 22 and having to defend a number of scrums and line-outs but from their very first excursion into the England half with ball in hand they earned a penalty and Gavin Hastings gave his side the lead.

Scotland's gameplan was clear to see, as they tried to keep the ball on the park and on the move, knowing that they weren't going to win many of the line-outs or scrums on England ball, whereas England were very happy to play the percentages and make the most of their traditional strengths. A huge clearance kick from Will Carling forced a hurried response from Hastings and after a couple of line-outs England won a penalty when Finlay Calder went offside; Webb once again missed a kick which should have been pretty routine for an international kicker.

It meant that England were getting little tangible reward for all their forward dominance, and in turn gave Scotland the encouragement that they could compete. The score was still just 3-0 at the end of the first quarter, with play largely taking place between the two ten-metre lines, although there was one occasion just before the half-hour when a great kick from Hastings saw Webb caught in possession by Iwan Tukalo resulting in a scrum deep in England territory. Once more the England pack took charge, though, scragging Armstrong as he attempted to clear up at the back of a messy scrum and forcing a turnover.

Hastings extended the Scotland lead to 6-0 just on the half-hour after Jeff Probyn was penalised for tackling David Sole without the ball at a line-out, but England pulled it back almost immediately. Rob Andrew kicked off, the ball was touched down for a 22 drop-out and then Derek White got in front of the kicker to give England a scrum, which they drove forward dynamically to win a penalty right in front of the posts. And that's how it stayed until half-time, despite a late and rather feeble effort at a drop goal from Chalmers.

The half-time figures showed a 50-50 split in terms of territory, with England ahead 57 per cent to 43 per cent on the possession stats. Chalmers tried a left-footed drop goal early in the second half which barely got off the ground and provoked a certain amount of jocularity in the stands and commentary box. England continued to hold the advantage in all the set plays but couldn't make it count on the scoreboard until one of the few flowing moves they managed to put together was stopped only by the Scots coming up offside, but Webb missed another simple kick.

From the very next passage of play, Webb had yet another chance, his fifth of the game, from the ten-metre line but pretty straight and yet again he missed. Webb, who had had a perfectly respectable 70 per cent success rate going into the game, was now one from five and his continued misses were in danger of costing his team a game which they were largely dominating. A beautiful kick from Rob Andrew into the corner gave the England pack the chance to rumble forward and gain the put in to a scrum just a few metres out. This resulted in a penalty so simple that even Webb could not miss, and the scores were tied at 6-6, 17 minutes into the second half.

Gordon Brown, working as a co-commentator for TV, complimented the 'awesome' power of the England front five, but still they could not put daylight between them and their tenacious opponents. Shortly after the hour, Scotland looked to have benefited from a dummy run in front of the ball only to win the penalty a moment later when England killed the ball. The kick was only 20 metres out, just to the right (from the Scotland standpoint) of the England posts and a 'gimme' for a kicker of Hastings's ability. He sliced it wide. And the whole of Murrayfield gasped, and put their collective heads in their hands.

Did Hastings's miss give England renewed belief? Possibly, though of course if their kicker had been performing to his usual standards they would have been two scores clear anyway by that point. They certainly charged forward, and won a scrum just inside the Scotland 22, but an accidental offside swiftly reversed the put-in and enabled Scotland to clear their lines. As the match got tenser, so the mistakes multiplied, with a plethora of knock-ons and misplaced kicks; England had probably the best chance when a switch of direction from Andrew gave Brian Moore a bit of space and Moore set Rory Underwood away down the left. With just inches to work in, Underwood beat Stanger, Weir and Armstrong and was almost at the corner flag before he was put into touch by Calder.

From the five-metre scrum, England tried to drive over but Scotland artfully pulled it down so Mike Teague picked up and tried to go, but was held up by Jeffrey. Another scrum, another wheel, so England came up with an alternative plan – quick ball from Hill to Andrew and a drop goal, calm as you like, right between the posts.

England led for the first time in the match, and though Scotland still had some eight or nine minutes to hit back they found themselves largely pinned down deep inside their own half and under huge pressure. England denied Scotland any semblance of an opportunity in those last few minutes, and in fact looked more likely to score again than they did to concede one. As Brown pointed out, Scotland looked 'dead on their feet'; coping with the England forward power had drained them and they could do nothing to muster one last chance.

It was horribly unfair that a player who had been Scotland's player of the tournament, one of the players of the year and whose standout performance had been largely responsible for Scotland's impressive win over Western Samoa in the quarter-finals was the one to miss such a crucial kick. Hastings was a fantastic player and has turned into an excellent ambassador for the sport, always willing to talk to fans and media alike; he deserved better from the biggest match of his career, though in truth England were worthy winners and would have been out of sight much earlier in the match had they kicked their goals.

Much was made at the time of England's limited gameplan, with McGeechan saying, 'England wanted to strangle the game; we wanted to keep it alive,' and New Zealand coach John Hart going much further in describing it as 'the ruination of rugby'.

England hooker Brian Moore defended his team when he was captured in the dressing room after the semi-final win, saying, 'Their whinge will be that we killed the game again, that we did nothing to contribute to a running game. There again, who gives a damn. Why do we have a responsibility to anyone else? If we were the [All] Blacks, they'd have said "awesome display of scrummaging power".'

Not for the first or last time, Moore had raised a very valid question as to whether a team, any team, has some sort of amorphous wider responsibility to the game. In the context of a World Cup semi-final, the answer surely has to be that they do not.

2 November 1991
Venue: Twickenham, London
Attendance: 56,208

England 6 Australia 12

England	Australia
Jon Webb	Marty Roebuck
Simon Halliday	David Campese
Will Carling (capt)	Jason Little
Jerry Guscott	Tim Horan
Rory Underwood	Bob Egerton
Rob Andrew	Michael Lynagh
Richard Hill	Nick Farr-Jones (capt)
Jason Leonard	Tony Daly
Brian Moore	Phil Kearns
Jeff Probyn	Ewen McKenzie
Paul Ackford	Rod McCall
Wade Dooley	John Eales
Mickey Skinner	Simon Poidevin
Peter Winterbottom	Willie Ofahengaue
Mike Teague	Troy Coker

Most casual observers, and many rugby fans, would have expected New Zealand to be lining up against England following their heavyweight Southern Hemisphere semi-final clash with Australia.

In many eyes, the defending champions were nigh-on unbeatable and had already recorded one win over England in the 1991 tournament whereas Australia had struggled past Western Samoa and almost suffered a shock defeat by Ireland. But the clues to an Australian victory were there if you dug a little deeper – in the two Bledisloe Cup matches between the nations that August, Australia had won 21-12 in Sydney before losing 6-3 in Auckland a fortnight later. Although the split series was sufficient for the Cup to remain in New Zealand hands, it showed that Australia weren't afraid of their more illustrious rivals.

Furthermore, there hadn't been the same buzz around the New Zealand camp as there was four years earlier. For a start, they seemed to have little rapport with the media or the fans and when they arrived in Dublin for the semi-final, they offered a stark contrast to the popular Australians who, despite knocking out the home team, went to great lengths to engage the locals. The Wallabies trained at Trinity College, located right in the heart of the city, and skipper Nick Farr-Jones, despite being injured early in the quarter-final against Ireland, allowed himself to be pictured with a pint of Guinness.

The All Blacks, on the other hand, appeared charmless and Vincent Hogan memorably wrote in the *Irish Independent*, 'They strolled into town with all the charmlessness of old. Frowns of stone, eyes glazed with frosty indifference, All Black teams have never been known for courting niceties. They carry themselves with the gaiety of gravediggers.'

Of course, it would have been quite reasonable for the All Blacks to respond that they were in Ireland for only a week, they had come to do a job and, once done, they would be on their way. But the malaise appeared to run deeper than that. From the start there were tensions in the New Zealand camp, caused primarily by the friction between their co-coaches. The New Zealand Rugby Union had seen fit, in its wisdom, to appoint John Hart alongside the incumbent Alex Wyllie in spite of the fact that they were polar opposites in terms of both character and approach. As the players' loyalty splintered and divided into two camps, it was clear that an error had been made – it is one of the very few times that New Zealand rugby has been divided in such a way, and it was to cost them their World Cup trophy.

It still took a momentous performance from Australia to defeat them, one which Michael Lynagh has since called 'one of the best 40 minutes of rugby we have played as a team in that first half. We were clinical, we took every opportunity against a very, very good side and went up to a pretty comfortable lead at half-time.'

David Campese was the star of the show, scoring one try after just seven minutes with an electric burst of pace and making the other for centre Tim Horan with a blind flip pass. With Lynagh converting and adding a penalty, it was 13-0 and New Zealand were playing catch-up from early on, and for once fell short. 'We probably had the best 20 minutes of Australian rugby, ever,' said Horan.

England, by contrast, had come through two huge physical battles, both away from home, against France in the quarter-finals at the Parc des Princes and Scotland in the semi-finals at Murrayfield. Would another away game have suited the England bunker mentality better? Possibly. Assailed on all sides by comments in the media and from opposing players and coaches – the Scottish players pathetically even turned up at Twickenham in kilts and Australian scarves and hats, Moore pithily commenting that perhaps Scotland hated the England team 'because we have figured out how to beat them consistently' – England took the fateful decision to play a more expansive game.

Were they influenced by all the negativity? It's impossible to say. Captain Will Carling claims that the players were all in agreement with the decision to change the strategy, whereas Brian Moore says that many of the forwards had serious reservations about it. But the management team of Roger Uttley and Geoff Cooke felt it was the way to go, particularly in light of that summer's defeat by Australia when they had been hammered 40-15 in Sydney.

Second row Paul Ackford recalled the impact of that result in Gerald Davies's *World Cup: Rugby's Battle of the Giants*, 'If the margin of defeat was bad enough, the manner was worse. We could not cope with the pace and continuity of the Australians and we could not dominate the ball for long enough to get our own style of game going. The next day we gathered in the team room for a debrief… we resolved that if we ever met Australia again we would match them for speed and ingenuity.

'The mistake we made was not to play that way from the start of the competition. In the group games and for the quarter-final and semi-final we reverted to type: catch and drive, bang up the middle, regroup, inch forward, secure the scrum and begin the whole process again. It had worked six months previously during the grand slam campaign and it worked once more. When it came to the big day we found we could not transfer the excellence of the unopposed training sessions to the intensity of a live match. Passes were dropped, opportunities went begging. Around half-time, when we started to get on top of the big Aussie forwards, we should have thrown the running rugby option out of the window.'

'History shows we made a mistake,' said Andrew. 'We should have stuck with the way we played the previous 18 months. If we'd focused on our normal game from the start, we would have been too strong for Australia. We still nearly beat them playing what was in effect an alien game for us.'

'We actually made more chances than them,' said Carling. 'We just weren't precise enough in finishing our chances off. There's a lot of talk about if we'd played a tight game, we would have won. I'm not sure I agree with that, we played a game which gave ourselves the opportunity to win the game, we just didn't take those chances.'

Remarkably, there was no score in the first quarter of the final. England had most of the possession and were winning plenty of ball but could not find a way through the Australian defence. In the 26th minute Lynagh slotted home a penalty and just four minutes after that Australia scored what was to prove the only try of the match. For once the Australian line-out operation got the upper hand, and the mighty Willie Ofahengaue burst through the England defences.

The Wallaby forwards managed to get up in support of the giant back-rower and forced their way over the line, with prop Tony Daly being awarded the score. Lynagh converted to put the Australians 9-0 up, and that was the way it stayed until half-time.

Finally on the hour England full back Jon Webb kicked his team's first points, but Lynagh restored the Australian lead to nine points in the 65th minute, and that was the way it remained going into the final ten minutes. England were still running the ball at every opportunity, however, and from one such occasion they created an overlap, which Campese prevented them utilising only by a deliberate knock-on of what might have been the scoring pass. Welsh referee Derek Bevan opted to award a penalty rather than a penalty try, and Webb calmly slotted home to narrow the gap to 12-6, but their best chance of a try had gone.

To this day there is a difference of opinion as to how vital that moment was. Nick Farr-Jones, who a few minutes later was holding the Webb Ellis trophy for his team, said, 'I can't believe people still go on about that, insisting that Campo cost Underwood the score. I don't know why as there's no way Underwood would have scored. He still had miles to cover and the defence would have got across.'

Maybe Farr-Jones wasn't fully au fait with the speed of the England wing; on replays it certainly looks more than possible that Underwood would have got over in the corner, although it should be pointed out that even if England had scored a try, and Webb had converted it, they would still have been behind with little more than five minutes left to play.

Moore's typically incisive view was, 'Campese has gone through this tournament telling everyone that he is the saviour of rugby but he proved today he is as cynical as the rest of us. There is no way that Rory would not have scored.'

David Miller, writing in *The Times*, admitted, 'I prefer watching Campese to listening to him. Having told England for a fortnight how to play, he then deliberately knocked on and proceeded to say afterwards that "attacking play doesn't win in rugby, defence does". Amid a splendid bunch, he was a shade too smug.'

Clearly it is hard to make an objective decision, but Bevan got his call right, I think. For all Underwood's pace, the play was too far from the Australian line for a referee to say that a try would 'probably' have been scored. 'Nobody in our team said a lot about it at the time,' agreed Rob Andrew. It is beyond dispute, though, that Campese's offence would be a yellow card every day of the week since that sanction was introduced.

The Twickenham crowd continued to offer unstinting support, and England continued to batter at the Australian door for the remaining minutes of the match, but they could not breach the defences. 'At the end, the team was exhausted,' said Farr-Jones. 'Against the All Blacks we felt we could have gone on another 40 minutes but England ran at us so many times, we had to make so many tackles, that it was a far more tiring game. I just lay in the bath for 20 minutes afterwards. I was so absolutely exhausted.'

'They definitely took us by surprise,' agreed John Eales, 'but when you're out there on the field you just play what's in front of you. A World Cup Final goes just like that, very quickly. Afterwards I just remember this overwhelming feeling of exhaustion, I sat down in a chair and just melted into it, it was all I could do.'

Australia had the best rugby team in 1991; they also had the best coach. Bob Dwyer was years ahead of his time and almost as soon as he took over from Alan Jones, in 1988, he had started to introduce a comprehensive programme covering conditioning, diet and psychology. He also took a more scientific approach – rather than just saying 'we must score' he encouraged players to work out what they needed to do to score, then execute that plan.

Although the world-renowned Australian Institute of Sport had opened in 1981, its rugby programme, centred on Brisbane, Sydney and Canberra, had only begun in 1988, but its impact was felt almost immediately. It enabled the rugby players to benefit from the input of experts in a number of fields, and to break a game of rugby down into its constituent parts and improve them little by little.

So it was that Australia finished the final behind on many of the stats, including possession and territory, but ahead on the only one that matters – the scoreboard. If they were a trifle fortunate in the final itself, they were undoubtedly worthy winners of the second Rugby World Cup.

25 May 1995
Venue: Newlands, Cape Town
Attendance: 51,000

South Africa 27 Australia 18

South Africa	Australia
Andre Joubert	Matt Pini
James Small	David Campese
Japie Mulder	Jason Little
Hennie le Roux	Dan Herbert
Pieter Hendriks	Damian Smith
Joel Stransky	Michael Lynagh (capt)
Joost van der Westhuizen	George Gregan
Os du Randt	Dan Crowley
James Dalton	Phil Kearns
Balie Swart	Ewen McKenzie
Mark Andrews	Rod McCall
Hannes Strydom	John Eales
Francois Pienaar (capt)	David Wilson
Ruben Kruger	Willie Ofahengaue
Rudolf Straeuli	Tim Gavin

Since the Rugby World Cup had started, siren voices from South Africa had been decrying its validity in the absence of the Springboks from the party. In 1991 some of their fans had even erected a banner reading 'You Are Not World Champions Until You Have Beaten The Springboks', a stance which was – and was designed to be – provocative.

It wasn't a stance borne out by the facts – since their re-admittance in 1992 South Africa had played four Tests against New Zealand and four against Australia posting just a solitary win, one draw and six defeats, three by each country. They had also been well beaten at Twickenham in a one-off Test, 33-16.

In any case, whatever South Africa's on-field claims of superiority, they had been prevented from competing not by some unreasonable attempt to keep them from winning, much less an outside agency, but because their abhorrent apartheid policies demanded their exclusion. Staggeringly is was a theme to which Louis Luyt, the unloved president of the South African Rugby Football Union, gracelessly returned at the post-final dinner. Having claimed that the cup was now in the hands of those to whom it rightly belonged, he added, 'We boasted in 1987 that the real World Cup could not be won in New Zealand because we were not there. It was the same in England in 1991. In 1995 we have proved that if we were there we would win.'

The All Blacks got up and walked out. It was an unsavoury end to the third Rugby World Cup, but fortunately what had gone before that moment was sufficient, just, to make up for it.

It had taken a giant leap of faith to award South Africa the 1995 Rugby World Cup. The decision was taken early in 1992 and the IRB then watched as violence engulfed the country – to the extent that little-known contingency plans had been drawn up by the governing body in case it was deemed too unsafe to take the tournament to South Africa.

Fortunately from the opening ceremony, which hit just the right note and at which the new national anthem 'Nkosi Sikelel iAfrika', or 'God Bless Africa', was sung by all with gusto, the Rugby World Cup 1995 was a triumph.

Of note is the fact that Australia fielded eight of the same players who took the field for the World Cup Final four years earlier, while Tim Horan, Troy Coker and Tony Daly were also all still part of the squad for South Africa 1995 but didn't play in the opening match for a variety of reasons. In the case of Horan, of course, this was because he was still recovering from more than a year out with a career-threatening knee injury. Of the 1991 winning team, back-row player Simon Poidevin had retired in the aftermath of that victory; full back Marty Roebuck and captain and scrum half Nick Farr-Jones had played on for a couple more years but decided another World Cup was a step too far.

Their replacements were not to be sniffed at, however. The full back slot saw Matt Pini and Matt Burke vying for the honours; the back row spot had gone to David Wilson, who came into the side in the summer of 1992 and would go on to make 79 international appearances; and the irreplaceable Farr-Jones had been replaced – it may have only been George Gregan's seventh cap, but he was to win a further 132 over the subsequent 12 years playing for his country. Bob Dwyer was still in charge too, and if little was known about him in 1991, by 1995 he was widely acclaimed as a visionary mastermind whose thinking was some way ahead of the game and who was constantly on the lookout for ways and means to improve his team.

In another coincidental note, the referee for the opening game was the highly respected Derek Bevan, who had officiated the final four years earlier.

It swiftly became apparent that South Africa had learnt fast from the defeats they had suffered since their return to the rugby fraternity. Having looked off the pace and one-dimensional, initially, they were a different beast in this opening match: dynamic and forceful, they brushed the defending champions aside, not quite with ease but powerfully and unrelentingly.

Not that it looked that way from the start. Indeed, Australia had the better of the opening exchanges and looked to be patiently building a platform while relying on the solidity of their defence to hold the Springboks at bay. An early exchange of penalties between Lynagh and Stransky, both for offside offences, were matched by another for each team, although in between Lynagh also missed a relatively simple one. The Australian line-out was supreme, over the course of the game they would win 22 to the Springboks' four, and that was the starting point for their first try.

When quick ruck ball from Gregan gave Lynagh time and space from just a few metres out, the fly half sold the whole South African defence a dummy and scooted over. He converted his own try – now worth five points, an increase introduced in April 1992 – to give Australia a 13-9 lead, the sort of margin they comfortably built on throughout their 1991 campaign when only three tries were scored against them in the entire competition, two by Argentina and one by Ireland.

On this occasion, however, South Africa upped the tempo and began to win a lot of loose ball in midfield, and suddenly Australia started to look rattled. Gregan was harried throughout, in particular by Ruben Kruger, a fantastic openside flanker who might well have been talked about as one of the all-time greats had he had more luck. Kruger, later named South African Player of the Year for 1995, suffered a broken leg the year after the 1995 RWC but fought back to play in the 1997 Test series against the British & Irish Lions, and was selected for the 1999 squad. Less than a year after the 1999 tournament, Kruger was diagnosed with a brain tumour and despite a couple of operations which seemed successful at the time, the tumour kept returning until, in 2010, it finally defeated him a couple of months before his 40th birthday.

South Africa re-took the lead when equally quick ruck ball on the South African right saw fly half Joel Stransky launch his back line swiftly and with both wingers suddenly appearing in the line, the Boks created an overlap for Pieter Hendriks, in for the injured Chester Williams, which he ran in for the simplest of tries. David Campese looked somewhat less interested in tackling his opposing winger than he did when running his own ball.

Into the second half and South Africa kept piling on the relentless pressure until from a five-metre scrum number eight Rudolf Straeuli picked up, gave a short pass to scrum half Joost van der Westhuizen and he turned it back inside for Stransky, running the angle to cut back and go over for a try which he converted himself to bring his personal tally up to 22 points.

Australia weren't finished and hit back with a try from hooker Phil Kearns, when Lynagh produced a lovely floated pass over the top of the South African rush defence for Kearns – hanging disreputably wide on the left, no doubt fellow hookers Brian Moore and Sean Fitzpatrick would have had a quiet word with him later as to what he was doing out there – to jog over. Despite Kearns getting right round under the posts, however, Lynagh missed a simple conversion which would have brought Australia back within a converted try of South Africa with about ten minutes to go. Instead the game rather fizzled out as the Australian midfield could make little impression in attack.

'Our concentration went,' lamented Dwyer after the game. 'We had trained so well but when we got out on the pitch we forgot all our training. Why we reacted the way we did, we'll never know for sure but by the end we did well to keep the score as close as we did.'

South Africa captain Francois Pienaar explained it thus, 'I think we were a bit more hungry than them. Some of their players faltered when we put pressure on them. When we ran out on to the field it was an unbelievable atmosphere and you knew the emotion around the whole occasion extended beyond the ground and across the whole country. We have improved since 1992 and we can improve some more.'

The rest of Pool A consisted of Romania and Canada, the latter particularly unlucky in that after their efforts in 1991 had earned them a place among the top eight seeds, they should nonetheless be drawn in a pool containing both the hosts and the holders (such a situation arose of course because South Africa weren't seeded having not previously taken part in the Rugby World Cup). Canada were once again to prove awkward opponents, but despite opening with a 34-3 victory over Romania, they weren't quite able to challenge either of the big two, losing 11-27 to Australia before finishing with a 20-0 defeat by South Africa.

This game, however, was the notorious Battle of Boet Erasmus. South Africa had very deliberately decided on a policy of fielding a second string team against Romania and Canada, though for the latter game coach Kitch Christie did draft in his captain, Pienaar. Whether the physical Canadians found this disrespectful or whether the second string South Africans felt they had something to prove, who knows. 'If they feel they'll walk all over us, then as captain I'm delighted,' said Gareth Rees in the build-up to the game. 'We'll find out if they've made a mistake.'

Whatever the cause, it proved to be a combustible mix which finally boiled over in the 70th minute. When Hendriks tackled fellow winger Winston Stanley it was more of a shoulder charge than a tackle, which sent Stanley into the hoardings. Canadian full back Scott Stewart took exception and ran in from some distance away and struck Hendricks from behind. Before Irish referee David McHugh could regain control of the situation, it had kicked off. James Dalton was the next on the scene and took out Stewart and then it rapidly became a free-for-all.

Once the dust had finally died down, McHugh seemed to have little idea where the real blame lay and sent off Rees and Rod Snow for Canada and Dalton for South Africa. Stewart undoubtedly should have joined them, as should South Africa replacement Hennie le Roux who can clearly be seen on the video throwing, and landing, several big punches. Hendriks could have gone too, for a combination of the original no-arms high tackle and for clearly kicking in the ensuing dust-up. Hendriks and Stewart were cited and later suspended for 90 and 60 days respectively. 'There were guys on our side who were at fault,' admitted Rees, 'but [the referee] completely missed the real culprits.'

Little remorse was shown by either side, with Rees declaring that he didn't regret getting involved while Christie tried to imply that the entire incident could be blamed on Stewart. 'You have to blame the third guy who came into the tussle, it was he who started the whole incident,' said Christie, ignoring the illegality of the original tackle.

'I couldn't believe that two of our players had gone and only one of theirs,' said Rees, which seems a less one-eyed take on events.

Victory confirmed South Africa as group winners, affording them an easier passage to the final whereas Australia now faced a quarter-final against their opponents in the 1991 final, England.

4 June 1995
Venue: Ellis Park, Johannesburg
Attendance: 35,000

Ireland 24 Wales 23

Ireland	Wales
Conor O'Shea	Tony Clement
Richard Wallace	Ieuan Evans
Brendan Mullin	Mike Hall (capt)
Jonathan Bell	Neil Jenkins
Simon Geoghegan	Gareth Thomas
Eric Elwood	Adrian Davies
Niall Hogan	Robert Jones
Nick Popplewell	Mike Griffiths
Terry Kingston (capt)	Jonathan Humphreys
Gary Halpin	John Davies
Gabriel Fulcher	Derwyn Jones
Neil Francis	Gareth Llewellyn
David Corkery	Stuart Davies
Denis McBride	Hemi Taylor
Paddy Johns	Emyr Lewis

Welsh rugby was experiencing a torrid time in the early and mid-1990s. Not only had the team failed to make the quarter-finals of the 1991 Rugby World Cup, but they had had a disappointing few seasons in the Five Nations Championship – fourth place with two wins in 1992, just one win (over England at home) and bottom place in the 1993 edition, and bottom again without a win in 1995. It all made victory in 1994, when they somehow topped the table with three wins out of four, look more of an anomaly than a revival.

Furthermore, their defeat by Western Samoa in the 1991 Rugby World Cup had condemned Wales to playing in the qualifying competition – the first Tier 1 nation that had had to suffer such an indignity. The first stage of qualifying saw Wales record big victories over Portugal (102-11) and Spain (54-0), and that at least ensured they would be at the 1995 World Cup. The final stage of qualifying was actually to determine which of Wales, Italy and Romania went into which group, and again Wales won both their matches. Not without the odd scare, however, as Romania pushed them to 16-9 and Italy to 29-19, despite Wales being at home on both occasions.

It was with a sigh of relief, then, that Wales lined up as 'Europe 1', in Pool C, where they would face New Zealand, Ireland and Japan. Even six months before the tournament started (which is when the European qualifiers were completed), it looked likely that the Ireland v Wales clash would be for second place in the group, and so it turned out.

Ireland had problems of their own. In spite of their laudable efforts to upset Australia at the quarter-final stage of the 1991 RWC, Ireland had finished rock bottom in the 1992 Five Nations, without a win, and although they had improved slightly to finish mid-table in 1993 (with two wins and two losses), they slipped to fourth in 1994 (when their only win came courtesy of a Simon Geoghegan try at Twickenham) and stayed in that position in 1995. Earlier that year a 16-12 win in Cardiff was Ireland's only victory in the Five Nations, and both teams' uncertainties were reflected in the number of changes they made between that March Five Nations clash and this one in Johannesburg less than three months later.

Wales retained just seven of the players who started the Five Nations match and of them one, Neil Jenkins, was moved from his regular spot at fly half into the centre. It was an experiment which had been tried on six occasions prior to the RWC but not for some 18 months and never again afterwards. Jenkins did play full back at times, most notably on the 1997 British & Irish Lions tour to South Africa, but never looked comfortable at inside centre. Wales were fielding different combinations in the front, second and back rows of the scrum, though it is only fair to point out that none of these players were wholly new faces, to the squad or the team.

Ireland had only changed five of their starting line-up, but nevertheless they too had different combinations in all three rows of the scrum from the March encounter. In Cardiff much of the damage had been done by Paul Burke, who had converted Brendan Mullin's try, kicked two penalties and added a drop goal for good measure. But Burke now found himself on the bench and Eric Elwood promoted in his place.

Perhaps that was why the match was so fractured and unsatisfactory. It got off to a blistering start when a high, hanging kick-off from Elwood was gathered in by his pack and they nearly drove over. The play ended with a penalty to Ireland, but Elwood missed it. No matter, just a few minutes later, from a line-out a few metres from the Welsh line, a solid catch by Neil Francis enabled Ireland to set up a rolling maul which quickly saw prop Nick Popplewell dip over. Elwood converted with just over five minutes on the clock.

It got even better for Ireland on 13 minutes when back row forward Denis McBride scored. The move began with another line-out, this time just past the Wales ten-metre line, when McBride ended up with the ball in his hands and he took the chance to run fast straight at the Welsh midfield defence. Although the Irish pack were quickly up in support, it appeared as if there was no way through for McBride, but suddenly he broke free and just sprinted over the line. With the ball placed right in between the posts, the conversion was once again easy pickings for Elwood.

But Ireland didn't score again for almost an hour, and Wales chipped away at the lead through two Jenkins penalties, sandwiching a drop goal from Adrian Davies, the man who was playing fly half instead of Jenkins. At 14-9 to Ireland a scrum inside the Welsh 22 led to several phases; at one point it appeared that the ball had been knocked by back row blood replacement Eddie Halvey when he was tackled on but nothing was given and Ireland were allowed to reclaim the ball and keep pressing forward. Eventually a break from Paddy Johns saw Halvey himself up in support for his first try for his country, just to the left of the posts. Elwood once more added the extras.

At 21-9 and with under ten minutes to play, surely it was game over. Except it wasn't. Wales threw caution to the wind and a moment of quick thinking from former captain Ieuan Evans gave them a glimmer of hope. Evans set Tony Clements away and the full back broke clear to put hooker Jonathan Humphreys in under the posts. Jenkins converted to make it 21-16. Suddenly Wales, for all the fact that they had been totally outplayed in the first quarter of the match, had the scent of victory. That appeared to have been snuffed out by an Elwood penalty, but again Wales fought back and Hemi Taylor went over for a second try, converted by Jenkins. Unfortunately for Wales, they had left it too late for a comeback and fell one point short.

Although both countries had dismissed Japan without undue alarm, neither had made a huge impression on New Zealand, but at least second place in the group gave Ireland a shot at the French in the quarter-finals – although the 25-7 defeat at Lansdowne Road, in Ireland, in the Five Nations match that March scarcely gave them much cause for comfort.

For Wales the future looked as bleak as the immediate past. A second successive defeat in the group stages was seen as a disaster, though at least Wales would be spared the indignity of having to play in the qualifying tournament again by dint of the fact that they were hosting the 1999 World Cup. The problem for Wales was that they were haemorrhaging players to rugby league where they got paid for their endeavours.

However, the union game was finally waking up to the challenge of professionalism. The threat posed in the Southern Hemisphere, and particularly Australia, was two-fold: the massive popularity of rugby league's Super League competition meant that large salaries were on offer, and a Sydney-based group calling itself the World Rugby Corporation was planning to implement a global professional game.

How far along the plans of the World Rugby Corporation had gone is open to dispute, but that they were potentially serious players is not. Notable Australian businessmen and entrepreneurs Ross Turnbull (also a former player) and John Singleton were involved alongside lawyer Geoff Levy. Kerry Packer was backing the idea and he certainly had form, having been behind the 1970s transformation of cricket with the introduction of the one-day game. In response to the growing threats, the Southern Hemisphere banded together to form SANZAR (South Africa, New Zealand and Australia Rugby), which would administer both Super Rugby and the Tri Nations competition – the Rugby Championship as it's now known, and include Argentina.

What began as a counter-measure to those dual threats morphed, probably inevitably, into a move to make the game open, and professional. It wasn't until 26 August 1995 that the International Rugby Board declared rugby union would henceforth be an 'open' game and all restrictions on players earning money either from playing or for complementary activities (such as sponsorship, advertising, endorsements, after-dinner speaking and so on) were removed. Whether the IRB would have taken such a step without the immediate threat of the union game collapsing in Australia is a matter of conjecture, but it levelled the playing field somewhat among the bigger nations (the Southern Hemisphere had always appeared to have a somewhat more relaxed, some would say 'enlightened' attitude to off-field earnings) and removed the threat of large-scale defection to either WRC or rugby league.

There was, and is, a question mark over whether the move to an open game has benefited the smaller nations in the same way. Arguably, it makes it even harder for those countries where there isn't a fully realised professional structure to compete. It has also led to talented individual players seeking fame and fortune in countries where the clubs can afford to recompense them, a theme of which more later.

Ironically, News Corporation (Rupert Murdoch's media organisation), which was backing Super League, signed a ten-year deal for exclusive broadcasting rights to both Super Rugby and the Tri Nations, starting with the 1996 season. The broadcast deal was announced on the eve of the 1995 World Cup Final, and it heralded a new age for the sport, one which would profoundly affect both the club and international scene in both the Northern and Southern Hemispheres. It would also enable Wales to become a competitive force once more, through the introduction of regional rugby (at the cost of the famous Welsh clubs of yore) and, latterly, dual contracts whereby the best players are part-funded by the Welsh Rugby Union so they can afford to stay in – or return to – Wales.

But all that was of little consolation in the immediate aftermath of this defeat by Ireland.

4 June 1995
Venue: Free State Stadium, Bloemfontein
Attendance: 25,000

Japan 17 New Zealand 145

Japan	New Zealand
Tsutomu Matsuda	Glen Osborne
Lopeti Oto	Jeff Wilson
Akira Yoshida	Marc Ellis
Yukio Motoki	Alama Ieremia
Yoshihito Yoshida	Eric Rush
Keiji Hirose	Simon Culhane
Watara Murata	Ant Strachan
Osamu Ota	Craig Dowd
Masahiro Kunda (capt)	Norm Hewitt
Kazuaki Takahashi	Richard Loe
Yoshihiko Sakuraba	Robin Brooke
Bruce Ferguson	Blair Larsen
Hiroyuki Kajihara	Kevin Schuler
Ko Izawa-Nakamura	Paul Henderson (capt)
Sinali-Tui Latu	Zinzan Brooke

With wins over Ireland (43-19) and Wales (34-9) already recorded, New Zealand could afford to take their foot off the pedal somewhat for their third group game, against Japan, and give the rest of their squad a run out. That is not the New Zealand way, however, and while only four of the starting XV against Ireland in the first match of the tournament also began against Japan, all six of the bench reserves from that first game were in the line-up and while the first-choice centre pairing of Frank Bunce and Walter Little were given the afternoon off, more than a few countries would have been happy to field their replacements – Marc Ellis and Alama Ieremia.

Jonah Lomu, of whom more later, was also given a break from wing duty, with Eric Rush taking his place. Rush only won nine caps for the All Blacks in the 15-man game, the emergence of Lomu effectively limiting his opportunities, but he was a legend on the Sevens circuit where he frequently captained the team to success, including the 1998 Commonwealth gold medal in Kuala Lumpur and the 2001 World Cup Sevens title, not to mention winning the World Sevens Series for the first six years after it had been introduced in 1999. Rush broke a leg in New Zealand's last group match in that 2001 competition, but fought back and won a second Commonwealth gold medal at the Manchester Games in 2002. His initial success came as a winger, but he later switched to playing as a forward, where he was equally proficient and he remains a respected and popular figure within the sport.

At half back there were rare outings for Ant Strachan, who played 11 times for the All Blacks, the last of which was the 1995 World Cup Final, and Simon Culhane, who had a solid club career with Southland but could never force his way past Andrew Mehrtens for the international side. More significantly, the great Zinzan Brooke was back at number eight having missed the first two group games through an Achilles tendon injury which had seen him sidelined for six weeks.

So for all the changes the All Black management team, headed by Laurie Mains, had made, it was still a pretty strong-looking team which took the field for the third and final group game against Japan.

Culhane kicked off and from Tsutomu Matsuda's clearance to just beyond his 22, New Zealand quickly moved the ball, Rush made inroads coming in off his wing on the left, and when the ball was moved from the resulting ruck, Rush had somehow extricated himself in time to get over to the right of midfield and make the extra man. The hint of a dummy and he was over under the posts with less than two minutes on the clock. Culhane kicked the conversion.

From the restart, Japan showed how they intended to play, running everything and trying not to get bogged down in the set piece. They even came close to scoring down their left, but Jeff Wilson just got a hand in to prevent what would have been the try-scoring pass. Full back Glen Osborne made a lot of ground on the counter attack and the ball was worked to Ieremia in the centres and he broke the tackle to keep the All Blacks on the front foot and cause panic in the Japanese ranks. The All Blacks were at the breakdown quickly and in numbers and formed a wedge which drove over with prop Richard Loe coming up with the ball. There were only just over six minutes on the clock when Culhane slotted his second conversion.

New Zealand's third try came from a simple hand-off and break in the centres by Marc Ellis. Suddenly there was clear space in front of him and Ellis easily had the pace to get home. Ellis's run did feature a superb sidestep off his left foot to fool Matsuda, but it's easier to pull that off in acres of space than in a tight corner, and Ellis had all the space in the world. It was 21-0 by the tenth minute.

Even when Japan managed to mess up a New Zealand scrum, Zinzan Brooke was still able to pick the ball up and hold off the tacklers until the support arrived. And that summed up one of Japan's problems: they just didn't have the strength or directness in their play to counter the ruthless All Blacks. This was epitomised by the fourth try when the pace and power of Wilson and Ellis down the right presented the latter with his second try of the game. A superb Culhane conversion from almost on the touchline again added the extras.

A slightly loose kick from Matsuda went straight to Culhane on his own ten-metre line and he countered back to the Japanese ten-metre line where a great interchange of passes put New Zealand away again. Play was spread to the right where it looked for all the world like Ellis was in once more, but a great covering tackle saw him stripped of the ball. Centre Yukio Motoki came away with it, but then in a moment of madness just threw it into space where instead of launching a Japanese counter-attack as he had clearly intended, the ball went to ground and Robin Brooke just bent down, picked the ball up and sauntered over the line from a few metres out.

Straight from the restart unheralded back row player Kevin Schuler, who was to play and coach in Japan himself once his New Zealand career had ended, took play deep into the Japanese half. That particular attack ended when New Zealand were penalised on the Japanese 22; but seconds later they were back in the same spot with their own line-out ball and they spread it from right to left. This time it was Ieremia who broke the gain line and the ball was shipped on to Ellis; he lost the ball in the tackle but it didn't go forward and Osborne was on hand to pick up the loose ball and stroll over. Culhane again nailed the conversion, this time from wide out of the left-hand side.

The game had just moved into the second quarter at this stage, and already Japan were looking at a huge defeat; they just couldn't stem the tide. A fabulous one-on-one tackle by Matsuda on Rush briefly prevented the winger scoring, but the forwards recycled and a great cut-out pass from Ellis put his fellow centre Ieremia in under the posts to give Culhane one of his simplest kicks of the day.

The next try was made by a break down the left wing from Rush who breezed past his opposite number, Lopeti Oto and once he was away, a try was always on, it was only a question of who would get up in support; it was Culhane. he dotted down under the posts then converted to take the All Blacks up over 50 points before the half-hour mark. From the restart Ieremia took play well into the Japanese half before offloading to Robin Brooke who passed superbly into space off one hand as he was tackled to put Wilson away down the right. Wilson weaved in and out to create enough space to go round the last defender for the ninth try.

The tenth looked like it would come from an Osborne break from a scrum in their own 22. Once again the moment the All Blacks were over the gain line, their running was so powerful and direct and their support play so efficient, a try always looked on. Japan kept them out from that phase of play, but from the next they spread the ball wide far too fast for Japan to cope with, leaving Ellis to jog in wide on the left.

Almost incredibly the next score went to Japan, a simple penalty for fly half Keiji Hirose after the All Blacks were penalised for not allowing release of the ball from a maul. Carried away, maybe, by this success, Japan tried to run it from deep but a floated missed pass provided easy pickings for Wilson who intercepted and ran in easily. And they scored again before the first half was up, Rush the latest to benefit from Japan's total inability to cope with the power and pace of the New Zealand midfield and the missed passes out wide. It left the half-time score as 84-3.

The second half started in the same vein, and good, quick handling in the backs gave Osborne the overlap. He made no mistake, though for once Culhane did, hooking his conversion from wide on the right. The All Blacks were relentless though and it took only a few more minutes for another try to arrive, Ieremia making the initial incision then looping round to become the extra man and laying on a simple try for Ellis. That took the score to 96-3 just five minutes into the second half, and then, bizarrely, a Japanese try followed. A succession of penalties as the All Blacks weren't getting back ten metres, led to some good driving play from Yoshihito Yoshida and when he was finally stopped there was Hiroyuki Kajihara on his shoulder, like all good flankers, to take the ball and plunge over.

With ten minutes of the second half gone, it led to the almost surreal stat of possession being equally split, 50-50 between the teams. The 12th try went to the forwards as the giant Craig Dowd went over to bring the 100 points up.

Although too lightweight to make much headway, the Japanese never gave up but the danger of New Zealand on the counter-attack was that they executed with such precision. A fantastic Osborne break was taken on by Ellis, Rush, Ellis again and finally finished off by Robin Brooke. That made the score 110-10 as the match entered the final quarter, and it was actually Japan who scored next when Matsuda made a break and found Kajihara on his shoulder for the flanker's second try of the game. Hires kicked the conversion to take Japan up to 17.

Maybe that was the worst thing Japan could have done, in that it seemed to fire the All Blacks up for the last section of the game. Some rather feeble tackling failed to prevent Ellis going over for his fifth try of the game from the halfway line, then Ellis turned creator with an astute grubber kick ahead for Wilson to collect and slide over, but the referee decided he hadn't grounded the ball correctly and disallowed it. It looked harsh, but scarcely mattered as from the drop-out the All Black forwards drove the ball back deep into the 22 and Ellis went over in the right-hand corner for his sixth try of the game. At that point there were only seven minutes left but a tired-looking Japan shipped three further tries. The first of these came when they stole Japan ball on their own 22 and Zinzan Brooke, Ellis and Osborne combined to put Rush away down the left wing for his hat-trick.

The penultimate score again came from turnover ball. A Japan try looked the most likely outcome from pressure on the All Black line but somehow the ball ended up on the All Black side and Ieremia, Rush and Osborne combined to put Wilson away on the right for his hat-trick. The final score was created by the beautiful running skills of Rush and Osborne and just when it looked like the free-flowing move had broken down, flanker Paul Henderson, captain for the day, seized on the ball and crashed over.

It's hard on Japan to pick out this match to highlight, but so many sporting records were set by New Zealand as a team (most points, most tries, most conversions) and by individual players (Culhane's 45 points and 20 conversions were both records, as was Ellis's six tries) that it couldn't be avoided. To redress the balance somewhat, it should be pointed out that Japan has figured in every Rugby World Cup to date. Invited to take part in 1987, the Brave Blossoms, as they are known, have qualified for the other six tournaments, and can boast an excellent record in the various qualification rounds. Japan have lost just one match in qualifying, when they were beaten 37-11 by Western Samoa in 1991; they have won their other 31 qualifying matches. In 1995, qualifying entailed wins over Taiwan, Sri Lanka, Malaysia and South Korea.

At the finals themselves, they have recorded only one win, against Zimbabwe in 1991, but have nevertheless often given a good account of themselves, drawing twice with Canada and in 1995 they pushed Ireland hard before losing 50-28, two collapsed scums leading to penalty tries highlighting Japan's biggest hurdle. More recently they have reached the fringes of the world's top ten and have recorded wins over Wales (23-8 in June 2013) and Italy (26-23 in June 2014).

Japan is a proud rugby nation and hosting the Rugby World Cup in 2019 will undoubtedly lead to another surge in popularity for the sport. The story of Japan rugby is far from finished.

16

3 June 1995
Venue: Olympia Park, Rustenberg
Attendance: 16,000

Ivory Coast 11 Tonga 29

Ivory Coast	Tonga
Victor Kouassi	Sateki Tuipulotu
Aboubacar Soulama	Peneili Latu
Jean-Baptiste Sathiq (capt)	Simana Mafile'o
Lucien Niakou	Unuoi Va'enuku
Max Brito	Tevita Va'enuku
Abubacar Camara	Elisi Vunipola
Frederic Dupont	Nafe Tufui
Ernest Bley	Kolau Fokofuka
Eduard Angoran	Fe'ao Vunipola
Toussaint Djehi	Edwin Talakai
Gilbert Bado	Pouvalu Latufeku
Somalia Kone	Falamani Mafi
Patrice Pere	Inoke Afeaki
Alfred Okou	Willie Lose
Isimaila Lassissi	Mana 'Otai (capt)

The rugby fraternity is always welcoming of new members and if there was a concern as to whether the Ivory Coast could possibly compete with the major rugby-playing nations, no one was disputing their right to have a go after they had battled through an arduous qualifying process.

It had begun 18 months earlier, on 26 October 1993, when the Ivory Coast had travelled to Tunis to face Tunisia in their first Africa Group B qualification match. They won 19-16 and when they beat favourites Morocco 25-3 four days later, they progressed to the final qualifying round where they would face Namibia, Zimbabwe and Morocco again, at a mini-tournament held in Casablanca in June 1994. With Namibia traditionally among the stronger African nations, Zimbabwe having played in the 1987 and 1991 World Cups and Morocco playing at home, Ivory Coast started as rank outsiders. Their odds got even worse when they lost their first match 17-9 to their hosts, but they fought back admirably to pip Namibia 13-12.

When the final round of matches came around all four teams had won one and lost one, and the margins had been so small that there was very little in the points difference. Ivory Coast scored a stunning win over Zimbabwe, 17-10, ruling their opponents out of the finals for the first time. Nevertheless a win for either Morocco or Namibia would see them win the group and go to South Africa the following year. Incredibly they fought out a 16-16 draw which left Ivory Coast a point ahead of both and in the main competition.

Ivory Coast, nicknamed Les Elephants, were only formed in March 1990 and had played their first international in May of that year, losing 22-9 to Zimbabwe. To qualify for the RWC only four years later was an impressive feat, and on that basis the African nation was warmly welcomed to South Africa. 'When we play in the World Cup, we hope most of all not to be ridiculed,' Ivory Coast coach Claude Aime Ezoua is quoted as saying in Alison Kervin's *Thirty Bullies: A History of the Rugby World Cup*. 'We will apply the option to play positively and I hope that people will see we are trying.'

Their first match was a rude awakening as to what rugby at the elite level was all about, however, as Scotland scored 89 points without reply against the outgunned Africans. Gavin Hastings scored four of his team's 13 tries and converted nine of them for a world record haul of 38 points – which lasted precisely nine days until the record books were rewritten by New Zealand's Simon Culhane. Their captain Athanase Dali, who got injured in the match and was replaced by Abubacar Camara in this game and for the rest of the RWC, said that he was surprised by how much better Scotland were than they had expected and admitted his team had a lot of work to do.

Ivory Coast could do little to stem the tide against Scotland, but they gave a much better account of themselves four days later when not only did they restrict France to 54 points, but also scored 18 of their own, including tries for fly half Camara and winger Aboubacar Soulama. Before the third match against Tonga, Dali received the awful news that his brother Maxime, who had represented Ivory Coast in the qualifying rounds for the 1991 Rugby World Cup, had died. Maxim had been suffering mental health problems for several years, but his death was still a big blow to the Ivory Coast squad as the Dali family were well-known and influential in rugby circles within his country.

The Tonga match was academic in terms of the tournament as both teams had lost to both France and Scotland and therefore had no possibility of progressing to the knockout phases. Nevertheless, it was important in itself so while France and Scotland were competing hard for the privilege of not having to face the All Blacks in the quarter-finals but rather Ireland, Tonga and the Ivory Coast prepared to battle for a win. There was no doubt that Ivory Coast saw a realistic proposition of a victory against the disappointing Pacific Islanders. In the very first minute of the game, a dreadlocked winger called Max Brito, who had made his debut coming on as a substitute against Scotland and impressed sufficiently to retain his place and make his first start against France, caught the ball on his own 22 out on the left wing and cut inside towards his support. A routine tackle from Tongan flanker Inoke Afeaki turned into something much worse as Brito was caught in a ruck and his head appeared to be forced forward, extending his neck.

As the players got up from the ruck, Brito did not. He stayed prone on the ground and required extensive treatment on the pitch before having his back and neck immobilised and being stretchered off. Tragically, despite emergency operations at the Unitas Hospital in Pretoria, Brito suffered damage to two of his vertebrae which left him paralysed below the neck. Brito was just 24 years old and an electrician by trade; in those days there was little medical insurance of the players, and the cost of Brito's treatment was met by an emergency fund to which all the countries contributed.

If there was anything good to come out of the tragedy which befell Max Brito it is that these days ambulances are on standby for all the World Cup matches and there are doctors, nurses, orthopaedic specialists and anaesthetists all present at pitchside. More recently still World Rugby has mandated a series of concussion and return-to-play protocols to try to ensure players who have suffered head injuries are properly examined and checked over before being allowed to play again, even if the player himself insists he is fine.

These protocols are having an effect and have resulted in some high-profile players missing some high-profile matches, most notably Irish fly half Jonny Sexton – arguably the best player in the world in his position in 2014 – having to sit out 12 weeks at the end of 2014 and start of 2015 following a series of four concussions over the course of the year. 'It is most unfortunate and I feel bad for the club [Racing Metro],' said Sexton, 'but I'm still not feeling 100 per cent and with injuries like this it's not worth taking any risks.'

England full back Mike Brown has also had to take time out in 2015 after being knocked out during the Six Nations clash with Italy in February. Brown said he 'didn't feel quite right' and that he was being cautious. Wales's George North was another to be sidelined not long after Brown after World Rugby's former medical adviser suggested he should not play again until the World Cup.

Club teams and international teams aren't always following the same agenda, and no one likes to lose one of their best players for a sizeable period, but there has been an outbreak of rationality where player welfare is concerned. In May 2015, World Rugby decided, after a successful trial period, that from the following August a player who suffers a head injury during a match can be temporarily replaced while he is assessed by a doctor. 'Allowing temporary substitution for a head injury has proven to be a massive step forward in protecting our elite players following a head injury,' announced Martin Raftery, World Rugby's chief medical officer. This removes the need for a team to get a player who has suffered a head injury back out on to the pitch before he has been properly assessed, and the upcoming World Cup will be played with this new protocol in place.

Of course it's worth reiterating that Brito's tragic injury was not a head injury as such, and questions were also raised at the time about the wisdom of third-tier nations such as Ivory Coast were in 1995 facing the might of the likes of New Zealand and South Africa. However, Tonga were themselves, if not minnows, certainly not a top tier nation. While on the face of it professionalism might have been expected to widen the gap between the top nations and those less well funded, in fact the increased involvement of medical experts, and advisers on diet, nutrition and training (including recovery periods) has filtered down throughout the sport and increased awareness at all levels. Thankfully the Rugby World Cup has not witnessed any catastrophic injuries even approaching the severity of Brito's in the four subsequent Rugby World Cups, but the possibility should not be discounted, hence the advances made in various medical protocols are to be warmly welcomed.

Brito has been largely confined to his bed, at his parents' home in Bordeaux, and can move only his head and upper body and, to a limited extent, one arm. In 2007 he was reported as saying that he had come 'to the end of my tether'; no one in rugby should be allowed to forget the tragedy that befell the exuberant young winger from the Ivory Coast. Ivory Coast fought back strongly from a half-time deficit of 24-0, outscoring Tonga in the second half by 11-5 to give the scoreline some respectability at 29-11. But it was a game rendered irrelevant by earlier results, and even more so by Brito's injury.

11 June 1995
Venue: Newlands Stadium, Cape Town
Attendance: 35,500

17

Australia 22 England 25

Australia	England
Matt Burke	Mike Catt
David Campese	Tony Underwood
Jason Little	Will Carling (capt)
Tim Horan	Jerry Guscott
Damian Smith	Rory Underwood
Michael Lynagh (capt)	Rob Andrew
George Gregan	Dewi Morris
Dan Crowley	Jason Leonard
Phil Kearns	Brian Moore
Ewen McKenzie	Victor Ubogu
Rod McCall	Martin Johnson
John Eales	Martin Bayfield
David Wilson	Tim Rodber
Willie Ofahengaue	Ben Clarke
Tim Gavin	Dean Richards

It was four years on from the final of the 1991 Rugby World Cup, and, incredibly, four years since Australia and England had met. It seems inconceivable these days, but the two countries had not played a single fixture against each other in the intervening years and it was a very different-looking England side which took the field for this World Cup game. Only two members of the pack – prop Jason Leonard and hooker Brian Moore – survived and the back five was completely changed. In the backs Dewi Morris had taken over from Richard Hill at scrum half and Mike Catt from Jon Webb at full back, but Rob Andrew, Will Carling and Jerry Guscott were all still there while Rory Underwood had been joined on the wing by his younger brother, Tony.

Australia, as we have already seen, had largely the same squad, with the notable exception of the great George Gregan at scrum half.

Roles were reversed from four years earlier – this time it was Australia who had lost their opening match and gone through to the knockout stages only as runner-up, though with games against Canada (won 27-11) and Romania (won 42-3), their place in the latter stages of the competition was never really in doubt.

As defending champions they probably still started as marginal favourites to repeat their victory of four years earlier. England for their part had looked rather scratchy and out of sorts in their opening fixtures, a try-less 24-18 win over Argentina courtesy of six penalties and two drop goals from Andrew, and a 27-20 win over Italy when at least both Underwoods scored tries. The 44-22 win over Western Samoa (who had also beaten both Argentina and Italy) was a marked improvement and featured two further tries for Rory Underwood alongside one from Neil Back and a penalty try.

'We hadn't played well in our first two pool matches,' admitted Martin Johnson, 'but we turned that round a little against Western Samoa. We tightened things up a lot in the forwards and managed to cross for a few tries.'

The Western Samoans went though too and earned themselves a crack at the hosts in their quarter-final, but all eyes were on the Australia v England game. David Campese, as is his wont, decided to crank up the tension and raise the stakes – as if they could be raised any higher – by repeating his tired old cliches about England being a boring side. Even the excellent Australian coach Bob Dwyer got caught up in it, saying he thought it could be the match of the tournament but adding, 'I do not necessarily equate "good" with "open",' while former scrum half Nick Farr-Jones said, 'Both teams will be well briefed on the need for discipline, but one also hopes, for the good of the game, that they remember who the trophy they are playing for is named after. William Webb Ellis grew frustrated with only being allowed to kick the ball so he picked it up and ran with it.'

Andrew, by contrast, contented himself with an understated comment, 'We don't want to be going home just yet.'

Let's be quite clear, the Australian claims are just so much guff. In a World Cup match, particularly a knockout match, no team has any wider responsibility than to try to win the game. At this stage in the competition neither players nor fans could give two hoots about a style of play, much less who the trophy is named after.

England, playing into a strongish wind, dominated much of the first half and scored the only try of the first period when Michael Lynagh, of all people, spilled the ball on the England 22. Andrew, Guscott and Carling combined to put Tony Underwood away and the flyer comfortably held off the Australian cover to score down the right wing. Andrew converted and at that stage England led 13-3. A Lynagh penalty cut the deficit to 13-6 at half-time, and within a minute of the second half Australia were level.

Ironically after all their noise about England's constant kicking, Australia's try came from route one rugby, albeit perfectly executed. Lynagh put up a massive up-and-under and winger Damian Smith got up the highest to catch the ball and roll over for the score. Catt was rooted to the spot and waiting for the ball to come down so he could mark it, but Smith had no intention of letting that happen and got up above Catt to seize his chance. While the England defenders – Tony Underwood was also on hand but appeared to leave the ball to Catt – were rather caught ball watching, it was a tremendous leap by the tall Smith who just evaded Tim Rodber's sterling efforts to get himself under the man and ball.

Lynagh's superb curling conversion from out wide on the Australian left tied the scores at 13-13 and after that it was nip and tuck for the rest of the game. Andrew nudged England ahead again when the Australians were penalised for bringing down a rolling maul, but within two minutes Lynagh had replied. Lynagh then twice put Australia ahead, firstly when Morris was adjudged offside, while Andrew twice levelled the game, the second time when there was just four minutes remaining. And so it stayed into injury time with the score having moved on to 22-22, with the tension building by the second, never mind the minute.

The New Zealand referee David Bishop penalised the Wallabies close to the halfway line. Catt punted it into the Australian 22 and from the line-out Martin Bayfield – previously a policeman, the 6ft 10in Bayfield has, since retiring from rugby, become a noted presenter, pundit and pitchside reporter as well as an acclaimed after-dinner speaker – claimed the ball and England drove forward on him. Morris delivered the ball to Andrew with the time and space to land the match-winning drop goal. The game was over two and a half minutes into injury time.

Andrew later told *The Times*, 'We had lost our way after a wonderful start when we were so hungry, so precise in all we did. But we kept making our tackles and we stayed calm.' Andrew recalled that Dean Richards, jogging up for that final line-out, asked him what he needed for a drop goal and he had replied a catch and drive to tie in the Australian back row, a formidable and experienced unit of David Wilson, Willie Ofahengaue and Tim Gavin. 'Martin [Bayfield] made a wonderful leap at the line-out, the forwards piled in behind, produced the ball and all I could hope was that the kick would go over.'

Watching, you can see that Andrew knew full well the kick was over the moment he hit it. Like all great kickers he knew when he had caught one right. Andrew simply turned to the crowd – he has since said that the Newlands crowd seemed to be fully behind England that day, making it sound like Twickenham – and raised his fists in triumph.

'No one knew whether it was the end of the game,' Andrew told *The Times*. 'There were people on the pitch and some of our boys were starting a lap of honour while the Australians were kicking off again in a last-ditch attempt to retrieve their position.' In fact there was time for the Australians to kick off again and they did so in a hurry, but the ball was swiftly returned deep into their 22 and time ran out on them.

Andrew's kick, and his all-round play, was lauded by his captain, Carling saying, 'I have never seen anything like Rob's kick. After the match he touched Dewi's bruised leg and cured it and later in the evening we found him having a walk in Cape Town Harbour!' Not quite, but as Andrew said, 'That it was the goal which knocked out the world champions made it all the sweeter.'

The Australians were no more gracious in defeat than they had been before the game, with Dwyer saying, 'When teams play England, they often end up wondering, "How did they beat us?" Well in our case it was the combination of the rolling maul and Andrew's kicking. It's up to each nation to play the way they want, but I don't like England's style and I don't find it exciting.'

I'll just note in passing then that England's try came from a running move from their own 22 while Australia's came from a precise kick by their fly half.

The match was also a vindication for captain Will Carling. Three weeks before the England squad had departed for South Africa, Carling had been relieved of the captaincy for referring to the Rugby Football Union's committee as '57 old farts'. Carling had questioned why, 'Everyone seems to do well out of rugby except the players. It has become more than a fun game [and] what gets me and a lot of players is the hypocrisy of the situation. Why don't we just be honest and say there is a lot of money in the game. It is becoming a professional game.' Which is just what the RFU committee didn't want of course, and what in its one-eyed way was trying to prevent. But Carling was right, a power shift was coming and this was about to develop into an example of it.

RFU president Dennis Easby told Carling he was sacked over the phone, though he magnanimously said Carling would still be allowed to play for England, just not captain them. Then the backlash began. First the crowd at that afternoon's Pilkington Cup Final, between Bath and Wasps, started chanting his name, then the media universally panned the decision, both for its timing and for not giving Carling a chance to explain, or even put his side of the story.

But the really significant development occurred the following week. The RFU found that none of the senior players were willing to take on the mantle of captaincy; in an impressive display of player power, they simply turned it down, one after the other. It painted the RFU into a corner from which there was no obvious escape route until Jon Holmes, Carling's astute agent, offered one. During a radio discussion show Holmes managed to get across the suggestion that Carling would be prepared to apologise and Easby accepted the peace offering and reinstated Carling.

What the whole episode showed beyond doubt is that Carling was right, and the era of the committee man was drawing to a close. In its place would come a properly professional game; the agreement for that was already in place, now it merely remained to see how it would work in practice.

18 June 1995
Venue: Newlands Stadium, Cape Town
Attendance: 51,000

England 29 New Zealand 45

England	New Zealand
Mike Catt	Glen Osborne
Tony Underwood	Jeff Wilson
Will Carling (capt)	Frank Bunce
Jerry Guscott	Walter Little
Rory Underwood	Jonah Lomu
Rob Andrew	Andrew Mehrtens
Dewi Morris	Graeme Bachop
Jason Leonard	Craig Dowd
Brian Moore	Sean Fitzpatrick (capt)
Victor Ubogu	Olo Brown
Martin Johnson	Ian Jones
Martin Bayfield	Robin Brooke
Tim Rodber	Mike Brewer
Ben Clarke	Josh Kronfeld
Dean Richards	Zinzan Brooke

Jonah Lomu. Two words destined to strike fear into the heart of any rugby player not representing New Zealand.

'Jonah was actually quite lucky to be there,' said All Blacks captain Sean Fitzpatrick. 'He was sent away to the Sevens team because he wasn't up to speed during the fitness camps ahead of our travelling to the tournament in South Africa. Laurie Mains, our coach, told him that Eric Rush would play in the final trial, but then in one of our final practice runs before that last trial Rushie pulled a hamstring and the call went out for Jonah to come back and join the team and he then played a massive part in that final trial.' And the rest is history.

Although not quite yet. If the All Blacks suspected they had a secret weapon in their camp, no one else did. Not, that is, until New Zealand's first group stage match on 27 May against Ireland in Johannesburg. At some 5,750ft above sea level, Ellis Park saw Ireland become the first team to find it hard to breathe against the human force of nature.

The unfortunate Richard Wallace, a 5ft 11in, 14st winger who won 29 caps for his country and went on the 1993 British & Irish Lions tour, was the first, but by no means the last, to be made to look slightly foolish in his attempts to stop Lomu.

Ireland actually started the game well, but in the second half New Zealand, and Lomu, took control. One barnstorming run carried him a full 80 metres and past four increasingly despairing attempts to drag him down; Lomu didn't score that try, he created it for Josh Kronfeld, but he did score two of his own as well. The other Ireland winger that day, Simon Geoghegan, recalls, 'That was the first time anyone had really seen Jonah. I would have liked to play against him but I was on the other wing. Whether it would have been a good thing or a bad thing,

I don't know. Probably bad! He's a very difficult boy to stop when he gets into his stride.'

Ireland captain Terry Kingston offered a more succinct opinion as to what his team would do when they next faced Lomu. 'We would get a shotgun for him,' he deadpanned.

Lomu had a more low-key match in the comfortable 34-9 win over Wales and was rested, along with many of the first-choice players, for the monumental win over a plucky Japan, as already detailed. So it was in the quarter-final match against Scotland that he next appeared.

Scotland can consider themselves a little unlucky to have been facing New Zealand, having lost a match to France which they had led for almost the whole 80 minutes. In a group also containing Ivory Coast and Tonga, the Scotland v France clash always appeared likely to be the decider, and so it proved. Scotland needed only a draw, having scored more points than their Five Nations rivals in their other two group games, and when they built a 13-3 lead at half-time they looked well set.

Scotland still led, by four inside the last five minutes, but then fell victim to that sort of sweeping move only the French are capable of, going left to right then back again in bewildering fashion before Emile Ntamack went over in the corner. Thierry Lacroix's touchline conversion, while irrelevant, gave France victory 22-19 and left Gavin Hastings declaring that he couldn't believe his side had lost the game.

It's hard to imagine now, but the New Zealand v Scotland quarter-final was not seen as a slam-dunk at the time. Although the All Blacks boasted the greater firepower, Scotland scored three tries of their own and, as ever, gave everything to the cause. Scott Hastings had said beforehand that he was going to sing 'Flower of Scotland' as loudly as he could before the kick-off and then crawl off the pitch afterwards having given his all and left nothing out there, and his country were true to his promise.

But still there was Lomu. A 60-metre run early in the game carved out a try for centre Walter Little inside the first five minutes and five more followed, including, inevitably, one for Lomu himself. It was Gavin Hastings's last game for his country and he finished it by converting all three of his team's tries (one by his brother, Scott, and two by Doddie Weir), and kicking three penalties. It was a brave effort by the Scots, but this was a new New Zealand, an all-singing, all-dancing model which was growing in confidence by the day.

Sunday 18 June, Newlands Stadium in Cape Town, 3pm local time (1pm back in England) and after the preliminaries were over, the Rugby World Cup semi-final between England and New Zealand was about to start, in front of more than 50,000. New Zealand were the favourites, but they were facing the only Northern Hemisphere team they were concerned about. England had height and power in the forwards and they were on a high after their nailbiting quarter-final win over defending champions Australia. It had all the makings of an epic match. What followed was arguably the greatest half of rugby that the World Cup has witnessed to date.

Andrew Mehrtens switched the kick-off from right to left where no English forwards were standing. No problem as captain Will Carling and winger Tony

Underwood were both there, but they collided and New Zealand, through Walter Little and Frank Bunce, were away and deep into the England 22. New Zealand got the put-in to a scrum following an England knock-on and switched play swiftly to the right where Jeff Wilson made ground before running out into touch. New Zealand kept the pressure on, however, and not long after play switched back to the left. This time Lomu did get his hands on the ball – and his feet on the England defence.

The pass from scrum half Graeme Bachop was a little loose, in truth, but Lomu gathered it, went round Tony Underwood, handed off the dive of Carling and simply ran over Mike Catt. Watching again in slo-mo, there wasn't much wrong with what Catt tried to do, it just wasn't sufficient to halt the juggernaut who steps into and over him and keeps going. There were two minutes on the clock. 'I remember the first try when Lomu ran over Mike Catt,' recalled Martin Johnson a few years later, 'and I thought, "It's going to be a long, long day".'

Rob Andrew, the hero of the previous week's quarter-final victory over Australia, took the restart and Robin Brooke soared to take it. Bachop's pass again was a little loose, and to no one in particular, but Walter Little picked it up, beat Jeremy Guscott and immediately the All Blacks were in a position to counter, even though still inside their own 22. Little passed to Glen Osborne, Osborne returned the favour on the halfway line, then it was back to Osborne and although he was held up just short of the line, Josh Kronfeld was on hand to take the pop-pass and go over for the second try within five minutes. This time Mehrtens added the extras from the touchline and New Zealand were 10-0 up with six minutes gone.

From the restart, England reclaimed the ball and Andrew went for a quick drop goal which drifted just to the left of the posts. A minute later, Bachop was penalised for an offside but Andrew hooked the kick horribly off to the left; Mehrtens did not make the same mistake on 13 minutes after Tony Underwood had been caught in possession and held on a little too long.

Robin Brooke continued to dominate the line-outs, winning New Zealand ball and spoiling England ball to an extent which made clean and useful possession hard to come by. After a bout of kicking between the two 22s, Zinzan Brooke decided it was time to make his mark on behalf of the family and from almost 40 metres out he launched a speculative drop goal which curled in and over.

Another Andrew penalty which should have been a gimme went begging, and clearly the pressure to try to keep England in touch was proving too much for him; conversely, confidence was flowing for the All Blacks, hardly surprisingly. Both teams were playing lots of rugby, but a Wilson break down the right required too many England defenders to snuff out the move and when Brooke launched a long pass into midfield, there was Lomu, on this occasion with only Andrew to beat and plenty of space to do it it in. No contest. Mehrtens extended the lead to 25-0, just two points shy of their worst-ever Test defeat.

Somehow England kept the All Blacks at bay for the remaining 15 minutes of the first half, even playing a certain amount of rugby in the New Zealand half, but it was a damage limitation exercise rather than anything more positive. Andrew did finally manage to kick a penalty, awarded for Kronfeld holding on in a maul. But more bad news for England came when a Carling pass gave Tony Underwood half a yard of space on the outside of Lomu; this was the position England expected to be able to exploit, but Lomu turned and quite easily caught Underwood, flinging man and ball into touch.

The commentators wondered whether England had the wherewithal to run the ball consistently or the cutting edge to score tries. To give England their due, they did their best to prove that they could run and score tries in the second half, playing some scintillating running rugby, albeit in a losing cause.

The second half began with Andrew kicking off and immediately giving away an offside decision from which Lomu scored again, his hat-trick. England were a little unlucky as a chip from Mehrtens didn't really look to be going anywhere, but a wicked bounce took it right into Little's hands, he passed to Kronfeld who played the linking role to perfection and put Lomu in at the left-hand corner. Carling's solid tackle was too late to stop the big man getting over. Inside two minutes of the second half the score was 30-3.

Initially England's attempts to run the ball looked a little cack-handed and ended with knock-ons or little mistakes, and when Tony Underwood was given the chance to run at Lomu, he never got past him, although it's worth mentioning in passing that one head-high tackle by the young giant would certainly have received a yellow card these days, if not a more severe sanction. Some of the running was rather aimless, and when they ran out of ideas, Andrew simply kicked.

Back to the game, and New Zealand's fifth try came from a superb piece of handling as Bachop made the break, floating an overhead pass out to Wilson on the right wing, whose pace caused England defensive problems. Wilson got the ball back inside to Osborne as he was tackled and the full back, who had an excellent game all round, passed to the supporting Bachop who scored. Mehrtens missed again, which at least meant that the New Zealand score was going up in fives rather than sevens.

Finally England managed to build up a head of steam through taking tap penalties, but even then the inspiration was missing and England's kicking, and kick-chasing, was not of the highest order. Former All Blacks coach John Hart said in commentary that England were 'going to have to do something in the backline, out open' and from a five-metre scrum on the right they did finally manage that. Tim Rodber made the initial incursion and although it looked like Catt had nowhere to go he went to ground and set the ball up and quick ball out to the left gave Rory Underwood half a yard of space. In the days of the TMO, he would surely have been adjudged to have put a foot in touch before he grounded the ball, but he wasn't and Andrew added the extras with his best kick of the match, curling it in at the last second from the left-hand touchline.

Mehrtens then made a rare mistake with his restart, failing to reach ten metres but from the resulting scrum back on the halfway line, New Zealand stole England ball and were immediately back on the edges of the England 22. They moved the ball swiftly from their right to left but Carling clung on to Little and killed the attack.

With 17 minutes remaining Brooke had to leave the pitch; did that perhaps enable England to gain an upper hand in the forward exchanges? It might have been marginal as Blair Larsen was a fine replacement, but it did appear that just a measure of control went out of the All Blacks' game from that point on.

New Zealand almost scored again following a slick interchange between Wilson and Osborne down their right, but the ball went forward from the last pass and England cleared their lines. England's second try came with 12 minutes to play when Dewi Morris and Andrew's quick passing put Carling away down the short side. The England captain tried a chip over the last defender and even though it didn't quite work out as planned it deflected back into his hands and he went over in the right-hand corner.

Almost unbelievably, Mehrtens again failed to make ten metres with his restart, but on this occasion it made no difference at all as Morris's pass fell into the arms of Bachop who flicked it on to Lomu and he handed off Tony Underwood and went round him on the outside, then stepped inside Catt. It was Lomu's seventh try of the tournament and set a new record, surpassing the six scored by Craig Green and John Kiran in 1987 and by David Campese and Jean-Baptiste Lafond in 1991. Mehrtens added the conversion to make the score 42-15.

England gained a penalty on the All Blacks' 22 straight from the restart and from a quick tap a good pass from Ben Clarke put Carling went over for his second. Andrew's conversion made it 42-22 with six minutes left, and then a weaving run out of defence by Guscott took play from the England 22 to the New Zealand 22 and it took a clattering tackle by Lomu on Clarke to prevent another England try.

The stats show that Mehrtens didn't run the ball once himself, but his kicking – those restarts apart – was top-notch and another huge clearance took play back into the England half. Two plays later and a half-break from Bunce and there was Mehrtens taking the ball from Bachop and hitting a drop goal.

England did manage to have the last word, Rory Underwood going over for his second try after a series of breaks by Morris, and Andrew converting with virtually the final kick of the game. It made Underwood the top try-scorer in Rugby World Cup history up to that point (and he is still England's leading try-scorer by some distance), though it was scant consolation for a well-beaten side.

'Jonah Lomu was a phenomenon,' said Johnson. 'He was just so huge, so quick and it was great for fans to watch him destroy teams. It wasn't good being on the receiving end though.' Carling's words made the same point, 'Jonah was the difference. If New Zealand didn't have him then the game could have been very different. We tried to stop him but we couldn't and that's sad for us but the man is unbelievable. It wasn't just his strength and speed, his balance was also special and he could step off either foot.' And more succinctly, with a smile, 'The man is a freak. He's awesome and the sooner he goes away the better!'

Even Australia coach Bob Dwyer was moved to say, 'How do you stop Lomu? I've no idea. I suppose an elephant gun might help.'

19

24 June 1995
Venue: Ellis Park, Johannesburg
Attendance: 62,000

South Africa 15 New Zealand 12 (aet)

South Africa	New Zealand
Andre Joubert	Glen Osborne
James Small	Jeff Wilson
Japie Mulder	Frank Bunce
Hennie le Roux	Walter Little
Chester Williams	Jonah Lomu
Joel Stransky	Andrew Mehrtens
Joost van der Westhuizen	Graeme Bachop
Os du Randt	Craig Dowd
Chris Rossouw	Sean Fitzpatrick (capt)
Balie Swart	Olo Brown
Kobus Wiese	Ian Jones
Hannes Strydom	Robin Brooke
Francois Pienaar (capt)	Mike Brewer
Ruben Kruger	Josh Kronfeld
Mark Andrews	Zinzan Brooke

The question on everyone's lips in the week between the semi-finals and final of the 1995 Rugby World Cup was how on earth could South Africa rein in the free-scoring New Zealand who had destroyed England in the semi-final with the breathtaking pace and power of their game? 'If New Zealand do not beat South Africa there will have to be a steward's inquiry,' wrote the *Daily Telegraph*'s John Reason and in the UK, bookies were anticipating a 15-to-20-point win.

The Springboks, by contrast, had survived their semi-final against France, but no more than that. Durban had witnessed rain of a volume rarely seen at that time of year, and purely in terms of the state of the pitch the match should have been postponed. But that would have caused all sorts of logistical problems and with both captains happy to give it a go, Welsh referee Derek Bevan settled for an hour and a half's delay then got the match under way.

The only try came when full back Andre Joubert ran back a loose Christophe Deylaud kick and gave his team good field position and Ruben Kruger was driven over the line by a dynamic drive from his pack. France looked to have scored a try of their own right at the death when, with the clock showing 38 minutes and 56 seconds of the second half expired, Abdelatif Benazzi appeared to have driven over, but Bevan decided, rather too quickly for some people's liking, that he wasn't going to give it. In the days of a TMO it no doubt would have been examined ad infinitum, but it looked like a try in real time, and still looks like a try in slow motion. However, there were few complaints from either the players or their coach, Pierre Berbizier, at the time, while captain Philippe Saint-Andre was more disappointed about the unexpected weather conditions, 'All week we worked on our gameplay, with lots of moves involving loops outside Philippe Sella, the outside centre, and lots of ways to counter-attack. We intended to play at speed. We wanted to play more open rugby because although South Africa were very strong, we thought we could beat them by playing it wide.'

France never really had the chance to do that, on account of the conditions, and South Africa rode their luck to reach the final.

Weather conditions were somewhat better for the day of the final, with clear blue skies for the 3pm (local time) kick-off, and after stirring renditions of the national anthems South Africa prepared to face an unusually intimidating Haka. 'Stuff the Haka,' said South Africa coach Kitch Christie. 'That's where it starts for them. Stuff the Haka and stuff the All Blacks, this is going to be our day.'

From the off, New Zealand displayed the same willingness to move the ball which had been so apparent in their semi-final display, with swift passing giving Frank Bunce an early run. Equally obvious, however, was the fact that the South African defence was going to be a completely different kettle of fish from England's; every time one of the All Blacks' dangerous runners got his hands on the ball, he had two or even three highly physical South Africans determined to shut him down.

First blood went to New Zealand, with Andrew Mehrtens slotting a fairly simple kick on six minutes after the South Africans had got themselves on the wrong side of a ruck, but his attempt at a drop goal shortly afterwards fell a long way short of his effort against England. South Africa's tactical kicking was also far better than Rob Andrew's had been – fly half Joel Stransky mixing long kicks with high ones, with chips and grubbers and long, raking touch-finders. A beautiful shimmy and half-break from Stranksy drew an offside against the All Blacks and he comfortably tied the game at 3-3.

Then Jonah Lomu was given his first opportunity to rumble up the middle, after taking an inside pass, and although Stranksy did well to bring him down, the Springboks were pinged for offside and Mehrtens put New Zealand back in front on the 14th minute. A period of South African dominance, including a huge scrum victory when they shunted the All Blacks backwards and a near-try when Ruben Kruger was driven over but couldn't get the ball down, ended with Stranksy tying the scores again in the 22nd minute.

Stransky missed a chance to put South Africa ahead for the first time when his penalty from the left just refused to curl in at the far post just before the half-hour. But good ruck ball not long after gave him oceans of time to hit a sweet drop goal and South Africa were ahead, 9-6, at half-time. One notable aspect of play was Andre Joubert's positional and covering play – wherever New Zealand kicked, Joubert seemed to be in the right place to collect it, and usually had the time to clear the ball.

The second half started in similar fashion, with New Zealand trying to play most of the rugby but finding the ball not quite going to hand and/or the South African defence keeping them out. There was no further score in the opening ten minutes of the second half, as the nip and tuck continued, though Mehrtens had a pot at a penalty from inside his own half which had the distance but faded away to the left. Lomu had another run, down the New Zealand left, but was not able to hand off Japie Mulder in the same way that he had Tony Underwood, and then Osborne tried the same move but Joubert just clung on to him. Mehrtens did drop an excellent goal to tie the scores up once more, at 9-9, then pushed another just wide. Small tried the same run down the South African right, but had no more joy than the All Blacks as he was unceremoniously dumped by Osborne.

The All Blacks continued to enjoy the edge on territory and possession, but couldn't get clear on the scoreboard. The official stats showed New Zealand with 62 per cent possession in the second half after the first had finished 51-49, in their favour.

South Africa did well to defend a line-out virtually on their line, with New Zealand penalised for dragging down the resulting maul, and for keeping their wits about them when a kick rebounded off their posts back into centre-field – Kruger was the first to it and he dived on the ball with little thought as to the physical battering he might get as a result. Mehrtens had one final chance to win the game, and the cup, for New Zealand with another drop goal; Bunce made a charge into midfield, Bachop set it back and Mehrtens had the time but not the accuracy, slicing it to the right.

And that was pretty much that. English referee Ed Morrison blew the final whistle and there was to be extra time for the first time in a World Cup Final. A five-minute break followed by ten minutes each way; interestingly if there was no further score, or the game was still level at the end of the extra time, New Zealand would have been declared the winners on the basis of the sending off of South Africa's James Dalton in the group match against Canada.

Mehrtens got extra time under way and play continued in much the same vein, with New Zealand getting the first penalty when Mulder was ahead of Stransky's kick. From just inside the Springboks' half, Mehrtens easily got the length and New Zealand were back in front, leaving South Africa needing a try or two three-point scores. Small had a glorious chance to leave Stransky one on one with Osborne but his pass was forward and suddenly it was noticeable that All Blacks were going down like flies. Right on the stroke of half-time in extra time the All Blacks were penalised for offside at a ruck and Stransky levelled with a simple penalty.

With seven minutes left South Africa got the put-in at a scrum after a New Zealand hand had knocked on an up and under and when van der Westhuizen set it back to Stransky he hit a calm drop goal from about 15 metres, his second of the match. New Zealand still had time to come back but replacement winger Marc Ellis failed to take a couple of slightly unsympathetic passes from Bunce breaks, and when the All Blacks were penalised for diving over in a ruck it gave Stransky another shot at goal, a simple one from the left about 15 metres out. Incredibly given Stranksy's performance, he missed, pushing it wide to the right, but there was virtually no time for New Zealand to launch another attack and South Africa had won, 15-12.

The lack of tries and the fact that defences ruled the day prevented the match from ever developing into a true classic, but it was never less than engaging and tense throughout. Whereas in the semi-final every loose ball had seemed to end up in Lomu's massive grip, in the final it evaded him time and time again and the All Blacks appeared a little rushed in their efforts to find him. 'We just couldn't get the ball to him as often as we had planned,' lamented captain Sean Fitzpatrick after the match.

In fairness to the aggressive, physical play of South Africa winger James Small, their most experienced player, he looked after Lomu well and by hook or by crook ensured that the Kiwi had few chances to run. Zinzan Brooke, whose kicking as well as his general play had been a feature of the semi-final, couldn't find quite the same brilliant level, especially in the second half after his fellow back-rower Mike Brewer had had to depart with injury.

One aspect of the final which was little commented on at the time, but came to light later was that the New Zealand squad had been badly affected by food poisoning in the camp. Was some sort of sabotage involved? Some in New Zealand, both within and outside the camp, thought it was too big a coincidence for there not to have been, but nothing has ever been proven. That the players definitely were ill is beyond doubt – Craig Dowd and Jeff Wilson were both sick at the side of the pitch during the game – and this might have had a bearing on their energy levels in extra time. 'Eighteen of us went down with food poisoning,' said Zinzan Brooke. 'That may be coincidence but I don't think so.'

There was a feeling that for the first time, the 'best' team had not won the Rugby World Cup, but perhaps there was a higher power in play that emotional afternoon. The iconic Nelson Mandela, wearing a Springboks number six jersey, presented the captain, and number six, Francois Pienaar, with the trophy. 'Getting the cup from Nelson Mandela was the ultimate,' said Pienaar, the perfect statesmanlike spokesman for the occasion. 'He is a guy with incredible humility and he has done phenomenal work in bringing our country together. In my opinion it was the catalyst for bringing the entire nation together for the first time in support of one team.'

Mandela thanked Pienaar for what the rugby team had done for South Africa, and Pienaar replied, 'Mr President it is nothing compared to what *you* have done for our country.' Sometimes even at the moment of a World Cup victory, there are more important things than sport.

20

2 October 1999
Venue: Netherdale, Galashiels
Attendance: 3,761

Spain 15 Uruguay 27

Spain	Uruguay
Miguel Manrique	Alfonso Cardoso
Oriol Ripol	Martin Ferres
Alvar Fernandez-Valderama	Pedro Vecino
Sebastien Loubsens	Martin Mendaro
Rafael Gutierrez	Pablo Costabile
Andrei Kovalenco	Diego Aguirre
Jaime Rivero	Federico Sciarra
Jordi Riba	Rodrgio Sanchez
Fernando de la Calle Pozzo	Diego Lamelas
Jose Ferraras	Pablo Lemoine
Jose Cabeza	Juan Carlos Bado
Sergio Vidal	Mario Lame
Jose Diaz	Nicolas Brignoni
Carlos Vidal	Martin Panizza
Alberto Navio (capt)	Diego Ormaechea (capt)

The 1999 Rugby World Cup saw the competition expanded to 20 teams, and although this led to the ill-fated (and not repeated) decision to introduce a quarter-final play-off round, in general it was a good idea to allow some of the minor nations to get a taste of World Cup rugby beyond the qualifying stages.

Two of these were Spain and Uruguay, the former having progressed through the European qualifiers and the latter from the Americas. Spain initially posted wins over Andorra, the Czech Republic, Germany and Portugal and then in the final stage repeated their win over Portugal, this time by 21-17, to snatch second place behind Scotland. Their 85-3 loss to a Scotland XV gave a few anxious moments as to how they would fare in the World Cup itself, but Spain were worthy qualifiers.

Uruguay had a more convoluted route, beating Paraguay and Chile to reach the final qualifying stages in the Americas. There they were well beaten by Argentina (55-0), but gave a good account of themselves against Canada (losing 38-15) and came quite close to snatching the last automatic place before losing 21-16 to the USA. It meant Uruguay faced a repechage stage against Portugal and Morocco. They comfortably beat Portugal home (46-9) and away (33-24), but the final game against Morocco was a more nervy affair. The South Americans had taken an 18-3 lead in Montevideo but faced a strong fightback from the Africans in Casablanca where it briefly looked like that lead could be overturned. Ultimately although Morocco won the second leg 21-18, Uruguay went through 36-24 on aggregate.

Drawn into a group containing defending champions South Africa and Scotland, Spain and Uruguay knew that their first match of the 1999 Rugby World Cup afforded both teams their only realistic chance of recording a victory. Uruguay had won a warm-up game in Italy 20-3, making them the favourites against an attractive but lightweight Spanish side, and the final margin of four tries to nil seemed to confirm that. It wasn't the whole story, however, as Uruguay struggled to subdue a game Spain.

The only try of the first half came from veteran number eight and captain Diego Ormaechea, which was converted by scrum half Federico Sciarra. Fly half Diego Aguirre added a penalty, but two penalties from Spain's Ukrainian-born fly half Andrei Kovalenco kept them in touch at 10-6 down at half-time. Two further penalties from Kovalenco in the first ten minutes of the second half actually put Spain ahead at 12-10, but Uruguay's much bigger pack then proceeded to out enormous pressure on Spain and after a number of scrums collapsed in prime attacking positions for the South Americans, English referee Chris White felt he had no option other than to award a penalty try. Aguirre converted to restore Uruguay's lead at 17-12, though Kovalenco's fifth penalty cut the deficit to two, and looked like making for an exciting climax.

It was exciting, but not for the expected reason. Uruguay full back Alfonso Cardoso made a spectacular 50-metre sprint down the left to score in the corner and almost straight from the restart replacement fly half Juan Menchaca intercepted a loose Spanish pass to do the same down the right flank to score in that corner.

Goodness knows what either team made of the venue – Galashiels in the Scottish Borders region – but they produced an entertaining match, and further good news for the International Rugby Board could be found in the fact that neither team suffered the sort of embarrassment which had befallen the likes of the Ivory Coast and Japan in the 1995 RWC. Spain did not concede a half-century of points to either South Africa (47-3) or Scotland (48-0), while Uruguay were even more competitive, losing 43-12 to Scotland and 39-3 to South Africa.

Uruguay had all the same assets that their better known cousins in Argentina did – a strong, well-drilled pack which could cause problems for better teams and a solid if one-dimensional team – while Spain liked to move the ball and could play some exciting rugby but were a bit too lightweight at the top end of the game. To date, it is the only Rugby World Cup for which Spain have qualified; in 2015 they finished fourth in the final European qualifiers, but some way behind Georgia and Romania (who qualified automatically) and Russia, who advanced to the repechage play-off. There they beat Germany, followed by Zimbabwe in the repechage final only to fall at the very last hurdle – beaten by Uruguay for the final place at the 2015 tournament.

The Spanish game is modelled on the French style, and they did boast some exciting backs, not least winger Oriol Ripol, who went on to have a successful career in the English Premiership at Northampton and Sale, scoring 100 points for the two clubs. The sport has been played in the country since 1923 and they joined the IRB in 1988, but it is still largely played only in the big cities, primarily Madrid and Barcelona. Development beyond those confines is possible but not yet imminent.

The reason behind the expansion to 20 clubs for the 1999 Rugby World Cup was the success story of the first three tournaments, and the fact that the game had gone open in the intervening years. As we have seen, the decision to take the game open was all but forced on rugby union as the only viable way to see off the threat posed by the Kerry Packer-backed WRC. The great Australian centre Tim Horan is quoted in Lance Peatey's book *In Pursuit of Bill* as saying, 'It would be interesting to know how long it would have taken for professional rugby to come along if the WRC hadn't turned up. The WRC probably brought it forward by about ten years or so. There was no way I thought rugby would go professional while I was playing, and that was why I was about to sign with rugby league for the last four or five years of my career.'

Legendary Australia coach Bob Dwyer recalls that Super League was a genuine threat to the future of rugby in his country, 'Australia really needed to do something to protect its playing stocks,' he said. 'The best players were like sitting ducks waiting for league to pluck them out and throw big money in front of them.'

Thankfully, Horan says, it only took a few matches of the inaugural Super 12 (as it then was) season for fans to be won over, and to realise that 'better rugby was going to be produced because players were being paid and could spend a lot more time training. The quality of rugby improved really quickly.'

As with the World Cup itself, the Southern Hemisphere was the driving force behind the changes in the game, but the Northern Hemisphere clubs weren't too slow to jump on the bandwagon, with the start of the Heineken Cup pan-European club competition being quick to attract fans and sponsors alike – and appeal to players. World Cup winners Francois Pienaar and Joel Stransky signed for Saracens and Leicester respectively within 18 months of their country's triumph. In stark contrast, the Five Nations countries dilly-dallied, saying they were going to watch and wait for a year. By the time they had decided on a course of action, more than a few of the big clubs were in the hands of wealthy individuals and as money was now an increasing factor in the game, so players were torn between loyalty to those who paid their wages and a desire to represent their country.

In spite of the growing conflicts, the home nations were able to put together a British & Irish Lions side strong enough to win the Test series in South Africa in 1997. Shortly after the Springboks were to become the dominant force in world rugby and, at a time when New Zealand were rebuilding, they posted a 17-match unbeaten run during 1997 and 1998; that Lions triumph was one of the great sports stories of the 1990s.

Despite the ructions in the Northern Hemisphere as the club v country rows escalated, England captain Martin Johnson nevertheless reiterated the sentiments of Horan. 'I loved it when we went professional,' he said, 'because you could actually train and do it properly without trying to fit it all in around work. We were able to concentrate on rugby alone, and the game was the better for it.'

One fear about the game becoming professional was that it might make it even harder for the second- and third-tier nations to compete right at the very top of the game, in the countries where the infrastructure and money wouldn't permit players to go full-time. Certainly it has proved difficult for the Pacific Islands, for example, to tour as readily as the richer countries can;

on an individual level, however, the picture is less clear-cut as professionalism has afforded Pacific Islanders the chance to play abroad, for top clubs, and earn money which will benefit their families and their countries. Ironically, the Islands have actually found it easier to maintain contact with their players when they are at big clubs in France and England than it ever was when they were scattered across a multitude of tiny islands across the Pacific, often without reliable communications systems.

As for upsets, well the Rugby World Cup has never had a plethora of those – there were none at the 1987 tournament – and the occasional thrilling win for an Island nation does not appear to have become less likely with the advent of professionalism. Long may that continue.

14 October 1999
Venue: Millennium Stadium, Cardiff
Attendance: 70,849

Wales 31 Samoa 38

Wales	Samoa
Shane Howarth	Silao Leaegailesolo
Gareth Thomas	Brian Lima
Mark Taylor	To'o Vaega
Scott Gibbs	George Leaupepe
Dafydd James	Inga Tuigamala
Neil Jenkins	Stephen Bachop
Rob Howley (capt)	Steve So'oialo
Peter Rogers	Brendan Reidy
Garin Jenkins	Trevor Leota
Dai Young	Robbie Ale
Gareth Llewellyn	Lio Falaniko
Chris Wyatt	Lama Tone
Martyn Williams	Junior Paramore
Brett Sinkinson	Craig Glendinning
Scott Quinnell	Pat Lam (capt)

In 1991 the joke doing the rounds after Western Samoa had beaten Wales at the Rugby World Cup was, 'Thank goodness we weren't playing the whole of Samoa.' In 1999, the Welsh got the chance to do just that. Samoa had officially changed their name from Western Samoa in July 1997, so by the time of the second World Cup meeting between the two countries, it was, indeed, the 'whole' of Samoa that Wales faced. And the result was just the same.

Samoa got the scoring under way quickly with an early penalty from full back Silao Leaegailesolo in the first minute, but with back-row stalwart Junior Paramore forced off through injury after just ten minutes, Wales took advantage with two first-quarter tries. First the forwards won a penalty try as their well-drilled pack proved too efficient for the Islanders, and Neil Jenkins knocked over the conversion from in front of the posts. Then winger Gareth Thomas went over out wide and although the conversion was missed, it put Wales 12-3 up.

But there was a disaster for Wales in the 22nd minute when a line-out almost on their own line went horribly wrong. Hooker Garin Jenkins missed Chris Wyatt who got fingertips to the ball but couldn't hold on to it as it drifted over his head and into the arms of Samoan second row Lio Falaniko, who only had to hold on and fall over the line for the simplest of tries. Leaegailesolo converted from quite wide on the Samoan left. Jenkins kicked Wales further ahead with two solid penalties so that shortly after the half-hour mark they led by 18-10.

Then Samoa hit them with two quick tries, both from their inspirational fly half Stephen Bachop. Straight after the second of those Jenkins penalties, Wales knocked on from the restart, handing Samoa a scrum about 30 metres out from the Welsh line and from a quick switch, they moved the ball swiftly from left to right with Bachop orchestrating and being on hand to take a return pass from his full back as he cut inside a fairly feeble attempt at a tackle by Jenkins to score under the posts. Leaegailesolo added the extras, and within four minutes, Bachop was at it again, this time from much further out.

A Wales scrum on the Samoan ten-metre line went as wrong as their line-out had in the first half as Scott Quinnell picked up from the back of the scrum only to pass the ball to no one in particular. Bachop was by far the quickest to pounce on the loose ball and his turn of pace almost brought the fly half union into disrepute as he streaked away and held off the cover with the greatest of ease. Leaegailesolo again converted to maintain his 100 per cent record, and Samoa were into a 24-18 lead.

All credit to the cool head of Jenkins as he kicked his third penalty two minutes into injury time to bring Wales back to just three points behind, and then tied the scores with another penalty just three minutes into the second half. But far from weathering the storm, Wales were almost immediately hit by Samoa's fourth try. Gareth Thomas made a great break, carrying the ball out of defence, and it was taken on by Mark Taylor. Taylor was stopped by a shuddering tackle, but offloaded well to Shane Howarth and Wales set the ball up again but from the ruck Jenkins's pass was telegraphed and Samoa's captain and number eight Pat Lam intercepted. It was an impressive run from Lam as he took it all the way from just outside his own 22 to dot down under the posts without the Wales defence getting anywhere near him.

After another Leaegailesolo conversion, Samoa led 31-24 but there was still over half an hour to play and, just after the hour mark, Wales again drew level with their second penalty try of the game and a Jenkins conversion to make it 31-31. It took Samoa scarcely three minutes to score their fifth try; this time Leaegailesolo took time out from his kicking duties to do some running – and pretty impressive it was too. Gareth Llewellyn dropped the restart, handing Samoa an advantage, and Inga Tuigamala and Lam both made ground before a beautiful piece of interplay between Lam and Brian Lima saw Lima gain half a yard of space down the Samoan right. He was tackled short of the line but had the wit to pop the ball up to the supporting Leaegailesolo to squeeze into the corner. Leaegailesolo got his breath back quickly enough to get up and strike a wonderful conversion from the right-hand touchline.

There were still almost 15 minutes left to play at that point, but bizarrely for a high-scoring match, there were no further scores in that time. Wales almost crossed for a try from short range in the dying minutes, but from a penalty advantage they opted for a scrum and although they drove forward Quinnell temporarily lost control of the ball and Bachop was able to hack it clear. Wales had one more chance, running a couple of penalties as Samoa defended desperately, but the Islanders held on and as referee Ed Morrison signalled the end of the match Samoa celebrated another famous victory.

'They had a day's public holiday the last time they won here in Cardiff,' ITV commentator Jim Rosenthal told TV viewers. 'I should think they'll give them a month off after that performance by the Samoans.'

Wales coach Graham Henry said caustically of his team, 'Frankly, I hope they don't get over the loss in a hurry. I want them to remember how bad it feels and gain new resolve. You develop as a team by absorbing the lessons of defeat rather than by pretending it never happened.'

It was in fact Samoa's third consecutive win over Wales as in between the two historic World Cup meetings, they had won a Test match in Moamoa, 34-9, in June 1994. Wales have managed to correct that somewhat in the years since, winning Tests in Cardiff in 2000 and 2009, and even recording a World Cup victory over the Islanders at the 2011 tournament, but leading by only five matches to four overall, and trailing 1-2 in World Cup clashes, Wales can hardly claim defeat by Samoa to be a massive upset.

And Samoa did, of course, boast some highly experienced as well as excellent players. In addition to Stephen Bachop, who had New Zealand caps as well as Samoan ones, there was Inga Tuigamala who not only had All Blacks caps but international rugby league caps too and played 90 times for Newcastle Falcons in the English Premiership, with whom he won the title. Trevor Leota too had hatfuls of Premiership experience, appearing on 146 occasions for London Wasps, where he was a cult hero, while Junior Paramore had played at Bedford in the lead-up to the World Cup and went on to make 82 appearances for Gloucester Rugby between 2000 and 2004.

Perhaps the most famous of them all was Brian Lima, who was ultimately to represent his country at five Rugby World Cups. He had spells playing club rugby in England, Wales, France and Japan as well as for the Blues in Super Rugby. Nicknamed 'The Chiropractor' for his bone-shuddering tackling, Lima was also a devastating runner and if occasionally his exuberance got the better of him, who can honestly say they didn't enjoy watching him try to rearrange his opponents' bodywork? Having been the youngest player at the tournament in the 1991 Rugby World Cup, Lima retired after the 2007 edition having won 64 caps for his country. He is the only Samoan so far inducted into the World Rugby Hall of Fame.

The only saving grace for Wales on this occasion, unlike 1991, was that even after this defeat they were guaranteed a place in the knockout stages. Slightly bizarrely, it had been decided that where teams finished level on points, positions in the groups would be decided by total points scored rather than by points difference. Wales would have topped Pool D regardless as their 23-18 win over Argentina followed by their 64-15 thumping of Japan had given them 118 points (and a points difference of +47), but if points difference had been the measure, then Argentina would have pipped Samoa to the runners-up spot by +32 to +25, and this thrilling victory by the Samoans would have been in vain. Instead it was Samoa who progressed by dint of scoring 97 points to Argentina's 83.

In fairness to Wales, they had played much more solid rugby than in 1991, and their opening-day defeat of Argentina was a good performance. After weathering something of a Pumas storm in the scoreless first 20 minutes, then seeing them go 6-0 up through two penalties from Gonzalo Quesada, Wales fought back and a Colin Charvis try was converted by Neil Jenkins who also added two penalties for a 13-9 half-time lead.

A Mark Taylor try, following a good move begun by full back Shane Howarth deep in his own half and carried on by wingers Dafydd James and Gareth

Rugby World Cup Greatest Matches

Thomas, was converted by Jenkins to increase the lead to 20-9. Three more Quesada penalties followed however, and although Wales had been in charge for large portions of the match they were ultimately grateful for the 23-18 win.

Argentina proved their worth by beating Samoa 32-16, fighting back strongly from a 16-3 deficit with 29 unanswered second-half points. However, they ultimately paid the price for not scoring enough against Japan, who they beat just 33-12. Quesada continued to kick goals at an impressive rate – 21 from Argentina's three matches at the 1999 Rugby World Cup, and his overall record of 486 points from 38 Test matches bears comparison with some of the best in the game in terms of his average, at just a shade under 13 points per match. Neil Jenkins, for example, Wales's all-time leading points scorer and Quesada's direct opposite number in the Wales v Argentina clash, notched up more than 1,090 points in his 87 Test matches (he's one of only five men to date to have scored more than 1,000 Test points), but his per-game average was 12.5.

Quesada did occasionally receive some barracking for his laborious style, and was nicknamed 'Speedy Gonzalo', but there's no gainsaying his metronomic ability. Interestingly, he preferred to build a mound of sand rather than use a kicking tee, saying, 'Each time I use a tee, I feel I am limiting my possibility to give the ball the orientation I want whereas with sand I can mould it how I want and choose the height I want using more or less sand.' Quesada has been coaching in France since his retirement as a player in 2008, most recently at Racing Metro and Stade Francais.

By the time of the Samoa game, Wales had also despatched Japan in clinical fashion, scoring nine tries in a 64-15 victory, which ensured them a place in the knockout stages. They had even avoided the perils of the play-offs having finished top of Pool D – the only team to top their group despite having lost a match, although it did leave them facing a tough quarter-final against Australia.

9 October 1999
Venue: Lansdowne Road, Ireland
Attendance: 3,000

Romania 27 USA 25

Romania	USA
Mihai Vioreanu	Kurt Shuman
Cristian Sauan	Vaea Anitoni
Gabriel Brezoianu	Juan Grobler
Romeo Gontineac	Mark Scharrenberg
Gheorghe Solomie	Brian Hightower
Roland Vusec	David Niu
Petre Mitu	Kevin Dalzell
Constantin Stan	George Sucher
Petru Balan	Tom Billups
Razvan Mavrodin	Ray Lehner
Tiberiu Brinza	Luke Gross
Constantin Tudor	Alec Parker
Alin Petrache	Dan Lyle (capt)
Erdinci Septar	Tasi Mo'unga
Catalin Draguceanu	Rob Lumkong

There may only have been 3,000 people at Lansdowne Road to watch the evening kick-off between two of the Rugby World Cup 'minnows', but that won't have bothered the eastern European nation, who chalked up the second World Cup victory in their history, having pipped Zimbabwe 21-20 in their first match, in 1987. Despite qualifying in both 1991 and 1995, the Romanians hadn't managed to notch up another win before this one.

The United States had a very similar track record, having won a solitary game in 1987, beating Japan 21-18, but failing to add to that in 1991. In 1995 they had missed out on a spot as the Americas were allotted just two places that year, which went to Canada (who qualified automatically by virtue of their quarter-final place in the 1991 tournament) and Argentina, who beat the USA in a two-legged play-off. With Argentina winning 28-22 in America and 16-11 at home, it was they who went through to the finals, 44-33 on aggregate.

It made the United States keen to leave their mark on the 1999 competition, and for the first half at least they appeared firm favourites. A try from captain Dan Lyle, who played in the English Premiership for Bath, was converted by scrum half Kevin Dalzell who also kicked a penalty for a 10-5 half-time lead. All Romania had to show for a disjointed performance was an opportunist strike from left wing Gheorghe Solomie, and their plight got worse less than a minute into the second half when the Eagles' left wing Brian Hightower scored the USA's second try.

But by this point the Americans had lost the inspirational Lyle to injury (it turned out to be a dislocated shoulder, which ruled him out of the rest of the tournament). Lyle was one of those players who, much like Sergio Parisse in more recent times, rugby fans would have loved to have seen playing in an international side which could have enabled him to do full justice to his talents. ESPN's Tom Hamilton quotes Lyle as saying, 'At Bath, when I played well I was accepted. It wasn't about "why is this American here?", perhaps there was a novelty factor to it, but I like to think I could play at that level. I knew in training or a game I had to be better than Lawrence Dallaglio, Neil Back or Richard Hill.' Lyle certainly made his mark, playing a key role in Bath's 1998 Heineken Cup win and staying at the club for seven seasons – not bad for someone who had signed a six-month contract.

The loss of Lyle may well have given the Romanians some encouragement, and they showed much greater appetite for the contest in the second half. First Solomie added a second try, and then the hard-nosed forwards – perhaps sensing confusion in the American ranks following Lyle's departure – grabbed the match by the scruff of the neck. They went over after a great line-out drive, with captain Tudor Constantin being credited with the final touch, although the Romanians themselves thought it should have gone to Adrian Petrache, and added a fourth which definitely went to Petrache. Constantin had missed much of the build-up to the RWC with an ankle injury which also prevented him from playing in the first match, against Australia at Ravenhill.

The third and fourth tries left the Romanians with a ten-point advantage, but the Americans narrowed the gap to seven and then had the chance to draw level just a couple of minutes from time when full back Kurt Shuman scored in the left-hand corner. It was a difficult conversion, though, and Dalzell's attempt went just wide, leaving his team two points adrift and no more time to recover the deficit. To add insult to injury, it is the only win that Romania have recorded in the seven meetings between the two countries.

It was agonising for the Americans, but equally it was hard for the neutral not to feel pleased for the Romanians who had struggled enormously since the sport had gone professional. Although the country had always produced some excellent players, the infrastructure for professional clubs just did not exist so ambitious young players who wanted to try to make a living from the game were forced to go abroad. More often than not this meant France, and French clubs were not known for the magnanimity in releasing players for matches for their country, much less for training. In fact, some even said they would dock players' wages, and this ruled out an estimated ten to 12 Romanians who would otherwise have been part of the squad for the 1999 Rugby World Cup.

Rugby in Romania was also closely, and unfortunately, associated with the hated Nicolae Ceausescu regime which had been overthrown a decade earlier in 1989. It was common for the players to be given sinecure roles in the army or police force, and therefore they tended to be, if not supporters of the regime, then at least not vocal opponents of it. Rugby equipment was the least of the country's worries as it tried to rebuild its economy and its political systems.

In their opening match, Romania had lost 57-9 to Australia, narrowly failing to prevent the Wallabies crossing the half-century mark. In wet and windy conditions, Romania fought hard but 24 points in the first half and a further 33 in the second tell the story of Australia's ability to score at regular intervals throughout the match. Victory over the USA, however, gave Romania renewed confidence for their match against Ireland and director of coaching John Phillips said, 'We came here with the sole ambition of winning against America and we've done that. Going in against Ireland we'll have a nice relaxed attitude, and who knows? We're certainly capable of winning.'

The World Cup qualifying match between Ireland and Romania had finished 53-35 in Ireland's favour and Romania clearly had high hopes of pushing them even closer than that but in the event Ireland won with something to spare, 44-14. Romania did manage a consolation try from winger Cristian Sauan, but Ireland scored five and with their fly half Eric Elwood adding the extras to all five, the result was never really in doubt.

The American Eagles also lost fairly heavily to both Ireland and Australia, although they did manage to cross the line in both matches. In their opening game they went down 53-8 to Ireland, with Irish hooker Keith Wood doing a passable imitation of his childhood hero Serge Blanco as he scored four tries. Elwood (2), Brian O'Driscoll and Justin Bishop got the other four between them. America were still just about in touch at half-time, at 24-8 down thanks to a try and a penalty, both scored by Dalzell. The second half was the Keith Wood show, however, as 'Woody' scored a hat-trick to add to his effort in the first half.

The USA's final Pool E match was against Australia at Thomond Park, the legendary home of Irish province Munster. Again the Eagles made a pretty good fist of the first half, going in 22-10 behind after a try by centre Juan Grobler, converted by Dalzell, and a 15th-minute drop goal from fly half David Niu. The Eagles thought they should have had another when lock Alec Parker got over the line but referee Andrew Watson ruled that he hadn't been able to get the ball down. The Wallabies, fielding a largely second-string side, had three tries of their own in the first half and added five more in the second, with winger Scott Staniforth scoring a double on his debut, but the one that really broke the Americans' resistance was a pushover try – credited to hooker Michael Foley – some five minutes into injury time at the end of the first half.

Two late tries at the end of the second half, both of which were converted by Matt Burke, usually a full back but playing on the wing in this match, put a gloss on the scoreline which was harsh on the USA at 55-19.

The US continue to be something of an enigma in world rugby terms. They are, famously, the defending Olympic champions, having won the competition on the last two occasions it was competed for, in 1920 and 1924. In the latter of these, they beat Romania 37-0 and then overcame hosts and favourites France 17-3. A pitch invasion followed the USA's win over France, and they had to be given police protection during the medal ceremony and these problems – coupled with the lack of interest (they were the only three teams who entered in 1924), led to the sport being dropped as an Olympic event. Despite numerous attempts to get it reintroduced, it has taken until the 2016 Games for it to happen, and even then it will be the Sevens version rather than the full 15-a-side.

And yet America have never really built on that Olympic success, nor have they been able to capitalise on the presence of thousands of very good college American footballers who weren't quite able to make it to the NFL. Dan Lyle told ESPN that his 'background in college football meant I knew how to study film [of games], I knew what a playbook was and how to lift weights so I knew the nuts and bolts of being a professional.' It seems logical to assume there must be any number of Dan Lyles out there who could make the switch, and if a concerted effort was made to introduce these excellent college athletes to rugby, their country could become a real powerhouse.

The sheer distances involved in the USA would make the setting up of a professional league a practical difficulty, as it is for their international coach when they try to gather squads together for training (their two successful Olympic campaigns drew almost entirely from players based in California), but World Rugby is ploughing £2.2m into US rugby every year in order to try to grow the game in the country. 'What is great in America is that if they get a sense that what they are going to see is the very best of that sport, they will be interested in it,' said Brett Gosper, CEO of World Rugby. 'I think what should appeal to Americans is a national team going up against another national team – you don't get that with many American sports. Rugby allows Americans to compete as a nation and that is part of its appeal.'

The USA do compete fully in the World Sevens Series and this year finished in the top ten, ahead of more established rugby nations such as Scotland, France and Wales. They also boast in Carlin Isles the sort of player who gets crowds on their feet. Described by renowned commentator Nigel Starmer-Smith as, 'I've never seen anyone that quick on a rugby field ever, XVs or Sevens. I don't think anyone else has either,' Isles is blindingly fast and has scored more than 50 tries in the Sevens format. Isles hasn't yet made the crossover into the full code, though has trained at top PRO12 team Glasgow Warriors and at 25 there is still time once he has fulfilled his dream of playing for the USA at the 2016 Olympic Games.

If the American public, and American sportsmen, could ever be convinced of the merits of the game, there seems little doubt that the USA has all the ingredients to become a successful rugby-playing nation.

EDEN PARK

The Michael Jones statue at Eden Park, Auckland, commemorating both a great player and the Rugby World Cup's first try scored by a player

Serge Blanco goes over for France's dramatic winning try against Australia in the 1987 World Cup semi-final

Two of Ireland's all-time greats, Brian O'Driscoll and Paul O'Connell (back view), during their country's famous win over Australia in 2011

Tony Woodcock, with captain Richie McCaw close behind, goes over for the winning try against France in the 2011 World Cup Final

Argentina 28 Ireland 24

Argentina	Ireland
Ignacio Corleto	Conor O'Shea
Gonzalo Camardon	Justin Bishop
Eduardo Simone	Brian O'Driscoll
Lisandro Arbizu (capt)	Kevin Maggs
Diego Albanese	Matt Mostyn
Gonzalo Quesada	David Humphreys
Agustin Pichot	Tom Tierney
Mauricio Reggiardo	Reggie Corrigan
Mario Ledesma	Keith Wood
Omar Hasan	Paul Wallace
Ignacio Fernandez Lobbe	Jeremy Davidson
Alejandro Allub	Malcolm O'Kelly
Santiago Phelan	Andy Ward
Rolando Martin	Kieron Dawson
Gonzalo Longo Elia	Dion O'Cuinneagain (capt)

A long with Romania and the USA in Pool E were Australia and Ireland, and on this occasion the Northern Hemisphere side could make little impression on their Southern Hemisphere rivals, losing 3-23. A penalty from David Humphreys (director of rugby at Gloucester as of the autumn of 2015) was Ireland's only reply to tries from Ben Tune and Tim Horan (both converted by Matt Burke) and penalties from Burke (2) and John Eales.

But if Ireland couldn't run Australia quite as dramatically close as they had at the 1991 Rugby World Cup, they at least despatched the USA (53-8) and Romania (44-14) without undue alarm and thereby progressed to the ingloriously named Quarter-Final Play-Offs, in other words, play-offs between the five group runners-up and the best third-placed side, those three ties producing three winners to join the five group winners in the quarter-finals. It was an awkward compromise, necessitated by the increase in the number of teams at the finals; it was a good move to expand the tournament, but the play-offs compromise was an experiment which was not destined to find favour.

Argentina were comfortably the best third-placed team, being the only one to have won two matches in the group stage, and the draw pitted them against Ireland, and not in Ireland where the Irish had played all three of their group games – nor in Wales where Argentina had played all theirs. Instead both sides had to travel to the Stade Bollaert-Delelis in Lens. A football ground (and home to RC Lens), the stadium had previously hosted matches in the 1984 European Championship and the 1998 FIFA World Cup, and is scheduled to host four games at the 2016 European Championship.

Both sides approached the game knowing that the prize was a winnable quarter-final against France who, despite wining all their games, had looked vulnerable against Fiji and had had trouble putting Canada away. What's more, that quarter-final match had been drawn to take place at Lansdowne Road so Ireland would have home advantage – in that year's Five Nations competition (the final Five Nations since Italy were to join in 2000) France had won in Ireland, but the scoreline of just 10-9 gave Ireland reasonable expectation of reversing that result.

Ireland got off to the best possible start, with Humphreys notching two penalties inside the first six minutes. A long left-footed clearance from Irish full back Conor O'Shea took play from one 22 to the other and although Argentina initially cleared the danger back to halfway they gave away a penalty for over-vigorous rucking and Humphreys kicked a mammoth penalty which cleared the bar with ease from the halfway line. Three minutes later, after Ireland had run the ball a few times, Argentina were penalised for a high tackle on Keith Wood, and Humphreys kicked his second three-pointer.

The next score, however, went to Argentina and Gonzalo Quesada proved he was perfectly capable of kicking penalties too when Ireland went offside. Ireland continued to play with considerable ambition, running much of the ball in an attempt to keep the Argentinians on the move and unable to play their more set-piece-oriented game. A third Humphreys penalty stretched Ireland's lead to 9-3, but Argentina were happier to play a more expansive game than they had shown up to that point, and from one great move the flanker Rolando Martin almost broke through the Irish defence and when the move was stopped illegally Quesada stepped up to strike a second penalty.

Jeremy Davidson was penalised for bringing down an Argentinian driving maul and Quesada brought his side level, but from the restart hooker Mario Ledesma impeded the Irish chasers, giving Humphreys a simple chance to put Ireland back in front. Right on the half-hour a fifth Humphreys penalty increased the Irish lead to six, and the second half started in similar vein. A Humphreys penalty for Argentine hands on the floor after just two minutes of play made it 18-9, and a couple of minutes later a huge garryowen had Argentina scrambling to get the ball clear, which they just about managed only for Humphreys to slot a calm drop goal from about 30 metres out.

At 21-9, Argentine hopes were starting to fade. Quesada edged them back into the game with penalties in the 46th and 55th minutes, the first when Justin Bishop was harshly penalised for not rolling away in the tackle when he looked to have effected a brilliant turnover and the second when a break from scrum half Agustin Pichot turned into a fantastic Argentine forward drive resulting in an easy kick for Quesada. Commentating alongside David Mercer, Australian legend Nick Farr-Jones voiced the opinion that, for all the brilliance of Humphreys's kicking, he would rather see Ireland keep the ball in hand a bit more as they had done in the opening stages of the match.

Although Farr-Jones stopped short of saying Ireland's inability to score tries would come back to haunt them, he said, 'You've got to give it to these Argentinians, they're still in it, they cling on to these margins and one score... and they could see their noses in front.'

In between those two Argentine penalties, Humphreys missed a much simpler drop goal attempt than the one he hit. However, another penalty on the hour, his seventh, harshly awarded against the Argentine pack for preventing release of the ball on the ground, maintained a nine-point lead for Ireland.

It looked likely that they had done enough to keep Argentina at arm's length, but still they couldn't quite get away and Quesada's sixth penalty in the 64th minute – after Argentina had again put together sustained pressure with a series of forward drives – once again closed the gap to six. A great attempt at a drop goal from Humphreys, to extend the lead to more than one score, bounced off the inside of a post and fell kindly for Argentina behind their line. Albanese very nearly ran the ball back out, but slipped at the crucial moment and was forced to concede a five-metre scrum. But an Argentine free kick enabled them to win the ball back and break out of defence.

More unexpected running rugby from Argentina saw Pichot appear twice in a move which took play up to just a few metres short of the Irish line after a neat inside flick pass from their captain Lisandro Arbizu to hooker Ledesma on the burst. It ended with a scrum to Argentina and from the set piece Argentina put huge pressure on the Ireland scrum then flung the ball wide with good long passes from Pichot and replacement Felipe Contepomi and a miss-move in the centres, using the blindside winger Gonzalo Camardon as the extra man, put Albanese over in the corner. Quesada nailed the conversion from out wide on the left, curling the ball in beautifully, and Argentina led for the first time in the match.

Ireland restarted with just a fraction over five minutes remaining, and a free kick almost immediately gave Argentina possession back. It was helter-skelter stuff for several minutes, with Ireland trying to move the ball and Argentina tackling for their lives to prevent Ireland opening the game up. The second-half stats showed Argentina moving ahead in terms of possession, 55 per cent to 45 per cent, and when their scrum produced a massive shove on the Irish ten-metre line they won the penalty which Quesada converted to go four points clear at 28-24.

There was no time for Ireland to hit back and even the phenomenal efforts of Keith Wood weren't sufficient. Wood was a ridiculously talented all-round footballer, and slightly unfortunate to be at his peak in the years just before Ireland developed into a genuine world force. At the 1999 Five Nations Championship they had avoided the wooden spoon only through dint of winning in Wales.

They had lost both their home games, to France and England, and been well beaten by champions Scotland at Murrayfield. In addition to his 58 caps for Ireland, Wood won five for the Lions, on the 1997 tour to South Africa and the 2001 tour to Australia, and throughout his career was an iconic player for club and country.

In fact, Wood wasn't brilliant in the set piece, his line-out throwing in particular could go awry, but in the loose he seemed to be ever-present, constantly showing himself to take a crucial pass, diving in where many wouldn't go and seemingly mopping up at every breakdown. He scored 15 tries for Ireland, an impressive tally (and a world record) for a hooker, and enjoyed running with the ball; he could even be found occasionally catching long kicks deep in defence and running the ball back. Chosen as the IRB's International

Player of the Year in 2001, Wood was inducted into the IRB (now World Rugby) Hall of Fame in 2014.

Wood was, however, devastated by this defeat. 'We didn't have an intelligent enough gameplan,' he said later.

Although Ireland and Irish fans might not agree, this result was an excellent one for the good of the wider international game. There was a feeling in the early years of the World Cup that the smaller nations weren't competing on equal terms – not only was the scheduling against them but they often weren't in a position to have camps or get their squads together some weeks in advance of a competition in the same way that the Tier 1 nations were.

There was also some concern that professionalism would widen the gulf, but in fact what happened was the best individual players from other countries found employment in a wide variety of countries which could afford to employ them. While the best Pacific Islanders inevitably went to play Super Rugby in Australia and New Zealand, the Argentinians were more likely to head to the Northern Hemisphere. Of the starting XV for the match against Ireland, only winger Gonzalo Camardon and flanker Santiago Phelan (who was forced to retire early through injury but was head coach of Argentina from 2008 to 2013) never played club rugby outside their own country. The likes of Diego Albanese, Lisandro Arbizu, Agustin Pichot, Mario Ledesma and Ignacio Fernandez Lobbe all became well-known figures at top clubs in France, England and Italy. Ledesma was an important part of the Clermont side which won the Top 14 title in France in 2010 while Fernandez Lobbe was among those recruited by Philippe Saint-Andre when the former French international was head coach at Sale, and was a key player in the team's 2006 Guinness Premiership title.

The impact in Argentina of their winning this match to reach the quarter-finals for the first time was huge – in nine previous matches they had won only once, against Italy in 1987. But they had been getting closer, and in 1995 had lost all three of their games by a margin of just six points; 24-18 to England, 32-26 to Western Samoa and 31-25 to Italy. Suddenly they had won three in a row, the country was going mad for rugby and the sport was firmly established in the national consciousness.

24 October 1999
Venue: Stade de France, France
Attendance: 75,000

England 21 South Africa 44

England	South Africa
Matt Perry	Percy Montgomery
Nick Beal	Deon Kayser
Will Greenwood	Robbie Flack
Phil de Glanville	Pieter Muller
Dan Luger	Pieter Rossouw
Paul Grayson	Jannie de Beer
Matt Dawson	Joost van der Westhuizen (capt)
Jason Leonard	Os du Randt
Phil Greening	Naka Drotske
Phil Vickery	Cobus Visagie
Martin Johnson (capt)	Krynauw Otto
Danny Grewcock	Mark Andrews
Richard Hill	Johan Erasmus
Neil Back	Andre Venter
Lawrence Dallaglio	Bobby Skinstad

England's 30-16 opening-game defeat by New Zealand had always looked likely to condemn them to a play-off, and despite scoring vast numbers of points against Italy (67-7) and Tonga (101-10), that did indeed prove to be the case. The All Blacks also had no problems against either of their group opponents, and sailed through as group winners, which involved them moving from Twickenham to Murrayfield and a likely date with Scotland, while England were somewhat fortunate to remain on home turf for their play-off against Fiji.

That Fiji were England's opponents rather than France was something of a scandal. In Pool C, both had won comfortable victories over Namibia and rather less comfortable victories over Canada. The upshot was that their match at Stade de Toulouse on 16 October was a straight fight to determine who would win the pool and who would be condemned to the extra game.

France won 28-19, but it is not a match which referee Paddy O'Brien will look back on with any fondness. A series of terrible decisions from O'Brien included a headbutt from prop Christian Califano which looked like a red card offence at the time, and doesn't look any less worthy of the sanction 16 years on. Even with 15 players on the pitch, France were outplayed for large periods of the game and when they took a quick tap penalty but threw a forward pass, O'Brien somehow decided they should get the chance to take the penalty again rather then deeming it an error and awarding Fiji the put-in at the resulting scrum. This time France opted for the pragmatic approach and kicked the three points.

Even worse was to follow in the second half, however, when full back Ugo Mola tried to run the ball out of defence from his own 22 and lost it in a big hit from his opposite number, Alfie Uluinayau. Flanker Seta Tawake Naivaluwaqa picked up the loose ball and strolled in to dot it down under the posts, but

O'Brien somehow saw a knock-on which no one else in the world did and awarded France a scrum. Then finally, with Fiji leading 19-13 and just over ten minutes to go, but under pressure on their own line, O'Brien awarded France a penalty try when it was the French hooker Marc del Maso who popped up in the scrum.

That put France one point ahead, but Fiji still had opportunities, only to see France seal victory with a breakaway try which contained more than one pass which looked suspiciously forward. Former All Black captain Sean Fitzpatrick, a close friend of O'Brien's who was in the ITV studio for the match, admitted, 'The Fijians will feel justifiably miffed.' The match could easily have finished 26-13 in Fiji's favour.

Instead they faced a tough assignment at Twickenham against a team they had never beaten. England took the tough decision to rest a number of first-choice players, but although Fiji only lost the try count four to three, the kicking of Jonny Wilkinson ensured that England were always in charge, building a 21-3 lead at half-time and steadfastly refusing to let Fiji back into it during a more even second half, which the home team edged 24-21 for a final score of 45-24. England progressed to a quarter-final against world champions South Africa, and Fiji went home, proud and a little unfortunate.

South Africa were still a good side, but there was a slight sense in England that they could be beaten. They had been good rather than imperious in their pool games, not wasting too much effort on racking up the points against Spain (47-3) and Uruguay (39-3) and although they scored more against a solid Scotland side, they also conceded plenty in their 46-29 victory.

England, however, for all their comfortable win against Fiji, had yet to show conclusively that they had recovered from another battering from Jonah Lomu. Four years on from Lomu's famous impression of a tank against them in Cape Town, England had put up a much stronger fight against the All Blacks but once again Lomu had made the difference.

It sounds inevitable from this distance, but in fact that was far from the case. Lomu had been diagnosed with a serious kidney problem at the end of 1996 – one which was to result in dialysis in 2003 and a transplant in 2004 – and had taken almost a year out of the sport. He had won a place on New Zealand's Northern Hemisphere tour at the end of 1997 but had failed to score against either England or Wales. The following year he notched only one try despite New Zealand racking up two big wins over England (64-22 and 40-10). He did play for New Zealand's 1998 Commonwealth Games gold medal-winning side in Kuala Lumpur, and in the 1999 Tri Nations Series he once more made an impression, mostly off the bench.

That cemented his place in the New Zealand squad for the World Cup, but prior to the England game, captain Martin Johnson admitted his team were more concerned about the impressive openside flanker Josh Kronfeld. 'We went out to try and minimise the impact he would have on the game,' recalled Johnson, 'but he was a real nuisance and we just couldn't get the better of him.'

In spite of that, England were playing well and were holding the All Blacks at 16-16 with 56 minutes on the clock, Phil de Glanville's try equalising that of Jeff Wilson and 20-year-old Jonny Wilkinson matching the far more experienced

Andrew Mehrtens kick for kick. Then Mehrtens fired a long ball out to Lomu who had a bit of space on the left wing and he was off, rampaging through the England defence as if the previous four years had vanished into the mist.

A third New Zealand try, from replacement scrum half Byron Kelleher, put the seal on a 30-16 victory which looks a little more comfortable than it actually was.

So to the Stade de France for England, and a Springboks team which boasted only three survivors from the World Cup-winning side of 1995, although two of those were the giant Os du Randt in the front row and the astounding fly half Joost van der Westhuizen, now captain of the side and one of the best scrum halves of all time.

But it was a much lesser-known figure in South African rugby, never mind world rugby, who was to be the key player in the match. Jannie de Beer knew that he was very much the second-choice fly half going into the 1999 World Cup; indeed, despite having played against the Lions in 1997 and having featured in that year's Tri Nations competition, new Springbok coach Nick Mallet had made it clear to de Beer that he preferred Henry Honiball and would always pick Honiball unless he should be injured. Then he was.

A hamstring injury ruled Honiball out of much of the tournament, and de Beer was brought in. England had made a change at fly half too – for once in his life coach Clive Woodward wobbled and reverted to the security of Paul Grayson over the youthful exuberance of Wilkinson. Not that Grayson did much wrong, he kicked his goals, six of them, including one from inside his own half, and at half-time England trailed just 16-12, the difference largely being a van der Westhuizen try.

When Grayson kicked his fifth penalty two minutes into the second half, the gap was down to a single point and most observers felt the stage was set for a final England push. Instead, a completely different story played out, one written by de Beer.

Just a minute after Grayson had dragged his side to within one point of South Africa, de Beer saw the opportunity for a snap drop goal. England full back Matt Perry got caught trying to run the ball out of defence and turned it over, van der Westhuizen found de Beer and with nothing much on, on account of England's defence being well aligned, the Springbok fly half slotted it over from close to the ten-metre line. It worked so well that one minute later he repeated the play. This time an England move from a tap penalty by Matt Dawson broke down inside the South Africa half and it was picked up by centre Robbie Fleck. He took play back inside the England half and when the ball was worked back inside from the wide right there was de Beer to hit a drop goal from beyond the ten-metre line to increase the lead to 22-15.

A Grayson penalty brought the margin back to four points with just over half an hour still to play, but then came de Beer's third drop goal. Quick ball came from a ruck in centre field and it was immediately obvious what the play was going to be, but de Beer stood so deep behind van der Westhuizen that the England defence couldn't get anywhere near him.

Wilkinson was brought on after 55 minutes and quickly picked up where Grayson left off, slotting over England's seventh penalty to keep them in touch at 25-21, but as the game moved into the final ten minutes, de Beer struck again. His fourth drop goal was perhaps the simplest of the lot as quick ruck ball in the centre of the field gave him the opportunity right under the posts from close to the 22. England were still only a converted try behind at that stage but de Beer's record fifth strike three minutes later increased the gap to ten as van der Westhuizen fed de Beer on the ten-metre line and over it sailed.

The heart had been knocked out of England, and they conceded two further kickable penalties – both of which de Beer nailed, in the 78th and 81st minutes – and in the dying seconds a try came when a high de Beer crossfield kick bounced wickedly and straight into the arms of Pieter Rossouw. Fittingly, de Beer's conversion was the final word of the match and a game which had appeared to be a close call had been taken convincingly out of England's grasp by the boot of a second-choice fly half.

'I have not seen a better kicking display in my whole life than what I saw today,' declared 1995 World Cup-winning captain Francois Pienaar. 'He was awesome. I've never seen anything like it and I don't think we will for a long, long time.'

De Beer himself has always been modest about his performance, preferring to bestow praise elsewhere. 'God gave us this victory,' he said in the immediate aftermath. 'I am just happy to be part of his gameplan. I thank the Lord for the talent he gave me and I thank the forwards for the ball they gave me.'

More prosaically he later explained, 'We studied the way England played and realised we would have a lot of time to [go for drop goals] and decided to use it as an option. The first one or two were from turnovers and not planned but after that the guys started calling for it. But I'd gone for drop goals before and wasn't convinced any of them would go over but it was one of those days when you are not going to score many tries.' Thanks to de Beer, they didn't need to.

25

30 October 1999
Venue: Twickenham, England
Attendance: 73,000

Australia 27 South Africa 21

Australia	South Africa
Matt Burke	Percy Montgomery
Ben Tune	Deon Kayser
Dan Herbert	Robbie Flack
Tim Horan	Pieter Muller
Joe Roff	Pieter Rossouw
Stephen Larkham	Jannie de Beer
George Gregan	Joost van der Westhuizen (capt)
Richard Harry	Os du Randt
Michael Foley	Naka Drotske
Andrew Blades	Cobus Visagie
David Giffin	Krynauw Otto
John Eales (capt)	Mark Andrews
Matt Cockbain	Johan Erasmus
David Wilson	Andre Venter
Toutai Kefu	Bobby Skinstad

After their somewhat disappointing defence of their crown in 1995, when they failed to make it past the quarter-finals, Australia had run a more low-key campaign in 1999. Three easy victories at the pool stage had given little clear idea as to how good they were, and even that season's Tri Nations results were a little unhelpful in as much as Australia had won both their home games and lost both their away games. They looked to have a slight edge over South Africa in that tournament as they hammered the Springboks 32-6 in Brisbane, and lost just 10-9 in Cape Town, a defeat which cost them the chance to fight for the title with New Zealand in the last match of the Series.

In the quarter-finals of the World Cup, Australia had coped with the Welsh onslaught, defending well until the Welsh storm had blown itself out, then striking hard and fast through their penetrative backline. A hint of controversy had arisen before the game when Wales decided to leave the roof on the Millennium Stadium open to the wind and rain in an attempt to take the Wallabies out of their comfort zone and deny them the chance to play their fast, open brand of rugby. The Australians were less than impressed by the decision, with star centre Tim Horan memorably describing it as, 'A bit like having a Ferrari in the garage but then going out to catch a bus. The weather spoiled the game when there was a great atmosphere and a great occasion. If you have a roof you should use it.'

What it didn't spoil was Australia's progress to the semi-final, as they weathered the elements and the opposition storm. Wales trailed just 10-9 at half-time thanks to three Neil Jenkins penalties in reply to George Gregan's sixth-minute try, converted by Matt Burke, and Burke's penalty, awarded when Wales went offside in desperate defence to prevent a second try.

Wakes threw everything at Australia at the start of the second half, but their three-quarters just didn't quite have the pace or the guile to make the breakthrough. Australia raised the siege and when Stephen Larkham put through a perfect grubber, all the speedy Ben Tune had to do was fall on the ball over the line. A late third try, a second for Gregan, gave the scoreline a flattering look as far as the Wallabies were concerned, but as Horan had stressed before the game, 'I wanted to make sure the team had it locked into their heads that when we play Wales if we lose, we are gone.'

That didn't happen and the Australians went through to face a titanic battle against South Africa. The Springboks were also coming off a big quarter-final win, and the performance of their forwards and half backs in that match must have given them confidence, in spite of not being able to match the Wallabies in the backs.

Jannie de Beer, drop-kicking hero of the quarter-final win over England, had retained his place in the starting line-up despite the return to fitness of first-choice fly half Henry Honiball. 'Henry was sitting behind me during the quarter-final and he said he didn't think he should play in the team even if he was fit for the semi-final because Jannie was doing so well,' said Springbok coach Nick Mallet. 'Both the guys were so team-oriented.'

Australian captain John Eales said, 'We were very aware of Jannie de Beer as a threat, but the important thing for us was to ensure we didn't focus too much on him and allow some other player an opportunity. It's very hard to contain drop goals so you can't concentrate too much on that, you need to focus on the other aspects of the game, the ones which lead to that player being put in a position to kick a drop goal.' Australian coach Rod McQueen spoke in similar vein, 'It's very difficult to defend against something like that. The answer is to play the game in their half. The answer is to deny him the opportunity to do it.'

It meant that South Africa lined up exactly as they had done against England six days earlier. Australia, who had had one day more to recover from their quarter-final exploits, made just one change, recalling Toutai Kefu at number eight in place of Tiaan Strauss.

It was to prove a titanic encounter, and one which amply demonstrated that a rugby match can be absorbing and intense even without a single try being scored. it was a manic start, full of kicking, but most of it very, very good. South Africa looked to keep driving it in using their tight forwards, and it won them the first shot at a penalty, albeit from inside their own half. De Beer's effort was true, but short. The Boks continued to apply the pressure but when the ball went loose Larkham and Horan went the length of the field only for Larkham to make a right horlicks of a relatively straightforward drop goal from well inside the 22 and in front of the posts.

Matt Burke followed suit in missing an easy penalty and the end-to-end play continued. De Beer failed with a snap drop goal, drifting it out to the right of the posts instead of drawing it in as he had against England on several occasions. The first score came when Tune and Larkham ran deep into the South African 22 and were awarded a penalty for their efforts when the South Africans infringed. Almost inconceivably there followed ten minutes of play with no further points scored until, in the 22nd minute, a superb Horan break took play deep into the South African 22 and at least two of their players were offside, so the three points it cost them would have been deemed an acceptable price to pay.

The two teams then exchanged soft penalties awarded for killing the ball on the floor. Van der Westhuizen almost scored the first try of the game from a superb break after dummying what seemed like the whole of the Australian team and going straight through the middle, but he was hauled down just short of the line and the Australians managed to clear. De Beer did pull three points back with another penalty on 36 minutes, but Australia once more extended the lead to six on the stroke of half-time.

It took only four minutes of the second half for de Beer to close the gap once more, to 12-9, when Tune hesitated under a high ball and was flattened. The resulting penalty was almost inevitable. Burke then got one penalty strike horribly wrong, and Australia paid the price when de Beer finally found his drop-kicking boots and bisected the posts to tie the game at 12-12 with almost exactly half an hour to go.

It was hard to tell who the Twickenham crowd was favouring at this stage, but little doubt that they were enjoying the game. England fans in the crowd, however, surely couldn't help feeling a little sick as de Beer missed his third out of four attempts at a drop, none of them as difficult as some of the ones he had kicked in the quarter-final.

It was well into the final quarter before the scoreboard was troubled again – although a quick tap penalty down the blindside almost saw South Africa score a try and then a swerving Robbie Fleck line break took him to within seven or eight metres of the try line only for the ball to be lost. Having survived several minutes of severe pressure, Australia broke upfield and were awarded a soft penalty which Burke kicked for a 15-12 lead; in the wake of that score an onscreen graphic showed South Africa with 64 per cent possession in the second half, and that certainly felt like a fair reflection of the balance of play.

A massive left-footed clearance from Joe Roff, a superb all-round footballer who later played in the Varsity match while studying PPE at Oxford, took play from one 22 to the other and seemed to spark a return to a period of Australian dominance, with a disallowed try and a series of drives close to the South African line and then Gregan got over but was penalised by referee Derek Bevan for an offence which was hard to discern either in real time or in the slow motion replays. Another splendid Horan break was only just stopped by van der Westhuizen, but the Springboks were penalised and Burke kicked an easy penalty, his sixth, to give Australia an 18-12 lead with five minutes left to play.

Three minutes later South African captain van der Westhuizen was faced with a tricky decision: a penalty in front of the posts offered the near-certainty of three points but only a couple of minutes left for the Springboks to score again, or he could go for the riskier but potentially more rewarding play of kicking for the corner. In keeping with the generally more pragmatic nature of South African rugby, he opted for the kick at goal and de Beer made the score 18-15 in Australia's favour.

But would they get another chance? Larkham restarted and the Australians gave away a stupid penalty for coming round the wrong side. Percy Montgomery took play into the Australian half, and suddenly there was panic in the Wallaby ranks. Suddenly the Australian handling was breaking down and passes were being flung everywhere. It was no huge surprise when South Africa were awarded another penalty, about 40 metres out and quite wide on the right. It was the sort of kick you would expect frontline international goal kickers to make, but with the added pressure of knowing it was the last chance for the defending world champions to stay in the competition, all credit to de Beer for nailing it and taking the game into extra time at 18-18.

Burke got extra time under way, and it quickly became apparent that both teams had decided to play the percentages and try their utmost not to give away kickable penalties. The Springboks had the best of the opening moments and fully deserved to go ahead through a simple de Beer penalty, but Australia hit back when a great Roff break resulted in an infringement from the retreating – but not very quickly – South African defenders.

The teams turned round after the first ten-minute period still locked together at 21-21. The second period of extra time brought an increase in caution, but suddenly out of nowhere Larkham hit a ridiculous drop goal: there looked to be nothing on as the fly half took the ball from his scrum half but he looked up and kicked a massive curling drop goal from only just a couple of metres inside South African territory.

Once again time was against the world champions, and this time they just couldn't conjure up a response. In their desperation to regain possession, they gave away a scrum penalty and Burke stepped up to extend the lead to six points at 27-21. And that was just about that. The world champions were out, and Australia were into their second Rugby World Cup Final.

De Beer had had a perfectly respectable game, but he had failed to recapture the magic evident in the quarter-final win over England. Larkham on the other hand picked this match to kick the first drop goal he had ever struck in an international match (it was his 29th cap), and a glorious one it was. In the end it made the difference between winning and losing a World Cup semi-final.

26

31 October 1999
Venue: Twickenham, England
Attendance: 73,000

France 43 New Zealand 31

France	New Zealand
Xavier Garbajosa	Jeff Wilson
Philippe Bernat-Salles	Tana Umaga
Richard Dourthe	Christian Cullen
Emile Ntamack	Alama Ieremia
Christophe Dominici	Jonah Lomu
Christophe Lamaison	Andrew Mehrtens
Fabien Galthie	Byron Kelleher
Cedric Soulette	Carl Hoeft
Raphael Ibanez (capt)	Anton Oliver
Franck Tournaire	Craig Dowd
Abdelatif Benazzi	Norm Maxwell
Fabien Pelous	Robin Brooke
Marc Lievremont	Reuben Thorne
Olivier Magne	Josh Kronfeld
Christophe Juillet	Taine Randell (capt)

'The danger of this French team is that they can wake up in the morning, feel good and produce something special,' warned New Zealand coach John Hart. 'They looked [earlier in the tournament] as if they had lost confidence but they found their way back against Argentina. That makes them dangerous again.'

Maybe so, and one always discounts a French team, any French team, at one's peril. But this stumbling, bumbling side, which had been given an almighty shock by Canada and which had been the beneficiary of a terrible refereeing performance against Fiji had only just begun to regain its mojo in the quarter-final win over Argentina. Yes, they had looked impressive in scoring five tries to two, and in playing in a recognisably Gallic fashion, but against that you had to set the fact that Argentina had already surpassed expectations, they had had only four days in between their great upset win over Ireland and the game against France – and two of those had been spent celebrating their best-ever Rugby World Cup performance.

New Zealand, as ever, had progressed serenely through the group phase – too strong for England in their only real challenge, and dismissing Tonga 45-9 and Italy 101-3 to win Pool B. Against Scotland in the quarter-finals, they had taken advantage of the fact that the Scots were still somewhat battered and bruised from their midweek battle against Samoa in the play-offs and scored 17 points without reply in double-quick time. The Scots hardly knew what had hit them, and if they fought back gamely thereafter – even outscoring the All Blacks 15-5 in the second half – the damage had already been irreparably done.

So it was that New Zealand went through to yet another semi-final and, surely, another final.

The day dawned clear and bright at Twickenham, with only a stiff breeze to disturb the players of France and New Zealand. After a passionate Haka, Scottish referee Jim Fleming signalled the start and Christophe Lamaison got the game under way. Lamaison immediately showed his intent with a little chip-and-go which caught the All Blacks offside, and the French fly half put the first points of the game on the board with a well-struck penalty from about 40 metres out. From the restart, the All Blacks were again offside – possibly showing their nervousness, but from the resulting scrum they got a penalty and it was the turn of Andrew Mehrtens to have a pot from just a few feet inside the French half, but he could only hit the post.

In the next passage of play the All Blacks survived the charge of a high tackle, and won another long-distance penalty, but this time Mehrtens pushed it wide of the right-hand post. An All Blacks free kick almost on the French 22, saw yet another offside decision and this time a simple kick from about 15 metres and almost dead in front of the posts was not missed.

Despite making mistakes, the French continued to play lots of rugby, running and offloading at every opportunity, but also kicking intelligently when the occasion called for it. Finally New Zealand got pretty much their first chance to run with the ball, and Jeff Wilson took it, scorching across the turf and only a last-ditch, one-on-one tackle from full back Xavier Garbajosa stopped Wilson. Garbajosa was yellow-carded, however, for hanging on for too long after his fine challenge. From the next play the All Blacks won another penalty and Mehrtens kicked it for a 6-3 lead.

From the restart, however, Abdelatif Benazzi got to the ball and flicked it back, and though Lamaison's resulting kick was too long, so was Wilson's 22 drop-out, which invited the elusive Christophe Dominici to go on a swerving run initially down the left but then cutting back infield and when he was bought down just a metre short of the line, Lamaison was one among a handful of Frenchmen there to take the ball in under the posts. Lamaison converted his own try and France were 10-6 ahead.

New Zealand reduced this to 10-9 almost instantly when French hands in a ruck gave Mehrtens a third penalty, and straight after that the French defence failed dismally to deal with a bouncing ball on their ten-metre line and in an instant the All Blacks were all over them like a rash. Quickly recycled ball and a cover flick-on from that cleverest of players, Christian Cullen, and the ball was in the hands of Jonah Lomu. Lomu just bulldozed his way through and over. Mehrtens missed the conversion, but with New Zealand back in front at 14-10 with 23 minutes gone, they then tried to play some territory and possession for the next quarter of an hour, but found it impossible to tie the French down.

One Olivier Magne break down the right-hand touchline was particularly impressive and when Magne chipped through, Wilson only just beat Philippe Bernat-Salles to the ball. Referee Fleming awarded a 22 drop-out when both real time coverage and replays made it look like Wilson grounded it in front of the line. As commentator John Taylor said, it could have been a try, it was at least a French five-metre scrum, but 'the one thing it was not is a 22'.

With half-time looming, Mehrtens added a fourth penalty after a series of French penalty offences, the last of which was hands in the ruck, to make it 17-

10 to New Zealand at the break. Mehrtens did actually have the opportunity to extend the lead still further with the final kick of the half, but his penalty attempt from the left-hand touchline just didn't curl in sufficiently.

It took only four minutes for the All Blacks to go further ahead and again it was Lomu who did the damage. The French actually started very solidly, kicking deep into their opponents' half and keeping the pressure on at a line-out and then on the All Blacks' 22 via an up-and-under, but again it ended in a New Zealand penalty and they cleared their lines. A swift interchange of passes between Wilson and Lomu and the big winger carved his way through the French defence. Garbajosa didn't look too interested and waved Lomu through and Lomu scored close enough to the posts to give Mehrtens a relatively simple conversion. The score was up to 24-10 and if that was slightly harsh on the French, it looked too big a gap to bridge.

Some French driving play from the restart took France deep into the All Blacks' half and when Lamaison saw that the ball had been slowed right down, he quickly dropped back into the pocket and slotted a drop goal from about 30 metres out. It gave Lamaison a full house with barely five minutes of the second half gone, and two minutes later he did the same thing again; Tana Umaga of all people turned the ball over in contact, quick ruck ball just outside the All Blacks' 22 and after a couple of phases of play the French were given a penalty right in front of the posts. It meant a free play, and Lamaison kicked a second drop goal to narrow the gap to 24-16 with half an hour to play.

Substitute number eight Olivier Brouzet rumbled forward from the restart and made some ground, and when Lamaison hoisted a high kick Umaga dropped it and knocked on. From the resulting scrum a few pick and drives from France and the All Blacks were penalised for coming round the sides. It was a simple penalty for Lamaison and the score closed to 24-19.

Three minutes later, another French penalty for offside, and Lamaison lessened the deficit to three points. There was still a sense that France were creeping their way back in rather than blasting it, but one minute after Lamaison's penalty, that all changed. Nothing much seemed to be brewing with play on the halfway line but a beautiful little left-footed chip over from Fabien Galthie bounced wickedly for the All Black defenders, and beautifully for Dominici who hardly had to break stride as he took the ball one-handed, beat the sole would-be tackler and went round under the posts. From seemingly nowhere France were in the lead, 29-24.

The All Blacks looked to be making ground, but were pinged for crossing and Lamaison booted the ball deep into the New Zealand half. From the line-out, the French drove on and Lamaison conjured up a superb chip over the flat New Zealand defence. Centre Richard Dourthe was the first to the ball – just ahead of Wilson – and got the try. Lamaison added an easy conversion to put France 12 points clear at 36-24.

The Twickenham crowd were right behind the French by this stage, but the All Blacks had not given up, with Wilson going close in the right-hand corner and the All Blacks almost seized the ball at the line-out but were penalised for going over the top. And then again a minute later for another crossing offence. It was a remarkable turnaround not only in the scoreline but in the balance of the game, as the penalty count started to even up: New Zealand had only given away two penalties in the whole of the first half but now they were up to seven.

An up-and-under from Lamaison was well taken by Wilson under enormous pressure, but when the All Blacks tried to run it out of defence they knocked on to give away a scrum out on their wide left. They compounded the error by going offside at the scrum and France, rather than going for the kick which would have put them more than two scores ahead, called on Lamaison to punt it right into the corner. The play was brave, but the France line-out was well read by New Zealand who cleared their lines.

The All Blacks chucked everything at the French, but a combination of determined, sometimes desperate, defending and the ball just not falling for them for once prevented them closing the gap. As often happens when you are chasing a game, the ball got forced once too often and Umaga, who hadn't had his finest 40 minutes in an All Black shirt, dropped the ball. Magne had the pace to break clear and the wit to hack the ball on rather than try to pick it up and Philippe Bernat-Salles had the pace to capitalise and dive over just ahead of the covering Wilson. Lamaision converted and France had turned a 24-10 deficit into a 43-24 lead.

There was still time for Wilson, who had had an excellent game in defeat, to pull back one try, and with that breakaway a few minutes earlier, it could have led to a nervy few seconds for France, but the 12-point gap gave them the necessary breathing space.

'The biggest upset in the whole of World Cup history,' Taylor called it at the time, and it's hard to disagree.

New Zealand had started the match as unbackable favourites, but France had done what only France can do, turning a game on its head through the sort of rugby that everyone likes to watch, and which was acclaimed by the Twickenham crowd.

27

6 November 1999
Venue: Millennium Stadium, Cardiff
Attendance: 72,500

France 12 Australia 35

France	Australia
Xavier Garbajosa	Matt Burke
Philippe Bernat-Salles	Ben Tune
Richard Dourthe	Dan Herbert
Emile Ntamack	Tim Horan
Christophe Dominici	Joe Roff
Christophe Lamaison	Stephen Larkham
Fabien Galthie	George Gregan
Cedric Soulette	Richard Harry
Raphael Ibanez (capt)	Michael Foley
Franck Tournaire	Andrew Blades
Abdelatif Benazzi	David Giffin
Fabien Pelous	John Eales (capt)
Marc Lievremont	Matt Cockbain
Olivier Magne	David Wilson
Christophe Juillet	Toutai Kefu

The third place play-off is primarily a marketing concept; none of the players really want to be there and it's more of a distraction than a blessing. On this occasion, however, it rates a passing mention – not because South Africa's 22-18 victory over New Zealand was a particularly great game, but because it was the final Rugby World Cup appearance of one Jonah Lomu. Despite his injury and illness problems, Lomu would win a further 25 caps for New Zealand, but his last would be in November 2002, some 11 months before the next World Cup got under way.

Lomu's 15 tries put him out in front on the list of all-time Rugby World Cup try-scorers which features such brilliant finishers as Vincent Clerc, Rory Underwood, Brian Lima, Shane Williams, Australians Chris Latham, David Campese and Drew Mitchell, Bryan Habana and fellow All Blacks Doug Howlett and Joe Rokocoko (the other players who have scored tries in double digits). Lomu was a slightly different beast, however. Yes he was fast, but he was also massive, built like a tank, and like a tank he frequently ran over opponents rather than round them. As the great Colin Meads once said when asked if he had ever seen a player of Lomu's stature before, 'Oh, yes, lots of times – just never on the wing!'

In May 2003, Lomu had to start dialysis three times a week, and just over a year later he had a kidney transplant. Incredibly Lomu still fought back and returned to rugby, but a serious shoulder injury, requiring surgery, ruled him out for the whole 2005 season.

A full, consistent comeback never materialised and once it became apparent that he was not going to be selected for his third World Cup – in 2007 – owing to his failure to get a spot at a Super Rugby franchise, he chose to retire from professional rugby, though he has played at amateur level and in charity events since then.

Lomu was appointed a member of the New Zealand Order of Merit in the Queen's Birthday Honours list in June 2007, and has also been the recipient of a special merit award from the International Rugby Players' Association. He will always be credited with bringing the Rugby World Cup to the attention of the wider sporting public, and his exploits, particularly in 1995, will always be a part of rugby history.

The 1999 Rugby World Cup Final itself was something of a damp squib. The French storm had blown itself out in a semi-final which was never to be forgotten but also, sadly, not to be repeated – France have yet to win the trophy, the only side to have reached the final on three occasions without winning at least once.

Australia had been ill-prepared to face France; all their assumptions had been based on meeting a much more familiar foe, one with whom they had shared the honours a few months earlier in the 1999 Tri Nations Series. Then Australia had been well beaten in Auckland in July, 34-15 (though they had outscored the All Blacks by two tries to one), but had turned that around to win 28-7 in Sydney thanks to a superb kicking performance from Matt Burke with seven penalties and a conversion of Mark Connors's try.

But suddenly their plans had to change. Australia coach Rod McQueen requested a rush job on information about the French, which proved tricky not just because there was so little time to compile it but because the French didn't play to set patterns so it was difficult to come up with a gameplan specifically geared to countering it. What the Australians did pick up on was the importance of the dynamic French back row whose power and pace was often the source of their ability to counter-attack. Their answer to this was to retain possession as much as possible so that the French back row were too concerned with tackling and defending to get on to the front foot.

France manager Jo Maso, for his part, accepted, 'It will be difficult to play two matches like last week, to get the state of mind back.' And so it proved. The zip, the panache, just wasn't quite there and even Christophe Lamaison's first-minute penalty did not get the juices flowing. Admittedly it was nip and tuck for most of the first half, with Lamaison twice putting France ahead, but there was little sign of the pyrotechnics which had lit up Twickenham the previous week. Burke's fourth penalty of the half, deep into time added on, stretched Australia's lead to six points at the break.

And that was still the margin with an hour gone, Burke twice putting Australia nine points up, but Lamaison twice pulling the gap back within a converted try. Surely France would get that try sooner or later and then everything would be up for grabs?

Sadly, no. The French were never able to curb their indiscipline in the way that they did so spectacularly against the All Blacks. Indeed Australia captain John Eales complained to South African referee Andre Watson about the French tactics, and several of his players appeared to have injuries around the eyes at the end of the game. France were continuously penalised and that prevented them getting any sort of continuity into their running game. Watson was a fussy ref who did not appear to have total control of the game, and spent long periods lecturing the two captains. It's something of a mystery how four years later he became the only man yet to have refereed two World Cup finals – his second such appearance proving even more open to criticism than his first.

Burke once more increased the Australian lead to nine with a finely struck penalty, long but straight, after 64 minutes, and still we awaited the French explosion. Instead, from the restart Tim Horan somehow rode a huge tackle from Abdelatif Benazzi and squeezed out a precious few metres to put Australia on the front foot. Some pick-and-goes, most notably from Burke, kept them there and took play up into the French 22. When George Gregan went on the burst, there was back row replacement Owen Finegan on hand as the link to flip the ball on to winger Ben Tune who just squeezed over in the right-hand corner.

A magnificent conversion from Burke from the touchline took Australia out to 28-12 and the match was all but won. At 16 points down, the fight had leeched out of France and in the dying moments of the match Eales made a great line-out catch on the French 22, Gregan flicked an inside pass to Finegan, and the big flanker's line was perfect. He ran straight at the French defence, and his strength was enough to get him over and down despite the close attentions of three would-be tacklers.

Burke's ninth successful kick from 11 made the final score a slightly harsh 35-12, and Australia had become the first country to win a second Rugby World Cup. They had also yet again won the trophy away from home soil – both New Zealand in 1987 and South Africa in 1995 had claimed it on home turf.

France captain Raphael Ibanez, who before the game had declared, 'We are French, we are always unpredictable and I don't know exactly what will happen in the final, I don't know what we will do,' now admitted, 'We didn't have the freshness or the frenzy.'

It was a shame from a neutral's point of view that France weren't able to recapture the organised chaos which had proved too much for New Zealand, but the tournament probably got the right winner. In games against Romania, Ireland, the United States, Wales, South Africa and France the Wallabies had conceded just a solitary try – to centre Juan Grobler of the US in Australia's 55-19 victory.

In his 14th and last Rugby World Cup appearance, the wonderful Australian centre Tim Horan was a worthy recipient of the Player of the Tournament award, though no doubt his second World Cup winner's medal was the more cherished prize. Horan won 80 caps for his country, scoring 30 tries, but perhaps the most remarkable aspect was the way he battled back from a career-threatening knee injury (which ruled him out for over a year in 1994, during which he missed nine matches), to play in the 1995 Rugby World Cup and then an even bigger part in the Wallabies' 1999 triumph, when he was 29.

'I was determined to get back,' he said of his knee injury. 'But not only does a player need to get physically fit, he needs to be mentally in tune too.' Horan was certainly that, and having played a key role in the semi-final win over South Africa – arguably his finest in the green and gold – he was strong physically and mentally in the final.

The other pivotal player for Australia was John Eales, a rugby player so good in every facet of the game that his nickname was 'Nobody', because 'nobody's perfect'. Born just over a month after Horan, on 27 June 1970, Eales was not only king of the line-out, but a mobile, hard-working second row with a phenomenal reading of the game. And he also kicked goals. A lock forward who kicks penalty goals is always going to have a novelty value, but Eales was no novelty act – he kicked 163 international points for Australia, 31 conversions and 34 penalties to set alongside his two tries, one against Scotland in 1992 and one against Argentina in 1995, both times in Brisbane.

Eales was also a highly thought of captain, with coach Rod McQueen saying, 'Some captains are borderline cases as far as talent is concerned so there is some debate as to [the captain's] inclusion in the team. John was always first picked. That made life a lot easier for me as a coach. He began as a good captain and ended as a great captain.'

Eales returned the compliment to his coach, saying of McQueen that he 'understood the importance of detail. We all felt confident that he would not miss anything.'

Amusingly, Eales, a staunch Republican, recalled the moment he was going to have to receive the William Webb Ellis Cup from Her Majesty Queen Elizabeth II. 'There is no easy way to win a final, but for a few minutes at the end we knew we couldn't get beaten so we were able to enjoy those last few minutes and look around and soak it all up. Straight after the game I turned to anyone who was there to celebrate and go crazy. Then I realised I was going to get the trophy from the Queen and I thought, "Better make sure you don't swear!"' He didn't.

Australia were not, perhaps, the most exciting team to win the RWC, their triumph was built on defence rather than a swashbuckling style. They were, however, worthy winners and as Eales summed it up succinctly, 'We had achieved what we wanted.'

28

1 November 2003
Venue: Docklands Stadium, Melbourne
Attendance: 54,200

Australia 17 Ireland 16

Australia	Ireland
Mat Rogers	Girvan Dempsey
Wendell Sailor	Shane Horgan
Matt Burke	Brian O'Driscoll
Elton Flatley	Kevin Maggs
Joe Roff	Denis Hickie
Stephen Larkham	Ronan O'Gara
George Gregan (capt)	Peter Stringer
Bill Young	Reggie Corrigan
Brendan Cannon	Keith Wood (capt)
Ben Darwin	John Hayes
David Giffin	Malcolm O'Kelly
Nathan Sharpe	Paul O'Connell
George Smith	Simon Easterby
Phil Waugh	Keith Gleeson
David Lyons	Anthony Foley

T he 2003 Rugby World Cup was due to be shared between Australia and New Zealand, but a contractual dispute broke out over the requirement for 'clean' stadiums, i.e. free from advertising and with the corporate boxes relinquished by the sponsors and/or companies which held them. New Zealand seemed much more apathetic or unwilling to comply with these regulations than their neighbours – perhaps they didn't really believe there would be consequences to their lack of action, but there were, and they were severe. New Zealand were stripped of their right to be co-hosts in March 2002, a decision ratified by the IRB Council on 18 April.

So it was that the 2003 tournament became a solely Australian hosted affair, giving the defending champions a boost in their attempts to retain the trophy in front of their own fans. Credit where it's due, the Australian Rugby Union took advantage of the fact that it suddenly had a larger number of matches than it had bargained on by taking them round the countryside. Adelaide and Launceston in Tasmania were just two of the beneficiaries of this policy, and they in turn produced sell-out crowds for such unlikely games as Argentina v Ireland and Namibia v Romania respectively.

Mind you, those attempts almost came to grief early on when, in the final Pool A match Ireland once again went within a whisker of a surprise win over Australia.

The progression of Pool A had been much as expected: the hosts and holders' opening-day 24-8 win over Argentina was harder fought than the final scoreline would suggest as the win was only confirmed by a late Joe Roff try, converted by Elton Flatley, with six minutes remaining. Felipe Contepomi had something of an off day with the boot, notching just one from five, which made it all the more

117

strange that head coach Marcelo Loffreda left Gonzalo Quesada, the top points scorer from four years earlier, on the bench throughout. A few more penalties at crucial moments might have made the difference and certainly would have exerted a little more pressure on the malfunctioning Wallabies. Loffreda did not make the same mistake against Ireland when he shunted Contepomi into the centres and restored Quesada at fly half.

After that wake-up call, however, the Wallabies had romped through a 90-8 demolition of Romania, with Flatley scoring the fastest try in World Cup history (timed at just 13 seconds) and converting 11 of the 13 tries scored, including a Mat Rogers hat-trick. Rogers was the latest rugby league star to switch to the union code and coach Bob Dwyer moved 1999 World Cup-winning star Matt Burke into the centres in order to accommodate Rogers at full back.

They then posted a ridiculous 142-0 win over the hapless Namibians, the biggest winning margin in World Cup history. Chris Latham's five tries in that match account for almost half his World Cup total of 11, placing him at the head of the Australian try-scoring charts with one more than the more accomplished finishers David Campese and Drew Mitchell. There were also hat-tricks for the great Matt Giteau and Lote Tuqiri, the Fijian-born former rugby league international.

Ireland hadn't found it quite such plain sailing, but had been in no danger against either Romania (45-17) or Namibia (64-7). Romania certainly started off in a spirited fashion and prevented Ireland crossing their line in the opening quarter, but once their defences were breached the floodgates opened. A quickfire double from full back Girvan Dempsey and a trademark 30-metre sprint from Keith Wood as the hooker added to his impressive try tally saw Ireland stretch away. Although Ireland didn't get anywhere near Australia's total against the Namibians, they still managed ten tries in heavy rain in Sydney.

It made the claims that it was the pool of death look ever so slightly silly, but Ireland coach Eddie O'Sullivan did have a point when he called it that as, at the time, Australia, Ireland and Argentina were all in the top seven of the world rankings.

Against Argentina, Ireland had had to dig deep; having lost to the Pumas four years earlier in the quarter-final play-off they were well aware of the danger they posed and were determined not to fall into the same trap. They nearly did, however, as despite a dramatic try just as the first quarter was drawing to a close – a trademark burst from captain Keith Wood setting up a score for Alan Quinlan – Ireland finished the half only 10-9 up on account of the unerring boot of Gonzalo Quesada. Argentina even took the lead with a long-range drop goal from Ignacio Corleto after 57 minutes, but it lasted less than three minutes before Ronan O'Gara put Ireland back in front. O'Gara extended it to four points after 65 minutes and although Quesada reduced the deficit to one with seven minutes remaining, the Pumas could not fashion another chance.

'They took their opportunities and we didn't,' was winger Diego Albanese's blunt assessment as a disappointed Argentina headed home.

'There was obviously a lot of pressure and we seemed to freeze somewhat out there,' said Wood after Ireland had just hung on. 'But there was a weight of expectation which has been building for four years.'

For Ireland it meant the opportunity to have a crack at Australia without qualification for the knockout stages being on the line; that was already assured for both teams. 'It's Australia we were always most worried about, of course,' said O'Sullivan. 'It makes them dangerous that they've had a bad season – I'd rather play them on form.' It sounds a little, well, Irish, in logic but we all know what he meant.

Australia having won only one of their four Tri Nations matches that year were not displaying the sort of form one would expect of the defending champions. They had, however, despatched Ireland in June of that year by 45-16, a punishing six tries to one defeat which had illustrated the size of the gap which still remained between the two hemispheres.

Does the scenario of both teams knowing they had already qualified for the next phase lead to a lack of cutting edge? If so, it was scarcely in evidence in this game. Australia lined up with just five survivors from their 1992 triumph – the half back pairing of George Gregan (now installed as captain) and Stephen Larkham, winger Joe Roff, Burke (playing out of position, as mentioned earlier), and second row forward David Giffin, perhaps wanting to be known as something other than 'the other lock', alongside John Eales.

The key to the match was Ireland's cussed refusal to allow Australia to open up a gap – it looked like the Wallabies might do that on several occasions, not least early on when a snap drop goal from scrum half Gregan was swiftly followed by a flowing move which put flanker George Smith in for a try on the left. Flatley almost took the lead out to ten points, but hit the far post with his conversion attempt and barely three minutes later O'Gara had pulled three points back when Australia went offside.

Flatley and O'Gara exchanged second-quarter penalties for a half-time score of 11-6 in Australia's favour. Flatley increased that to 14-6 when prop John Hayes was pinged for offside. But with just a fraction over half an hour to play, Brian O'Driscoll made his World Cup mark. Ruck ball looked like it was being moved right, but play switched to the left, substitute winger John Kelly gave O'Driscoll just inches of space and the great man was round the outside of Wallabies wing Wendell Sailor and over in the corner. 'He only had inches to play with, but that's all that players of his calibre need,' said the TV commentary.

The conversion was from right out on the touchline, but O'Gara still nailed it, and it was a one-point game.

Irritatingly for Ireland they swiftly conceded another offside penalty for Flatley to kick, but then it was the O'Driscoll show again as he picked up a ball off his toes and seeing that absolutely nothing was on in either direction, he just calmly knocked off the coolest of drop goals to bring it back to 17-16 with about 12 minutes still to play.

David Humphreys, on for O'Gara, lined up a drop goal in the dying seconds, but his effort went wide of the posts. 'We were very close to having it,' said Ireland captain Keith Wood afterwards. 'We are not happy because we came here to win so we are disappointed, but not too disappointed because we have a quarter-final in a week's time.' Wood's Australian counterpart Gregan said, 'We're happy to have got through that. We didn't play the way we wanted, but that was a lot to do with the way the Irish performed. They put us under pressure and had most of the field position but we hung in there and won a tight match, which is always a good thing to do.'

It condemned Ireland to the runners-up spot and a match against the in-form France, while Australia gained what looked, on paper, like the easier draw, against the runners-up in Pool B, which looked to be between Scotland, Fiji, the United States and Japan. The result was hard on O'Driscoll who, quite apart from his two world-class scores, also topped the match charts for both tackles and carries. It was O'Driscoll's second of his four Rugby World Cup 2003 appearances – in total he played 17 RWC matches in his career, and that would have been a few more had Ireland qualified for the latter stages – two semi-final appearances with Ireland and O'Driscoll would have been up over the 20-game mark and closing in on Jason Leonard's record of 22.

It wasn't to be in 2003, however, as France launched a first-half blitz against Ireland. Tries from Olivier Magne (after just three minutes), Christophe Dominici (29) and Imanol Harinordoquy (33), all converted by Frederic Michalak, and two Michalak penalties gave France an unassailable 27-0 lead at half-time. It got worse for Ireland when Jean-Jacques Crenca added a fourth and with another Michalak penalty and conversion the score was up to an embarrassing 37-0 before Kevin Maggs finally got the Irish on the scoreboard.

A determined French side weren't averse to some cynical play to slow the ball down and prevent the Irish playing the sort of front-foot rugby which might have got them back into the game. Eventually former French captain Raphael Ibanez received a yellow card for a professional foul, killing the Irish ball while lying on the ground. O'Driscoll tried his hardest to drag Ireland back into the match, scoring two tries, both converted by David Humphreys, but the damage was already done, France winning 43-21.

That quarter-final defeat was to be Wood's last match for his country, an ill-fitting end to a fabulous career. O'Driscoll, however, would come again after that. And again.

29

1 November 2003
Venue: Sydney Football Stadium, Sydney
Attendance: 37,137

Fiji 20 Scotland 22

Fiji	Scotland
Norman Ligairi	Glenn Metcalfe
Aisea Tuilevu Kurimudu	Simon Danielli
Epeli Ruivarda	Gregor Townsend
Seru Rabeni	Andrew Henderson
Rupeni Caucaunibuca	Kenny Logan
Nicky Little	Chris Paterson
Moses Rauluni	Bryan Redpath (capt)
Isaia Rasila	Tom Smith
Greg Smith	Gordon Bulloch
Joeli Veitayaki	Bruce Douglas
Apenisa Naevo	Nathan Hines
Ifereimi Rawaqa	Stuart Grimes
Lula Maimuri	Ross Beattie
Koli Sewabu	Cameron Mather
Alifereti Doviverata (capt)	Simon Taylor

The demise of the unloved, unlamented quarter-final play-offs, introduced in 1999 and swiftly discarded after that tournament was completed, was never going to give rise to complaints – from anyone. It did mean, however, that there was no hiding place in the group stages; instead of sneaking through and having a shot at redemption, teams knew they had to finish in one of the top two positions. Third wouldn't hack it.

In the event, the Tier 1 nations did make it through, largely at the expense of the Pacific Islands, with Canada and Argentina also missing out. In Pool B, though, it came down to a straight fight between Fiji and Scotland. Fiji had taken a bit of a hammering from France in their opening match on 11 October, losing 61-18, and had just sneaked past the United States by a single point, 19-18, but even then they had been outscored two tries to one. Fortunately in Nicky Little they had, for once, discovered a fly half who could kick as well as run and his four penalties in addition to his conversion of Apenisa Naevo's try just gave his country the edge. A more comfortable 41-13 win over Japan set Fiji up for a winner-takes-all contest with Scotland.

The Scots, for their part, had looked good in scoring five tries against both Japan, who they beat 32-11, and the US, who they beat 39-15. France were a different matter, however, and they absolutely destroyed Scotland 51-9, keeping their Six Nations opponents tryless while scoring five of their own.

It turned the Fiji v Scotland clash into a shoot-out for a quarter-final spot. Sydney Football Stadium was the venue and Englishman Tony Spreadbury was the referee on a sunny afternoon, for a 4pm kick-off local time.

With just a minute and a half gone, Scotland's players – and fans – were left in no doubt as to where the main danger lay. Little hoisted a high crossfield kick from right to left and while Scotland watched and waited for it to come down, the dangerous winger Rupeni Caucaunibuca jumped high and aggressively for the ball. Luckily for Scotland he knocked it on rather than claimed it. Scotland hit back, combining a more structured approach while still trying to keep the game moving, and a rampaging run by in-form number eight Simon Taylor ended in a Scotland penalty. A rare miss from Chris Paterson followed as the normally metronomic Scot hit the far post from wide, but not too far, out.

From the very next play, Fiji turned the tables, driving on and earning themselves a penalty which saw Little push his first attempt past the near post. Fiji did well to tidy up a particularly scrappy line-out, but weren't able to make anything of it, and play continued in a slightly disjointed fashion with neither side gaining a clear advantage in the early phases.

But with about 12 minutes on the clock, Fiji put together a solid drive from another line-out take on their right, and Fiji moved the ball right to left, Little wrapped around in midfield to provide the 'extra' man and with both wingers appearing on that side of the pitch, the Fijians were able to create a little space. A little space was all Caucaunibuca needed; he was still about 25 metres out and there appeared to be sufficient cover, but he swerved out past the first line of defence, then just the hint of a shimmy back inside made Kenny Logan hesitate for a millisecond and Caucau stepped on the after-burners to scorch down the touchline and had enough pace and strength to prevent himself being forced into touch before he dotted down in the corner.

Referee Spreadbury asked for another look, but the replay made it pretty clear that he got the ball down cleanly without putting a foot in touch or clipping the corner flag on his way. Little added the extras with a superb conversion from right out on the touchline.

'Have we just seen the best winger in the world?' asked the commentary team.

From virtually the next play, a similar move saw Caucau in possession again and this time he tried a little chip ahead and it was only the covering Logan – across from his station on the left – who just averted the danger. Next the Fijians broke down the right wing; Scotland lost the ball in attack following a heavy tackle and Aisea Tuilevu Kurimudu, Tuilevu as he was known, was away. Once again great cover defence got to Tuilevu and Scotland full back Glenn Metcalfe managed to get his knee on to the touchline moments before the ball was touched down.

The bulk of play continued to take place in the Scotland half, with the Fijians recycling the ball quickly and keeping the Scots under pressure throughout. Another great high kick went loose and Seru Rabeni almost latched on to it before Taylor was able to tidy up. Then Rabeni attempted a drop goal, which missed but while the Scottish defenders stood watching, Caucau almost burst through on to the bouncing ball, and if the bounce had been kinder, might well have got his fingertips to it; even referee Spreadbury could be heard to say 'unlucky' as he awarded a 22 drop out.

Scotland finally got a relieving penalty and Paterson took play from one 22 to the other which at last gave them a measure of territory. A hurried sliced clearance from scrum half Moses Rauluni kept Fiji under a bit of pressure and eventually resulted in a simple penalty in front of the posts after the Fijians had come in from the side at a ruck. From the restart, Paterson put in a beautiful bouncing kick midway into the Fijian half, and the end result was exactly the same, with the Fijians pinged for coming in at the side again, and Paterson pulled the score back to 10-6, with half an hour gone.

Paterson then made a glorious break down the right, Fiji missed a couple of tackles and when the ball was spread left it looked like Scotland had the space, but the Fijian defence tightened up and just held out. It was starting to look as if Scotland had weathered the storm and were starting to exert a measure of control, but the first half had a sting in the tail when the Fijians ran the ball out of their own 22 and from nothing the ball got to Caucau and he ghosted inside replacement winger James McLaren, then back out and was away. The chances of the only remaining defender, Metcalfe, stopping Caucau one on one were zero, and so it proved.

'Give it to Caucau and he is go, go, gone,' said the commentator. 'White magic at Aussie Stadium.'

Caucau was never the most sleek, muscle-toned winger, but his speed was complemented by fantastic balance, and the ability to step off either foot and go in or out while running at full pace. Almost inconceivably, Caucau won just eight caps for his country, but he frequently didn't report for duty with the national team and served a one-year ban in 2005; on another occasion he couldn't find his passport! At club level, however, he proved a huge success, moving to Agen in France's Top 14 after the 2003 RWC for whom he scored 65 tries in 108 matches over the next five seasons. He left under a cloud in 2008, but returned to score 13 tries in the 2009/10 season which saw Agen regain a place in the Top 14, but was released by the club after failing to report for training at the start of the following season. Caucau's highlights reel is sensational, it's a shame it isn't a lot longer.

It meant the half-time score was 14-6 to Fiji, and Scotland had some work to do if they were to pull the match round. They knew they had to score first, and they duly did so when Fiji were penalised for 'slow retreat', i.e. not getting back behind quickly enough for Spreadbury's liking. Paterson was down receiving treatment for a knock to the back of the head, but got up in time to slot his third penalty of the game and reduce the deficit to 14-9.

Scotland started to play more of a percentage, territorial game – less popular with the fans but almost certainly the right way to go about this particular match. Henderson made good ground through the middle as the Fijians appeared to have gone slightly off the boil and then Scotland had a series of plays only a few metres out from the Fiji line. But when the Scots were penalised for obstruction, Fiji needed no second bidding to charge out of defence and take play back up almost to the halfway line.

Caucau kicked through and was taken out fractionally late and high, though nothing was given, though the Scots were penalised for holding on in the tackle and Little kicked deep into the Scottish half. 'How much petrol is left in this Fijian tank?' asked the commentators, worried that they might run out of energy. Fiji were harshly penalised at a maul and Scotland kicked to the corner from where they won an offside decision, giving Paterson a simple little chip over for 14-12 and Scotland were within a score of Fiji with 56 minutes on the clock.

The next penalty was for the same offence as most of the others – coming round the side of a ruck and playing the ball when offside. Paterson was afforded another simple kick from a fraction outside the 22, and Scotland were into the lead for the first time. But Caucau, who'd had no opportunities in the second half, caught his own high kick to put his team on the front foot and from the resulting breakdown Scotland flanker Cameron Mather gave away the daftest of penalties. Despite being warned by Spreadbury to leave the ball, Mather continued to try and play it and was frankly lucky not to be yellow-carded. Little, who hadn't had a penalty shot since missing early in the first half (though he had, of course, converted both tries), calmly put the Pacific Islanders back in front from 40 metres.

There were almost exactly 15 minutes left to play when Scotland restarted the game, and a kicking duel ended with Fiji advantage at a line-out inside the Scotland 22. But they couldn't steal the Scotland throw and then were penalised for going over the top. The giant lock Ifereimi Rawaqa almost got away down the Fijian left but just didn't have the pace to hold off the covering Metcalfe. From the line-out, Fiji were penalised for offside, allowing Scotland to get out of the dangerzone. Then a Little up and under was knocked forward by Logan – pretty much the only thing he did wrong in the entire match – and prop Bruce Douglas instinctively played it, giving Little another straightforward penalty, which he kicked for 20-15. Suddenly the Scots needed more than a three-pointer as the game entered its final five minutes.

There had been notable signs, however, that the Fijians were tiring fast, and some great Scotland mauling and rucking saw lock Api Naevo sent to the sin bin for what didn't look any worse a foul than numerous others. Scotland drove over from the linnet with Tom Smith the last man up with the ball, and although it wasn't Paterson's easiest kick of the day, he slotted it.

There were still two minutes left to play, but Fiji had no further chances and it was Scotland who progressed, though there was no doubt who the man of the match was.

30

28 October 2003
Venue: Aussie Stadium, Sydney
Attendance: 28,576

Georgia 12 Uruguay 24

Georgia	Uruguay
Irakli Machkhaneli	Juan Menchaca
Malkhaz Urjukashvili	Alfonso Cardoso
Tedo Zibzibadze	Diego Aguirre (capt)
Irakli Giorgadze	Martin Mendaro
Archil Kavtarahvili	Carlos Baldassari
Paliko Jimsheladze	Sebastian Aguirre
Irakli Modebadze	Juan Campomar
Goderdzi Shvelidze	Rodrigo Sanchez
David Dadunashvili	Diego Lamelas
Avto Kopaliani	Pablo Lemoine
Zurab Mtchedlishvili	Juan Carlos Bado
Sergo Gujaraidze	Juan Alzueta
Giorgo Chkhaidze	Hernan Ponte
Gregoire Yachvili	Nicolas Grille
Ilia Zedginidze (capt)	Rodrigo Capo Ortega

If you were looking for a simple clue as to the growth of the Rugby World Cup as a tournament, you need look no further than some of the crowd figures. In 1987, 18,000 spectators turned up to watch the spectacular semi-final between France and Australia in Sydney; in 2003 well over 28,000 turned up to watch Georgia v Uruguay in the same city.

For Uruguay it was a second appearance in the finals, having reached the same stage four years earlier. On that occasion they had beaten Spain 27-15 to record their first victory in the finals, and had given a good account of themselves in losing 43-12 to Scotland and 39-3 to South Africa.

In 2003 they had qualified via the Americas section, where they faced Canada, the USA and Chile. Uruguay won all three of their home games, beating Chile 34-23, Canada 25-23 and the USA 10-9; if their away form gave cause for a few concerns (they lost 10-6 in Chile, 28-24 in the USA and 51-16 in Canada), they nevertheless had done tremendously well to pip the USA and avoid the repechage.

Georgia, for their part, were making their first appearance in a finals, and a reflection of their struggles was that their pre-tournament camps had to be cancelled because of a lack of funds.

But the eastern European nation was fanatical about its rugby and their presence in Australia was well deserved after they had beaten Russia to get there, 17-13 in a rugby-mad Tbilisi. Georgia had been well beaten in Dublin, 63-14, against an Ireland side which suffered the ignominy of having to play in the qualifying competition, but they didn't care, they set up camp in France and knuckled down to the serious business of showing the world what they could do on a rugby pitch.

Head coach Claude Saurel, a former France international, had been in charge since 1999 having been asked to advise on rugby in the country two years earlier. He found he personally was having to pay for tracksuits for his squad and for video equipment to improve their training, and that his team's budget for the competition was some way behind that of the other teams. Alison Kervin, in her excellent *Thirty Bullies: A History of the Rugby World Cup*, reports that the players were on an allowance of £13 a day. 'We are light years behind England,' said Gregoire Yachvili, the French-born flanker whose brother Dimitri was to win 60 caps for France and score 373 international points. 'We might not have tackle bags, body armour or a scrum machine, but at least we have a ball and a pitch.' Instead Saurel arranged for his forwards to push against tractors.

The next problem they faced was the refusal of the French teams, for whom the majority of them played, to release the Georgians for the World Cup and consequently many of them had to go without pay for the duration of their involvement in the tournament.

In their first game, Georgia were comprehensively outplayed by England, going down 84-6, though they had started brightly enough. They next lost 46-9 to Samoa and 46-19 to South Africa. They looked to be learning on the job and improving fast, and in the game against South Africa, prop David Dadunashvili got their first-ever Rugby World Cup try – his country would have to wait until 2007 for the next.

Uruguay had managed to score some tries, but suffered just as heavy beatings, losing 72-6 to South Africa in their opening match, then 60-13 to Samoa, though Rodrigo Capo Ortega (known as Capo) and Pablo Lemoine, both of whom played their club rugby in France, scored for the South Americans.

So it was that going into the match between Georgia and Uruguay, both teams knew that it was their only realistic opportunity to chalk up a victory during the 2003 competition. ITV's World Cup coverage paid the match the respect it was due by televising the whole 80 minutes live on ITV2, and with its first-choice commentary team of John Taylor and Steve Smith. That it was a somewhat scrappy match with little continuity is only to be expected, perhaps, but it was nevertheless a landmark occasion.

Georgia had the first real chance, an offside penalty which was pushed just wide of the right-hand post by Paliko Jimsheladze. The European side then had the chance to rumble over from a driving maul, but Uruguay did well to defend it and won a clearing penalty for holding on. The first points came from yet another offside decision, affording Juan Menchaca a relatively simple chance from about 36 metres out which he converted for 3-0 after 14 minutes. Georgia continued to press, however, and from an extended period of possession after the restart Jimsheladze had another chance, but over-compensated and hooked it past the left-hand post.

A third opportunity was a much straighter kick, and the left-footed Malkhaz Urjukashvili slotted it home from about the same distance as Uruguay had scored theirs earlier. That concluded the first-quarter sparring, with neither side claiming a clear advantage, but a great line-out steal almost saw scrum half Juan Campomar scamper over down the blindside. Uruguay kept up the pressure, however, and after moving the ball swiftly from left to right, winger Alfonso

Cardoso was the man over and he touched down easily. Captain Diego Aguirre kicked a fine conversion to make the score 10-3 after 24 minutes, and that's how it stayed until the interval.

Uruguay seemed to be gaining a measure of control towards the end of that first half, but missed a penalty opportunity and, in the last five minutes, two decent drop goal attempts, one of which went wide, the other on target but dropping just shot of the crossbar. Aguirre had another left-footed shot from a similar position that he nailed the conversion earlier, but on this occasion he just didn't draw it in enough and hit the post.

'It's been very, very nervous,' said World Cup winner Francois Pienaar in the studio at half-time. Certainly too many handling errors and an inability to retain possession by either side made the game a disappointing spectacle. Georgia came out fired up and took the game to Uruguay but once again failed with a difficult penalty attempt barely a minute into the second half. When they got another chance from a very similar position, out wide on their right, the 19-year-old replacement Merab Kvirikashvili took over kicking duties and hammered it through.

It was just reward for the positive start Georgia had made to the second half, and minutes later scrum half Irakli Modebadze almost wriggled through. 'It's a different game second half,' said Steve Smith on commentary, and an obvious offside gave Georgia the opportunity to close the gap still further, which they took decisively to make the score 10-9 with exactly half an hour remaining.

Sadly for Georgia, a handling mistake deep in their own 22 resulted in a period of pressure on their line and when Uruguay got their driving maul set there was a sense of inevitability about their getting over the line. Hooker Diego Lamellas was the last man up. Aguirre kicked a fine conversion from wide out on the right and for all Georgia's excellent third quarter they found themselves trailing 17-9. With not too many signs of a Georgian try on the horizon, it was always going to be hard for them to turn the game around for a second time, but they gave it their all and a fourth penalty, again by the young Kvirikashvili, brought them back to within five points at 17-12. That came at the end of a flowing move and a fine kick ahead by Kvirikashvili which saw him taken out by a late shoulder charge by Nicolas Grille which should have seen a yellow card issued.

At that point there were 12 minutes left on the clock and the force seemed to be with Georgia, and they tried everything to get the try they needed, but Uruguay shut the game down effectively. An impressive drive from a line-out looked likely to result in a third try for Uruguay only to find them penalised for obstruction. Uruguay had the bit between their teeth, however, and were not to be denied. In the 78th minute, a break from man of the match Aguirre saw him slice through the defence, offload to Campomar and when the scrum half was tackled there was replacement back row forward Nicolas Brignoni on hand to take the ball and plunge over. A simple conversion from Juna Menchaca made the final scoreline 24-12, somewhat harsh on Georgia who had played a full part in the game.

'We came here determined to do our best,' said Laurel, 'to give it a go and see how we go against the strong teams.' Georgia would be back, and they would be stronger.

Rugby World Cup Greatest Matches

Unfortunately for Uruguay their joy at winning a World Cup match for the second tournament running was somewhat diluted when they lost their final group game 111-13 against England. Although Lemoine got his second try of the competition, they were simply overwhelmed in every facet of play as England recorded 17 tries, five of them from Josh Lewsey, with 13 of the 17 being converted. It was a bit of a return to earth for the South Americans, who then failed to qualify for either the 2007 or 2011 finals. They are back for 2015, however, under their head coach, one Pablo Lemoine. After winning 49 caps for his country, Lemoine retired in 2010, and since 2012 has been in charge of his national team as they return to the World Cup stage. It would be great for the sport if Uruguay could become a genuine world power alongside their fellow South Americans of Argentina.

31

18 October 2003
Venue: Subiaco Oval, Perth
Attendance: 38,834

England 25 South Africa 6

England	South Africa
Josh Lewsey	Jaco van der Westhuyzen
Jason Robinson	Ashwin Williams
Will Greenwood	Jorrie Muller
Mike Tindall	De Wet Barry
Ben Cohen	Thinus Delport
Jonny Wilkinson	Louis Koen
Kyran Bracken	Joost van der Westhuizen
Trevor Woodman	Christo Bezuidenhout
Steve Thompson	Danie Coetzee
Phil Vickery	Richard Bands
Martin Johnson (capt)	Bakkies Botha
Ben Kay	Victor Matfield
Lewis Moody	Corne Krige (capt)
Neil Back	Joe van Niekirk
Lawrence Dallaglio	Juan Smith

The great Joost van der Westhuizen was the only survivor from the South African team which lost the dramatic extra-time semi-final to Australia in 1999. And if the pack had a hard-edged, accomplished look to it, the line-up in the backs did not appear half as intimidating as it had in 1999. England, on the other hand, boasted five players in the starting line-up who had also started in their 1999 quarter-final defeat by those Springboks – captain Martin Johnson, back-row players Neil Back and Lawrence Dallaglio, prop Phil Vickery and centre Will Greenwood.

More significantly, though, in the squad were Richard Hill, Jason Leonard, Martin Corry, Danny Grewcock, Joe Worsley, Matt Dawson, Mike Catt, Paul Grayson and Dan Luger, all of whom had been part of the 1999 campaign. As had head coach Clive Woodward. It all added up to a vastly experienced squad which had claimed three of the four Six Nations titles since the previous World Cup, including a grand slam in 2003. They had also beaten all of the Southern Hemisphere's 'Big Three' in the 2002 autumn internationals – including a fearful 53-3 hammering of South Africa (who had also lost in both France and Scotland on that tour).

England set their stall out early on that day, running back the South African kick-off and going on to score seven tries; all South Africa had to offer in response was physicality, often illegal. The game was undoubtedly slanted by the 23rd-minute sending-off of South African lock Jannes Lubuschagne for a late, no-arms challenge on Jonny Wilkinson but England had already scored their first try by then. Unsurprisingly, not many Springboks survived the rout, though, so the game provided few pointers to this World Cup clash 11 months later.

It was certainly a more cagey affair, as World Cup games tend to be, and with both teams still to play the dangerous Samoa, they knew that defeat in this match could prove costly. At the very least it was likely to lead to a more hazardous route through the knockout stages, starting with a likely quarter-final against New Zealand, so there was no question of either side putting out a second string. The crowd may have been less than half that of the one at Twickenham the previous year, but the atmosphere was crackling with electricity. The first penalty chance went to England when centre De Wet Barry was penalised for holding on and from 40 metres out but pretty much dead straight, Wilkinson notched the points. England were trying to move the ball and Jason Robinson almost broke right through with one of his trademark shuffles, followed by a barnstorming run from hooker Steve Thompson, but Mike Tindall lost the ball forward in contact. Tindall almost made amends with an in-and-out dummy and step but was just forced into touch short of the goal line.

Moments later, Tindall was almost in at the other corner, the left. Robinson again had the Springboks chasing shadows in midfield and when Wilkinson switched play and looped a ball over the defence it looked like Tindall was in until a wonderful cover tackle came in from flanker Joe van Niekerk.

With quarter of an hour gone it had been all England, but then Lewsey failed to gather a bomb and knocked on in the process, giving South Africa pretty much their first piece of decent possession. Louis Koen had an attempt at a drop goal charged down by Will Greenwood, but South Africa managed to re-gather and Juan Smith went on a storming run down the right and at the breakdown England were penalised for handling in the ruck. Koen slotted the kick for 3-3.

Koen, who like the great Wales full back Leigh Halfpenny played in a scrum cap but removed it to kick, failed with a long-range effort from the halfway line – he had the accuracy but not the distance. South Africa, having been comprehensively outplayed in the first 15 minutes, had worked their way back into the match and England started to fret and look a little anxious and when Thompson lost the ball forward the Boks had the chance to counter-attack but took the ball back into the forwards rather than spreading it wide to where they had an overlap.

A scrum penalty on the South African 22 did enable Wilkinson to put England ahead again, but then Lewis Moody was pinged for a high tackle and Koen hit the post from 47 metres. England did a good tidying-up job, but were still getting little change out of the Victor Matfield/Bakkies Botha-controlled line-out. This was only the sixth time the two had played together, but even so there were signs of the partnership developing into a great one. Ultimately they would set a second-row world record of 63 matches in tandem – and it might well have been considerably more but for Botha serving the odd suspension. To say Matfield provided the skill and athleticism and Botha the beef and enforcement would be doing Botha something of a disservice, but there was nonetheless an element of truth in the caricature. Botha retired from international rugby in November 2014 having won 85 caps for his country, won in the World Cup and against the Lions. Add his club triumphs in Super Rugby, Currie Cup, Vodacom Cup, European Cup and Top 14, and Botha is one of the most successful players in the history of the game.

Koen, meanwhile, had drawn South Africa level again before the conclusion of the first half. He missed two which should have been sitters for an international kicker, but when Tindall was penalised for an early tackle, Koen finally slotted one, albeit unconvincingly, from the 22 and almost straight in front of the posts.

'Clive Woodward knows his whole dream is on the line,' said commentator John Taylor as the teams ran out on to the pitch for the second half. 'I think England need a big 15 minutes here, they ended up just on the wrong side of the possession and territory stats in that first half.'

Martin Johnson called the first line-out to himself and set up a driving maul – it didn't make that much ground but it did suck in a few defenders and England spread the ball wide to good effect as Greenwood, Lewsey and Robinson combined to take play into the South African 22. Then it was switched back the other way and Johnson charged up through the middle and caught the Springboks offside; a simple chance for Wilkinson to put his team back in front, 9-6.

Thompson put a pretty good kick through and chased it himself, but Jaco van der Westhuyzen just tidied it up before he got there, and a wonderful pick-up from off his toes by van Niekerk enabled him to make lots of ground, and Matfield and Botha almost combined to get over in the right-hand corner, but the latter was forced into touch just short. Barry was perhaps a little fortunate to escape a yellow card for a late charge on Robinson, but his immediate hands-up mea culpa probably saved him.

From an attacking scrum just inside the South African 22, England were unable to find a way through but gained another penalty right in front of the posts and Wilkinson increased the lead to six. England were coming under increasing pressure from the huge Springbok forwards, but the South Africans seemed to have few ideas in attack and rarely looked capable of crossing the England line, playing lots of good rugby in the centre of the park but never really getting in behind the England defence.

Then with 62 minutes gone, Koen had to stoop low to collect a pass from his scrum half and the split second that cost him enabled Lewis Moody to charge down his kick on the ten-metre line. Greenwood was the first to the loose ball, and a carefully controlled kick on took the ball over the line. The centre was in acres of space and comfortably got to the ball for the 28th try of his international career. Wilkinson converted and suddenly the score was up to 19-6. In a tight game, that always looked likely to be enough. Clive Woodward certainly seemed to think so as the cameras pictured him looking happier and more relaxed than previously.

Four minutes later Ben Cohen made an excellent break up the middle, spinning past Koen and bouncing off the tackles. The ball was set back so precisely that it gave Wilkinson ample time and space to drop a goal and further increase England's lead. England had by now nudged ahead on the possession stats, and were also beginning the disrupt the South African ball, particularly at the line-out where on two consecutive occasions the Springbok ball was thrown right over the back.

In fact, England were looking stronger the longer the game went on and when Josh Lewsey ran back a loose clearing kick, the move was taken on by

Dallaglio then Greenwood, Kyran Bracken had a quick look up to see where his half back partner was and provided the perfect ball for Wilkinson to slot over another drop goal from about 30 metres out and take the score to 22-6.

There were only five minutes remaining, and although South Africa had an attacking line-out just five metres out, they didn't make much of it and Dallaglio – who had had a monumental second half – stole the ball at a ruck. And that was pretty much that. The victory over the Springboks wasn't one of England's finest performances, and Clive Woodward afterwards spoke of relief more than anything. But it was resilient and, ultimately, it was a fairly comfortable victory over one of the world's superpowers – and the team which had knocked England out of the previous World Cup. Defence coach Phil Larder was especially pleased by the second-half shut out, and by not allowing the South Africans a try.

In Peter Burns's book *White Gold: England's Journey to World Cup Glory*, Larder is quoted as saying, 'There are three areas of defence that I look at. There's technique, some of which can only be improved when you work at 100 per cent so throughout a Test week we will build from 50 per cent to 100 per cent. The second thing is organisation but then the thing that really makes a defence as good as ours is the third thing: enthusiasm and desire. The only way to get that enthusiasm and desire is to go full-on. Obviously there is a danger of picking up injury so we keep it short. But it's essential. The fear of being unprepared is greater than the fear of picking up injuries – and that comes from the players.'

'What won the last World Cup?' asked France coach Bernard Laporte rhetorically. 'Defence. Australia had one try scored against them four years ago. Who has the best defence now? England. It's the best part of their game.'

32

2 November 2003
Venue: Telstra Stadium Australia, Sydney
Attendance: 80,000

New Zealand 53 Wales 37

New Zealand	Wales
Mils Muliaina	Garan Evans
Doug Howlett	Shane Williams
Leon MacDonald	Mark Taylor
Aaron Mauger	Sonny Parker
Joe Rokocoko	Tom Shanklin
Carlos Spencer	Stephen Jones
Justin Marshall	Gareth Cooper
Dave Hewett	Iestyn Thomas
Keven Mealamu	Robin McBryde
Greg Somerville	Adam Jones
Brad Thorn	Brent Cockbain
Ali Williams	Robert Sidoli
Reuben Thorne (capt)	Jonathan Thomas
Richie McCaw	Colin Charvis (capt)
Jerry Collins	Alix Popham

The New Zealand v Wales Pool D match was undoubtedly one of the best group stage fixtures in the history of the Rugby World Cup. And yet, nothing that Wales had done up until that point had given any real indication that they were capable of producing such a performance.

Their campaign had started with a comfortable enough 41-10 win over Canada, in which they scored five tries to one and Iestyn Harris converted all five and added two penalties for good measure. But the Welsh had really struggled to put Tonga away – indeed they were outscored on the try count, three to two. However, solid kicking from Stephen Jones coupled with a fine display from flanker Martyn Williams, who not only scored one of the tries but also kicked a drop goal, saw them edge through 27-20.

Wales's next challenge was to subdue Italy and having lost 30-22 to the Italians in that year's Six Nations, they went into the game all too well aware that defeat could see them knocked out. With Italy having also beaten both Tonga and Canada, their heavy defeat by New Zealand would not prevent them taking the runners-up spot if they beat the Welsh. Wales again scored tries – three more of them on this occasion – but the kicking of fly half Rima Wakarua always kept Italy in touch and the final margin of victory was only 27-15.

The neutral did fear for Wales against the All Blacks given that the latter had beaten Italy 70-7, Canada 68-6 and Tonga 91-7. It looked as if Wales's main target would be to keep the score below 50. In the event they did end up shipping over 50 points, but spectacularly, amazingly, they scored 37 of their own.

The All Blacks ran the ball straight from the kick off and Joe Rokocoko made ground down the left; the ball was recycled right and Doug Howlett and Ali Williams made further territory down the right, into the Wales 22. The ball was lost in contact, but New Zealand got the scrum put-in and the ball was spread quickly wide and Rokocoko was in down the left after just three minutes, with centre Leon MacDonald adding the extras. The width and pace the All Blacks were putting on the ball was extraordinary and it seemed unlikely that Wales would be able to live with them. They broke again straight from the restart with MacDonald and Howlett set free down the right by Carlos Spencer's pass and Wales scrum half Gareth Cooper was just able to collect Howlett's chip ahead.

There was then a long delay for treatment to Wales full back Garan Evans, who suffered a nasty neck injury. The unlucky Evans had just been recalled to the Wales set-up, some four years after he made his debut, but he had to be stretchered off and never won another cap. He was replaced by the experienced Gareth Thomas, who looked solid under the high ball and put in some useful clearing kicks.

The delay if anything seemed to affect New Zealand more than Wales, and after 15 phases Thomas would have scored but lost the ball forward as he was reaching for the line. The look on his face told you everything you needed to know as he failed by millimetres to become Wales's joint record try-scorer. Wales had the bit between their teeth, though, and continued to take the game to the All Blacks. A great chip and chase by Stephen Jones enabled him to gather his own kick and lay it off to Tom Shanklin, who made ground, and with the New Zealand defence splintered, Mark Taylor went over and Stephen Jones levelled the scores.

Welsh joy was short-lived, however, as Rokocoko went past Colin Charvis, round Thomas and held off Shane Williams for his second try of the night. MacDonald made it 14-7, and we had still played only 15 minutes. From the restart, New Zealand went straight back on to the attack, but it was a great break from Welsh flanker Jonathan Thomas which led to the next score as the All Blacks went offside and Jones kicked a simple penalty. Next the New Zealand back row got heavily involved as Jerry Collins and a young Richie McCaw made about 35 metres between them, while captain Reuben Thorne provided the link to set the backs away.

At the breakdown it looked like referee Andre Watson had waved play on, but he then penalised Wales, Justin Marshall took a quick tap and put centre MacDonald into the gap for the third New Zealand try. He converted his own try to make the score 21-10 and Jones kicked off again and immediately New Zealand moved the ball; it was the back row causing all the problems, but when prop Greg Somerville failed to hold an unsympathetic pass from Williams, Thomas ran clear all the way up to the New Zealand 22.

New Zealand's fourth try came from an unusual source – a crossfield kick from Spencer found the unlikely figure of second row Ali Williams loitering with intent on the side right and he barely had to jump to gather the kick ahead of the diminutive Shane Williams. A good time to score your first try for your country. MacDonald kicked his fourth conversion and the lead was up to 28-10 going into the final ten minutes of the half.

Gethin Jenkins came on to replace Adam Jones while Rodney So'oialo was a blood replacement for Collins, who was having a sensational match for the All Blacks. Then Shane Williams stepped his way past Ali Williams and Brad

Thorne, hit the accelerator and took play into the New Zealand 22; it looked like the move might break down, but Tom Shanklin just got there is time to support and move the ball on to Sonny Parker, who went over. Jones converted.

Some harum-scarum rugby was finally brought to a halt when Collins was penalised for a high tackle and despite only a couple of minutes remaining in the half, Wales bravely kicked for touch, won the line-out and drove on. Captain Charvis picked the ball up from the base of the ruck and dived over the top, getting a clear touchdown over the back of the New Zealand forwards. Jones converted again and it was 28-24 to the All Blacks at half-time.

Could the game possibly remain as open in the second half? It started with a rare mistake from Spencer, an all-fingers-and-thumbs attempt which proved that even the best of the best is capable of taking his eye off the ball for a moment and looking/thinking about what he's going to do with it. A scrum penalty saw Stephen Jones comfortably reduce the arrears to a single point with a kick from just about on the halfway line. A rueful-looking Spencer got play under way again only for a marvellous Welsh move see them score their third try. Brent Cockbain stole a line-out, Ceri Sweeney (on the bench as fly half cover but on for the injured Taylor) made a scorching break through the middle, brushed off Spencer, exchanged passes with Charvis and when Sweeney went to ground the ball was moved quickly to the wide left where Shane Williams had an easy run in. Jones converted and it was 34-28 to Wales.

Now a major shock was on the cards, but with barely six minutes of the second half played, Wales had a long time to hang on. Spencer and Howlett almost immediately launched an attack down the right which Wales could only slow up illegally. Spencer kicked to the corner about five metres out and quick ball was once again the undoing of Wales. The fly half looped round to give Howlett a bit of space, and that was all he needed but with MacDonald missing for the first time in the match, hooking the ball left of the posts, Wales retained a one-point lead.

Sweeney, like Thomas, was proving an excellent replacement and hit a huge clearance from one 22 to the other and although New Zealand looked to have won the ball it was scrappy and went loose and the All Blacks gave away the penalty – a simple one for Jones. Wales led 37-33, but from the restart Shanklin knocked on horribly to put his team under pressure and only desperate defence kept Spencer and Howlett out again. Another All Black penalty and another kick to the corner, but when Mils Muliaina got over the line, the Welsh defence brilliantly managed to hold him up. The resulting five-metre scrum came to nothing.

A series of pick-and-drives seemed certain to end in an All Black try, but yet again Wales held it up over the line. This time from the scrum, however, Spencer had space to go either way and he simply carved round the outside of Stephen Jones, for whom he was too quick. How good was Carlos Spencer? New Zealand coaches never seemed to entirely trust him, often opting for the more reliable goal-kicker in Andrew Mehrtens. But excellent player though he was, in my opinion Mehrtens never had that spark of genius which Spencer possessed. The fact that Brian O'Driscoll told me Spencer was his idol and that his skills were 'ridiculous' tells you all you need to know about how good Spencer was.

MacDonald hit the far post with his conversion attempt, just not pulling the ball in quite enough, but nevertheless the All Blacks were back in front at 38-37. Jonathan Thomas made a great break through the middle but ran out of support, and then Sidoli was penalised for a high tackle on Howlett, though it looked a harsh call given that the speedy winger was ducking into the challenge. Spencer took play up to just outside the Wales 22, and the next passage of play resulted in a five-metre scrum to the All Blacks from which Marshall had too much pace for the otherwise excellent Jonathan Thomas and scooted round outside him before flicking the ball to Howlett who went in for an easy try. On replay the final pass was clearly forward, but referee Andre Watson didn't even bother to ask to check it, and New Zealand moved 43-37 ahead with about 11 minutes left to play. MacDonald got his kick hopelessly wrong which meant the gap was still less than a converted try.

Wales went looking for the try they needed, but the All Blacks had tightened up their defence and there was no way through. Instead the All Blacks counter-attacked and won a penalty which MacDonald stroked through, and for the first time in a long while, New Zealand had some breathing space at 46-37. Wales's fine effort was spent and they conceded one final score, when they just ran out of tacklers and Mauger went over for the eighth try of the game. MacDonald converted and the score was 53-37, an end result which did not do justice to Wales.

This game concluded the pool stages of the 2003 RWC, sending New Zealand through to face South Africa, and Wales to face the Auld Enemy, England.

33

9 November 2003
Venue: Lang Park, Brisbane
Attendance: 45,250

England 28 Wales 17

England	Wales
Jason Robinson	Gareth Thomas
Dan Luger	Shane Williams
Will Greenwood	Mark Taylor
Mike Tindall	Iestyn Harris
Ben Cohen	Mark Jones
Jonny Wilkinson	Stephen Jones
Matt Dawson	Gareth Cooper
Jason Leonard	Iestyn Thomas
Steve Thompson	Robin McBryde
Phil Vickery	Adam Jones
Martin Johnson (capt)	Brent Cockbain
Ben Kay	Robert Sidoli
Lewis Moody	Dafydd Jones
Neil Back	Colin Charvis (capt)
Lawrence Dallaglio	Jonathan Thomas

Wales had made ten changes between the game against Italy and the one against New Zealand in the pool stages and the assumption was that they were protecting a number of first-choice players who were being saved for the quarter-final. In the event, however, the team which took the field in Brisbane against England bore a striking resemblance to the one which faced the All Blacks – Gareth Thomas and Iestyn Harris replaced the injured Garan Evans and Sonny Parker at full back and centre respectively, while in the forwards Dafydd Jones came into the back row in which Jonathan Thomas switched from six to eight. And that was it.

A more intriguing question was how Wales would approach the game tactically. Would they embrace the all-action running style which had been so impressive against New Zealand or would they revert to a tighter gameplan? Wales's attempt to shut England down in the Six Nations earlier that year had failed and although the home side had had the better of much of the game, England had been content to score heavily in the early stages of the second half and otherwise soak up the Wales pressure, for a 26-9 win.

Clearly the onus was on Wales to do something different from that occasion, and they certainly did.

England scrum half Matt Dawson made the first clean break and almost inevitably it ended in referee Alain Rolland penalising Wales for offside. Jonny Wilkinson should have put England into an early lead, but hit the post from a simple chance. Next it was the turn of Wales who broke into England territory and Robert Sidoli actually got over the line but Lewis Moody – with a little help from Wilkinson – hit him at the crucial moment and the big lock lost the ball forward.

The first scrum of the game ended with an England penalty, but Wales ran the ball back and the move only died when Shane Williams's chip through was a little too heavy and bounced into touch and goal. The resulting scrum again saw an England penalty and then some efficient tight play saw them gradually move the ball into Welsh territory but Moody was penalised for going over the top. From the line-out the ball went straight to Neil Back and he put in a strong run, but Dawson chose the wrong option and the ball was lost. When Jason Robinson and Back were harshly pinged for obstruction, Stephen Jones did exactly the same as Wilkinson and hit the post with the sort of chance he would normally have snapped up.

The game then entered a scrappy period with lots of handling errors on both sides and both sides trying to make ground through their packs, but eventually Back won England a penalty with one of his trademark steals, and Wilkinson opened the scoring in the 18th minute.

England were playing some enterprising rugby at this stage, but kept spoiling all their good work by losing the ball in possession and making numerous handling errors and when Wilkinson went for a snap drop goal he pulled it past the left-hand post. Next, the England centres did well, Mike Tindall and Greenwood ploughing into the Welsh defence and gaining another penalty. But they took a quick penalty instead of kicking a simple three points and failed to gain anything from it.

A few minutes later a loose kick aimed at Ben Kay, of all people out wide on the right, was snaffled by Williams and he was off, beating Kay easily and passing to Cooper who ran straight and hard. The England defence tried to recover but were all over the place and the move was taken on by Gareth Thomas and Williams again who flicked a superb pass back inside for Stephen Jones to put Wales ahead 5-3. Jones surprisingly failed to convert his own try, getting no curl on the ball having set it off towards the far post.

With 32 minutes on the clock, the stats showed England with around two-thirds of both territory and possession, and Wales were having to make far more tackles – would that have an impact later in the game? For now, though, a line-out drive saw Colin Charvis go over and take Wales to 10-3, though Jones again missed a reasonably straightforward conversion, kicking wide of the right post. There were five minutes left in the first half and England were looking shaky and needed desperately not to concede any more points before the break, which they managed after coping better with another line-out close to their line.

Into the sanctity of half-time, and what was said in the dressing room? A few choice words, no doubt, as well as some more tactical comments. 'There were some pretty harsh words at half-time,' admitted England coach Clive Woodward, 'and some colourful language, but we got the message across.' A score of 10-3 wasn't a huge deficit, for all Wales's efforts, and it took England just four minutes to tie things up.

Charvis was penalised on the halfway line for coming in at the side, and Wilkinson kicked to inside the Wales 22, but once again, they couldn't gather their own line-out ball. However, the clearance kick only found Robinson and he accelerated through the first line of defence. Once he was in behind it always spelt trouble for Wales and Robinson sprinted on and on before drawing the last defender and passing to Greenwood who was hugging the right-hand touchline.

Greenwood scooted in and Wilkinson kicked a fine conversion from out wide to level the game up. A moment later a Tindall clean break took him up to within metres of the line, a Dawson dart saw him stopped just inches short and Greenwood even got over but couldn't get the ball down – at which point Rolland went back for an earlier penalty and Wilkinson put England back in front at 13-10.

And then England started to exert some relentless pressure and Wales were pinned back in their own half for long periods through England's possession play. Almost inevitably Wales were penalised for a succession of offsides, trying to slow the ball down and playing it on the floor. A straight, 30-metre penalty made it 16-10; a tougher, wider one from England's right proved no more challenging for Wilkinson who by now had his eye firmly in and took the score out to 19-10 and more than one score in front.

And when Wales did have some ball, they found the England defence had tightened up considerably – a massive hit by captain Martin Johnson on Dafydd Jones killed the Wales momentum in one promising-looking move, and Mike Catt's presence gave his team more variety and a right-footed kicking option which took some pressure off Wilkinson. Wales's running, while still attractive to watch, was starting to look a little more aimless and unthreatening as a result of England's solid defence.

A fly-kick by Catt didn't come off, but his tactical punting deep into Wales territory kept turning the defence and put England almost permanently on the front foot for much of the middle period of the second half. A Wilkinson break was taken on by Lawrence Dallaglio and a panicking defence gave away another simple penalty; and as the final quarter started it became 22-10. Catt made a clean break from the restart, taking play deep into the Wales 22, but his pass just couldn't find a supporting player and Dawson knocked on while trying to collect the loose, bouncing ball.

Wales at this point had made 155 tackles – twice the England total – and still the England forwards were exerting huge pressure on their counterparts. A ridiculous offside at the back of the line-out by replacement second row Gareth Llewellyn resulted in another Wilkinson penalty and still Wales were scoreless in the second half and now playing catch-up rugby.

To give Wales credit, there was one final rage against the dying light; just as the game entered its final ten minutes hooker Steve Thompson was penalised for not rolling away and Jones kicked his team up to the England ten-metre line. Replacement scrum half Dwayne Peel made a great break from a breakdown and then appeared again in the move as Wales made it almost to the England line. A crossfield kick saw Shane Williams and Dallglio collide and Martyn Williams pounced on the loose ball over the line. A soft try which Iestyn Harris converted to bring Wales back to 25-17, though it was interesting that Wales had had to resort to that method of scoring when in the first half they had put together flowing move after flowing move.

Harris had another penalty chance from about 40 metres out but sliced it horribly and it ended up almost closer to the corner flag than the posts. Now

Wales seemed to be getting all the penalty decisions, but mostly around the halfway line; Harris punched one deep into England territory and Sidoli made a great jump but England's defence easily shut down the short side. Another penalty and Peel took a quick tap from nowhere near the mark, but Wales never really looked like breaking through as they had in the first half.

In injury time Wilkinson kicked a brilliantly nonchalant drop goal from almost the ten-metre line with the last action of the match to finish things at 28-17, and England moved on to the semi-finals.

'We just couldn't get any ball in the second half,' lamented Wales coach Steve Hansen. 'We kept getting penalised and that took away our momentum, and Jonny kept popping the penalty kicks over as he does and in the end that's what broke the camel's back. But the team hung in there and kept trying and I think it was a great effort.'

'In the second half we pretty much dominated,' felt England skipper Martin Johnson.

'If we play France like we did today, we've got no chance,' said Woodward of the upcoming semi-final.

In the event, England and France's plans were pretty much ruined on account of the atrocious weather. High winds and driving rain dictated that it would be a game of territory and possession, and England were much better equipped to play that way. Specifically, Wilkinson was much better suited to that sort of a game than the talented but more mercurial Freddy Michalak, whose place-kicking technique faltered under the pressure of the need to keep the scoreboard ticking over.

Despite scoring the only try, through Serge Betsen, France's inability to kick their goals cost them dear, and though even Wilkinson wasn't immaculate for once, he notched five penalties and three drop goals for a 24-7 victory which took England through to their second World Cup Final.

34

15 November 2003
Venue: Telstra Stadium Australia, Sydney
Attendance: 82,400

New Zealand 10 Australia 22

New Zealand	Australia
Mils Muliaina	Mat Rogers
Doug Howlett	Wendell Sailor
Leon MacDonald	Stirling Mortlock
Aaron Mauger	Elton Flatley
Joe Rokocoko	Lote Tuquiri
Carlos Spencer	Stephen Larkham
Justin Marshall	George Gregan (capt)
Dave Hewett	Bill Young
Keven Mealamu	Brendan Cannon
Greg Somerville	Ben Darwin
Chris Jack	Justin Harrison
Ali Williams	Nathan Sharpe
Reuben Thorne (capt)	George Smith
Richie McCaw	Phil Waugh
Jerry Collins	David Lyons

Australian hooker and two-time Rugby World Cup winner Phil Kearns once said, 'You can go to the end of time, to the last World Cup in the history of mankind, and the All Blacks will be favourites for it.' He did not add, however, that the Wallabies subscribed to the view that they were therefore unbeatable.

The All Blacks had undoubtedly started the 2003 competition as favourites, or at least joint-favourites with England. Nothing that had occurred during their romp through the group stages of the tournament had done anything to disturb that assessment, and if Wales gave them a bit of a hurry-up, most of the All Blacks seemed to feel that that was exactly what they had needed to avoid any hint of complacency.

Even South Africa – admittedly not a vintage South African side – had really presented few challenges in the quarter-finals. New Zealand had recorded a very similar scoreline against the Springboks that England had, winning 29-9 and scoring three tries to nil in the process. The highlight was the third try, which came from Carlos Spencer passing between his legs to the unmarked Joe Rokocoko on the left wing, a moment of genius improvisation which got the result it deserved.

The rest of the game was largely one of unexpected dominance by the All Blacks forwards who established an early stranglehold and never relaxed it to record their first win over the Springboks at a World Cup.

Australia, meanwhile, had been a little fortunate to pip Ireland to first place in Pool A, and then had endured a scratchy first half against Scotland which they finished at 9-9. Although they scored three tries in the second half and pulled away to win 33-16, Australia hadn't convinced many neutral onlookers that they had the wherewithal to upset the All Blacks and the scene looked set for the much-anticipated England v New Zealand final.

We should have known better, of course. Woe betide those who write the battling Aussies off, particularly when they are the defending champions and determined not to surrender their crown. Already that year had witnessed their fighting qualities when, having been absolutely battered in Sydney in the Tri Nations, in losing 50-21 to New Zealand, they had pushed the All Blacks all the way in the return fixture in Auckland, losing just 21-17 even though the title was already won and lost by then. Nevertheless, if Australia's attitude made it likely that they would not get overrun again, it was hard to see how they could actually win.

Australia began the semi-final in an unexpected manner, running the kick-off back from deep rather than simply clearing it, and it soon became obvious that their gameplan, devised by coach Eddie Jones and his team, was to keep the ball in hand as much as possible and not kick away possession which would allow the All Blacks to run the ball back at them. A combination of not allowing the dangerous All Blacks back three the time or space to counter-attack and to target the mainline in attack was put into effect. 'You've got to hit the line hard,' explained Jones, 'and that's what our forwards did. The result was good ball. We wanted to get that go-forward.'

The Wallabies benefited from the perfect start when a Spencer pass was intercepted by Stirling Mortlock who ran in behind the posts from 80 metres, putting them seven points to the good within the first ten minutes. Throughout the game, Mortlock ran hard at Leon MacDonald, who though an accomplished player was really a full back filling in for the injured Tana Umaga in the centres. At 6ft 3in and a touch over 16st, Mortlock had four inches and over a stone in weight on MacDonald and part of the plan was for him to try and use those physical advantages.

Despite being under pressure, though, the All Blacks still managed to find a way to score – as they usually do – when Reuben Thorne worked his way over. A turnover in midfield was snapped up by Justin Marshall, who instantly fed Spencer and a short pass to Thorne put him over. MacDonald converted and the All Blacks trailed just 13-7 at half-time. But they still couldn't really get anything going, and Mortlock continued to cause havoc in the second half, often ably assisted by former rugby league winger Lote Tuqiri. Jerry Collins was penalised for hands in the ruck inside his own 22, giving Elton Flatley an easy chance to put his side further ahead at 16-7. Flatley added his fourth penalty after Stephen Larkham had carved his way through and MacDonald was caught offside.

MacDonald responded to his own mistake by notching a penalty to reduce the arrears to nine again at 19-10, but it remained the Australians who were playing most of the rugby despite the efforts of Richie McCaw who had a monumental match in defeat. There was one moment when the two dangerous wingers did combine – Doug Howlett making the extra man to put Joe Rokocoko away down the left-hand touchline. Rokocoko's superb balance kept him inside the line despite running at full pelt and when the move broke down, English referee Chris White awarded a penalty under the posts.

There were still more than 20 minutes to play, but New Zealand just couldn't get up a head of steam, robbed of momentum by errors. Flatley extended the lead to 12 again when replacement Brad Thorne was caught offside. Gregan pushed a drop goal attempt wide, but play was brought back for a simple penalty chance and Flatley kicked it with the minimum of fuss.

The Wallabies then shut up shop and backed their defence to keep New Zealand at bay. Flatley had the chance to extend the lead still further after Byron Kelleher (a 48th-minute replacement for Marshall at scrum half after Marshall had been injured by a late tackle from George Smith) got on the wrong side of a ruck, but for once he missed to give the All Blacks one final chance, but the 12-point deficit always looked a bridge too far, and so it proved. On the day, the Wallabies deserved their win, as Spencer was quick to acknowledge. 'Hugely disappointed, but we were beaten by the better side on the night,' he said. 'They played rugby and we didn't. They shut us down and we felt like we didn't get any ball, and ball we did get we turned over.'

Australia had forced New Zealand to make so many tackles early in the match, particularly targeting the likes of Collins and Thorne, that when it came to the final quarter, the All Blacks didn't have their usual zip which enabled them to put many teams to the sword late on. 'New Zealand just didn't fire,' was all legendary All Blacks hooker Sean Fitzpatrick could offer.

There was one moment of supreme sportsmanship in the heat of battle which should not go unacknowledged. Australian prop Ben Darwin heard a crack when a scrum collapsed early in the second half and cried out 'neck' several times; immediately opposition prop Kees Meeuws stopped pushing and that might well have saved Darwin from life in a wheelchair – or worse. Sadly Darwin was forced to retire as a result of his injury, on doctors' advice, but at least he could walk out of the hospital a few days later unaided. After a successful career in coaching, Darwin founded and runs a sports analytical company called Gain Line which is becoming a major player in the business of analysing the factors which lead to successful sports teams.

That made it the fourth Rugby World Cup in a row in which New Zealand had failed to live up to the tag of favourites. Fitzpatrick maintained that, man for man, the All Blacks had the better side, even claiming before the semi-final that in a combined team he would probably have only George Gregan from Australia. Stirling Mortlock, Elton Flatley, Justin Harrison and George Smith – to name just four – might well have had something to say about that, but as a general point Fitzgerald, who has developed into an excellent commentator on TV, had put his finger on the same issue which Phil Kearns had encapsulated. New Zealand always started as the favourites for the tournament, but they did not seem to have mastered the art of the sort of winning rugby that a World Cup campaign required, while their Antipodean rivals had progressed to their third World Cup Final in four tournaments.

With an air of inevitability, the All Blacks proceeded to look awesome in the third place play-off game against France, dominating the French to win 40-13, scoring six tries to one. Mils Muliaina and Doug Howlett both moved into the top four all-time World Cup try-scorers for their country as the All Blacks returned to the form of flowing, running rugby with which most fans associate them. It was all very impressive, but too little too late. Coach John Mitchell's record stood at 23 wins and four defeats in 28 games – a better win percentage than his three immediate predecessors, Laurie Mains, John Hart and Wayne Smith – and he had overseen New Zealand's unbeaten 2003 Tri Nations triumph, during the course of which they had scored 50 points away to South Africa and Australia. But World Cup failure saw Mitchell invited to reapply for his own job – usually a polite way of saying 'on yer bike, son', and so it proved on this occasion as he was replaced by Graham Henry.

The All Blacks became the butt of teasing which described them as peaking in between World Cups rather than *for* them. The great John Kirwan once described winning the World Cup as an exercise in 'handling episodes' and explained that the team which best handles the crucial episodes will win. In which case, the episode which saw Mortlock run in an early interception try was clearly one which could have been handled better.

More simply, history has shown us that World Cups are won on defence and while New Zealand's defence is consistently good, on occasion that of South Africa, Australia and England is even better.

35

22 November 2003
Venue: Telstra Stadium Australia, Sydney
Attendance: 83,000

Australia 17 England 20 (aet)

Australia	England
Mat Rogers	Josh Lewsey
Wendell Sailor	Jason Robinson
Stirling Mortlock	Will Greenwood
Elton Flatley	Mike Tindall
Lote Tuquiri	Ben Cohen
Stephen Larkham	Jonny Wilkinson
George Gregan (capt)	Matt Dawson
Bill Young	Trevor Woodman
Brendan Cannon	Steve Thompson
Al Baxter	Phil Vickery
Justin Harrison	Martin Johnson (capt)
Nathan Sharpe	Ben Kay
George Smith	Richard Hill
Phil Waugh	Neil Back
David Lyons	Lawrence Dallaglio

It was a damp evening at Stadium Australia when England and Australia took the field for the 2003 Rugby World Cup Final and the venue was packed with local support, but England took succour from the fact that that summer they had gone on a short tour Down Under and recorded victories against New Zealand and Australia.

The win over the All Blacks made the headlines, not least because halfway through the first half England had Neil Back and Lawrence Dallaglio in the sin bin, but the thin white line held firm, with Mike Tindall joining the pack and the forwards putting in a sterling defensive shift.

But the 25-14 win over Australia the following week was just as significant in that the World Cup was to be played entirely in Australia, and the Northern Hemisphere teams' records there were not all that impressive, to say the least. England came out for that Test match in Melbourne as fired up as they ever had been and scored three first-half tries, through Will Greenwood, Mike Tindall and Ben Cohen, to dominate the Wallabies. The Wallabies hit back, inevitably, and mounted a worthy rearguard action, but the damage to the myth of Southern Hemisphere pre-eminence had been done.

England, with a vastly experienced squad, were not daunted by the prospect of facing Australia in the final, nor were they going to make the same mistake that their 1991 side had in changing a winning gameplan. New Zealand sports columnist Mike Laws had memorably said of them, 'They're battle-hardened Vikings – all scars, snarls and, in Lawrence Dallaglio's case, snorts. The rest of the pack were simply giant gargoyles – raw-boned, cauliflower-eared monoliths that intimidated and unsettled. When they ran on to the field it was like watching a tribe of white orcs on steroids.'

That 'white orcs on steroids' mantle has stuck, and indeed has passed into legend as a description of one of the most fearsome packs which has ever taken to a rugby field and as such they were to fear no one.

Under the watchful eye of Andre Watson, in charge of his second successive Rugby World Cup Final, Jonny Wilkinson got play under way in an incredible atmosphere. 'It's one of the first times I wasn't really able to hear Jonno's team talk,' said Wilkinson. 'We were in our huddle and I still couldn't hear the guy next to me despite being about two yards from him.' Both sides showed an inclination to run and both had an early chance but failed to find their man with the final pass. Then, with two minutes gone, we got our first look at a scrum, generally reckoned to be one of England's key facets of play, but the evidence from that early engagement was unclear.

The first penalty of the game was given away by prop Trevor Woodman, who saw fit to have a sly punch at the back of a maul, but Australia decided it was too far for any of their kickers so opted to punt it into the corner and from the resulting line-out they won a free kick for England having too many players in it. Opting for a scrum, the Wallabies came under a bit of pressure, but George Gregan got the ball away and Stephen Larkham hit a high right-to-left crossfield kick and in the battle of the former rugby league wingers Lote Tuqiri was able to climb above Jason Robinson – hardly surprisingly as he had seven inches on him – and fall over the line. It was an excellent kick, and it's a very hard tactic to defend against, especially if you have a mismatch in height and weight.

Elton Flatley hit a fine conversion attempt which bounced off the inside of the left-hand post and somehow stayed out.

Robinson decided the best way to make amends for being outjumped was to do what he did best and run, which he did to make some ground, and after several phases England won a penalty against David Lyons when the big number eight went over the top and Wilkinson had his first shot, straight but fully 47 metres out. No problem.

Neither team seemed to be having much difficulty winning their own set-piece ball initially, but England stole two line-outs, the second leading to a penalty which gave them some much-needed possession. England went through the phases, with Lewsey making a few little breaks, but in slippery conditions both sides had trouble hanging on to the ball. Shortly after Watson had warned both sides about playing men without the ball, Larkham did exactly that to Cohen, getting a boot in the face for his trouble, and Wilkinson put England ahead at the end of a first quarter in which they had had 70 per cent of the possession.

An Australian fumble led to Richard Hill hacking through and Matt Dawson picked up and flicked it on to Ben Kay all the big second row had to do was catch the ball and dive over but he took his eye off it and dropped the ball virtually on the line. From virtually the next play England won a scrum and a huge forward drive resulted in another England penalty and Wilkinson extended the lead to 9-5. From the restart, England were incorrectly penalised for a knock-on but in general they were getting the decisions because they were the team on top in the set piece and at the breakdown.

Dallaglio made an outside break, turned the ball back inside to Wilkinson who made a few metres before turning it back outside to Robinson on the wide left and Robinson scooted in from about 18 metres, cleverly sliding in low for the last few metres when it looked as if the cover might just get to him. Wilkinson missed a difficult kick from almost out on the touchline and England went in to the break leading 14-5.

The second half, however, was a slightly different story. Somehow England, despite appearing to be in charge of most phases of the game, found themselves getting on the wrong side of the referee and giving away penalties on a regular basis. The first was for a Dallaglio offside when he thought it was open play but Watson decided a ruck had already formed, the second for Vickery who looked to be on his feet when playing the ball but was told he couldn't. In between Flatley missed a long-range effort for an obstruction which probably merited no more than a scrum put-in.

It wasn't so much that Watson's calls were wrong, but they were 50-50s, and they all seemed to go the same way. As commentator John Taylor said, the pattern of play was such that an England score looked more likely than an Australian one, but that isn't what happened. Some of the scrum penalties certainly appeared counter-intuitive: England's scrum was well on top, it seems unlikely that they would want to start collapsing, and when England were driving forward and Australia's front row popped up, it seemed inconceivable that it could be an Australian penalty.

England still had sufficient ball to put the game to bed, but just dropped the ball or knocked on at the vital moment. With nine minutes remaining, Wilkinson took matters into his own hands, dropped back into the pocket and slotted a drop goal. Except he didn't, he hooked it marginally wide of the left-hand post. Then Dallaglio stole a line-out but England were penalised for a forward pass which clearly wasn't – as both Clive Woodward and the crowd could see from the replay.

Watson's biggest call, however, was to award a fourth scrum penalty to Australia, this time against Woodman for not engaging. Commentator Taylor described it as a 'massive call' and opined that Watson 'was showing a little bit of anger' towards England and had taken the opportunity to penalise them. The stats showed that a dominant England scrum had been penalised four times to Australia's once. Taylor later admitted, 'I was totally perplexed. England appeared to have a clear advantage – Australia were going backwards under extreme pressure – but whenever the scrum went down it was England who were penalised. Aware that my audience was all back in Britain I have to confess I allowed myself a little bias but I remain convinced Watson got it horribly wrong.'

Credit to Flatley, who calmly kicked the penalty to tie the scores at 14-14 with the final kick of the 80 minutes.

England brought on Jason Leonard and Mike Catt at the start of the first period of extra time, and almost immediately Wilkinson had the chance for a 44-metre penalty after an Australian line-out offence. He put England back in front, 17-14. It was the first penalty shot Wilkinson had had since the first half of the match, but there were still 19 minutes to play. Some experts thought that England's ageing team might begin to tire in extra time, but there were few signs of that happening as they continued to make most of the running, and even to play the more creative rugby.

Wilkinson had another drop goal attempt but sliced it wide, and Iain Balshaw, on for a hobbling Lewsey, had a couple of good runs, but still they couldn't put Australia away. And then, with two and a half minutes to go, Dallaglio was penalised for coming in from the side, and Flatley, coolness personified, tied the scores up once more. There were less than two minutes remaining when England restarted, a Dawson dart into the 22 and what looked a perfect set-up for Wilkinson, but instead Johnson came thundering in to take it on just a little bit further. He laid it back carefully so that Dawson, who had extricated himself from the move and was back in position at the base of the ruck, could provide the pass to Wilkinson that would give him the time and space, except that it was on his 'wrong' foot. No matter, this time he hit it straight and true. There's a great picture of George Gregan running towards Wilkinson, knowing what is coming, but knowing that he can't get there in time to prevent it. The clock showed 19 minutes and 32 seconds, so England still had to gather the restart, which they did, and Mike Catt booted it safely into the stands.

Thank goodness the best team won and the referee was not destined to become the story.

Watson has since defended his decisions and gamely tried to explain each and every one of them, but world opinion has not supported him. The *Irish Times*, which could hardly be called pro-English, described him as 'frankly, awful'. Fortunately, England had still found a way to win. 'Every decision seemed to go against them, and yet they still won,' said Woodward. 'And that is the sign of a champion team.' Which England now were, the first Northern Hemisphere team to become rugby world champions to boot.

One notable postscript to England's triumph is that the players say they had no idea how big a story their World Cup campaign was becoming back in England. It was only when the victorious squad arrived back home that they grasped the full impact of their victory. 'Mind-blowing,' Dawson called it, while Wilkinson said, 'I'm overawed by the support, it's hugely humbling and massively uplifting. The guys all appreciate that more than they can put into words.'

There followed a victory parade in London – one to which this writer took his young children, bunking off school for the day – and it was left to Clive Woodward, the coach whose attention to detail and determination to make England the best team in the world had paid off to sum it all up, 'These are just extraordinary scenes. I never thought I would see something like this on the streets of London. This is probably the day when the fact that we have won the World Cup has sunk in and we are all very grateful for the support we have received.'

14 September 2007
Venue: Stade de France, Paris
Attendance: 77,500

England 0 South Africa 36

England	South Africa
Jason Robinson	Percy Montgomery
Josh Lewsey	JP Pietersen
Jamie Noon	Jaque Fourie
Andy Farrell	Francois Steyn
Paul Sackey	Bryan Habana
Mike Catt	Butch James
Shaun Perry	Fourie du Preez
Andrew Sheridan	Os du Randt
Mark Regan	John Smit (capt)
Matt Stevens	CJ van der Linde
Simon Shaw	Bakkies Botha
Ben Kay	Victor Matfield
Martin Corry (capt)	Schalk Burger
Tom Rees	Juan Smith
Nick Easter	Danie Rossouw

Somewhat surprisingly, South Africa had not had a particularly successful Tri Nations series in 2007. Although they had beaten Australia 22-19 in Cape Town in the opening round, they had narrowly lost 26-21 to New Zealand in Durban the following week. The Springboks had led 21-12 with only a little over ten minutes remaining in that match, only to be hit by late tries from Richie McCaw and Joe Rokocoko, both converted by Dan Carter. The pattern was repeated in Australia when they were two tries to the good after just eight minutes, and when fly half Derick Hougaard added a penalty to his two conversions, the Springboks held a 17-point lead before the end of the first quarter. But Australia gradually reeled them in, keeping the Boks scoreless from that point on, while they themselves scored 25. In the final week a slightly dispirited South Africa lost 33-6 in Christchurch, but there were signs that this team could produce tries as well as the traditional power and kicking game.

England, meanwhile, despite bold claims that they would use the 2003 Rugby World Cup win as a springboard to even better things, had not been able to back up that intention. Two third places and two fourth places in the subsequent Six Nations Championships had done little to inspire future generations. In the 2006 autumn internationals, England had been well beaten by New Zealand, had lost to Argentina (for the first and, to date, only time at home) and had split a rare double-header with South Africa. England won the first game 23-21, but the Springboks reversed the result the following week to claim a 25-14 win.

Each scored three tries across those two games and the teams looked well matched, if unlikely to trouble the business end at the World Cup the following year. The way the game developed, therefore, was something of a surprise.

Pool A had opened with a not entirely convincing win for England over the USA, with only a couple of Olly Barkley penalties to show for their efforts in the first half an hour – against one from American fly half and captain Mike Hercus. But a burst of activity in the 15 minutes before and after half-time saw the defending world champions score tries from Jason Robinson, Barkley and Tom Rees, two of which were converted by Barkley for a 28-3 lead after 50 minutes. After that, England sat back and attempted little, even allowing the USA to close the gap slightly with a try from their replacement prop, the Tongan-born Matekitonga Moeakiola, converted by Hercus to give a final scoreline of 28-10. 'There was a lack of physicality and energy,' admitted coach Brian Ashton, 'but I've no idea why. I can't put my finger on it. The last 20 minutes were very disappointing from our point of view.'

South Africa, by contrast, had run riot against Samoa. Leading just 9-7 with half an hour gone, the Springboks suddenly switched on the afterburners and with tries from Habana and Montgomery (who also converted his own try) stretched the half-time lead to 21-7. They scored six further tries in the second half with Habana going on to score four, while Montgomery added his second and Jaque Fourie and J.P. Pietersen weighed in with one each also to make the final score 59-7. Admittedly, as results in the rest of the pool matches would show, Samoa were not quite the force that they had been in previous World Cups, but it was still an impressive display from the Springboks to put them away so ruthlessly and comprehensively.

So to the much-awaited England v South Africa game. Andy Farrell kicked off in a tremendous atmosphere in Paris, and the opening skirmishes looked exactly that but from a line-out on their own ten-metre line, the Springboks made a tremendous blindside break through the dangerous winger J.P. Pietersen up to the England ten-metre line. Paul Sackey did his job in bringing down Pietersen, but the support was there from scrum half Fourie du Preez who took play deep into the England 22 and although he stumbled he had the wherewithal to find Juan Smith, up in support like any good back-row forward, to go over. Percy Montgomery kicked the conversion to give South Africa a sixth-minute 7-0 lead.

South Africa made a mistake and knocked on from the restart, giving England a swift chance to hit back, but from the scrum England were penalised and once more South Africa carved their way through, this time courtesy of their other winger Bryan Habana, and only a desperate England turnover saved them. Another penalty, this time for Matt Stevens not rolling away, gave Francois Steyn the chance to kick a fine long-range penalty to take the score up to 10-0 after 11 minutes.

A loose ball was hacked deep into South African territory and could easily have resulted in a penalty in front of the posts as it appeared that there were two England players to the one South African defender. The play ended with Mike Catt's attempted drop goal which was struck very well but went just past the near post. England had plenty of the ball and territory, but no cutting edge, and only a last-ditch clawing tackle from Lewsey stopped Jaque Fourie scoring a second South African try right at the start of the second quarter. The resulting scrum (for a knock-on) brought an England penalty and chance to clear their lines.

Bizarrely, both Montgomery and Steyn tried difficult drop goals when retaining possession looked the better option and when Jason Robinson called a mark, took a quick tap and went scything upfield, it looked like it might end in a score, but for the most part South Africa remained on top – epitomised by a charge down from fly half Butch James as Farrell took fractionally too long to get a kick away. It seemed as though England had partially weathered the storm and were going to get to the sanctity of half-time trailing just 10-0, but two quick scores suddenly doubled the Springbok tally.

First, Stevens was penalised for blocking at the side of a ruck – it looked a little harsh in that he was doing nothing different from hundreds of other forwards over the years at the breakdown, but Joel Jutge is a good referee and he felt Stevens was too obviously looking to block South African players rather than have anything to do with the ball. Montgomery slotted the kick. But second was the real disaster, and it was somewhat unlucky in that loose South African play somehow saw the ball end up in the hands of du Preez and he went from one 22 to the other before drawing Robinson and putting Pietersen clear. Montgomery kicked the conversion and instead of trailing by ten at half-time England found themselves behind by 20.

England obviously had to be the first to score in the second half, but they weren't; instead it was another well-struck Montgomery penalty which took the score out to 23-0. The next England attack saw Ben Kay of all people trying a left-footed chip for Sackey, but Pietersen held it comfortably. Robinson had a good game for England in attack and defence but when he was unable to get a pass away in his own half, the Springboks piled through and moments later England were penalised for pulling down the maul, and Montgomery kicked his third penalty to take the score up to 26-0.

Robinson had another chance when it looked like he might get all the way round the outside of the South Africa defence but pulled a hamstring and went down like he had been shot. From the same sequence, England did have an opportunity when Mathew Tait, Robinson's replacement, was taken out illegally going for a high ball in what looked a borderline decision. England kicked to the corner but from the next phase of play a poor Andy Gomarsall pass saw Catt knock on. The errors continued to mount as England just could not get their game going, although a lot of that was credit to South Africa's defence. When England's play broke down they forced the play and then made silly mistakes whereas when the Springboks made similar errors, they took a deep breath and kicked to the corners to keep the pressure on.

A classic example was a casually lost line-out shortly after the hour, and from the scrum du Preez cut back from left to right, had the defence at sixes and sevens and his pace drew in Sackey from the wing, whereupon he calmly flicked a lobbed pass to Pietersen on the wing and he cantered in for his second, and South Africa's third, try. Montgomery added the conversion for 33-0.

Barely a minute later, another Springbok charge out of defence saw Rossouw kick through to deep into the England 22 but the back row just didn't have the pace to get there. There was time for one more Springbok penalty, Montgomery doing the business with his fourth three-pointer to go with his three conversions.

The stats showed that the world champions had turned over the ball twice as often as South Africa and although they had had plenty of possession, they had very little idea of what to do with it and only even looked like scoring a try once the game was already lost. It was the only time that England had failed to score a point in a Rugby World Cup match. It was a shattering blow and one which had several commentators and rugby writers sounding the death knell for English rugby.

'England have endured some grim nights since lifting the World Cup four years ago,' wrote *The Guardian*'s excellent Robert Kitson. 'But nothing on this scale. Not only did they never remotely look like beating South Africa, they barely looked like scoring a point.' Chris Hewett in *The Independent* wrote, 'The paucity of their effort was shocking. England offered next to nothing apart from the odd soft-shoe shuffle from Robinson … they showed nothing that was of the remotest concern to the South Africans, leaving aside the odd driving scrum.'

England still faced two tough games against the Pacific Islands teams of Samoa and Tonga, both of whom would have been licking their lips after watching this performance and eyeing up the possibility of pipping England for second place in the group. At least both Jonny Wilkinson and his deputy Olly Barkley would be fit again for the Samoa game eight days later.

37

16 September 2007
Venue: Stade de la Mosson, Montpellier
Attendance: 24,000

Samoa 15 Tonga 19

Samoa	Tonga
Gavin Williams	Vungakoto Lilo
Sailosi Tagicakibau	Tevita Tu'ifua
Elvis Seveali'i	Sukanaivalu Hufanga
Seilala Mapusua	Epi Taione
Alesana Tuilagi	Jospeh Vaka
Loki Crichton	Pierre Hola
Steve So'oialo	Enele Taufa
Justin Va'a	Soana Tinga'uihat
Mahonri Schwalger	Ephraim Taukafa
Census Johnston	Kisi Pulu
Joe Tekori	Inoke Afeaki
Kane Thompson	Paino Hehea
Daniel Leo	Hale T Pole
Ulia Ulia	Nili Latu (capt)
Semo Sititi (capt)	Finau Maka

A lthough the Pacific Island nations have always been well represented at the Rugby World Cup, it was only at this sixth tournament that two of them actually met for the first time.

Fiji were the first of the Islands to make an impact – invited to the first Rugby World Cup, they had thrilled fans with their unique brand of running rugby and had got through to the knockout stages where they had given eventual runners-up France quite a fright before going down in the quarter-finals. They had qualified for three of the subsequent four tournaments – missing out only in 1995 – and in 2003 had very nearly pipped Scotland for a place in the knockout stages yet again.

In 1991 the baton had been picked up by (as it then was) Western Samoa who, smarting at not being invited to the inaugural competition, had made up for it in spectacular style by beating Wales at Cardiff Arms Park in what was their first RWC match. A narrow defeat by Australia followed by a big win over Argentina had seen Western Samoa qualify for the knockout stages at the first attempt and though they ran out of steam in their quarter-final against Scotland they had thrilled us all with their ball handling and their massive hits. In 1995 and 1999 (by 1999 they had dropped the 'Western' and henceforth were know purely as 'Samoa') they again got past the group stages, but in 2003 the draw was unkind to them, placing them in a group with both England and South Africa and for the first time they failed to negotiate the group phases.

Tonga, for their part, had taken a little longer to make a mark. Invited in 1987, they failed to win a game against group opponents Canada, Wales and Ireland, and in 1991 Western Samoa and Japan had taken the two Asia and Oceania qualification spots on offer. Tonga returned to the party in 1995 but despite beating Ivory Coast comfortably enough, they were unable to make much impact on either France or Scotland, losing 38-10 and 41-5 respectively. It was a similar story in 1999 when they lost 45-9 to New Zealand and took a real beating at the hands of England, losing 101-10 in a 13-try rout. However, they managed a fine 28-25 win over Italy to at least give them some hope for the future.

The question in 2007 was whether either of these Pacific Islands nations could mount a real challenge in a Pool A containing the reigning world champions in England and one of the favourites for the competition in South Africa.

Before that could be answered, there was the small matter of a domestic dispute to be settled.

Tonga had the advantage of having already got a win under their belts, having beaten the United States 25-15 in their opening match. Finau Maka made a dramatic debut, the Toulouse number eight being driven over for the opening try inside two minutes. With fly half Pierre Hola adding the conversion and two penalties, Tonga were 13-0 up before the half-hour mark and still 13-3 ahead at half-time. The United States gradually pulled themselves back into the match, and even took a measure of control in the second half, reducing the margin to five points thanks to prop Mike MacDonald (who won the man of the match award).

But just when it looked like the US could turn the game round completely, a breakaway try from winger Joseph Vaka, benefiting from a break by his captain Nili Latu taken on by full back Vungakoto Lilo, stopped the comeback in its tracks. Eagles back-row forward Louis Stanfill did score his side's second try, converted by the ever-reliable Mike Hercus, but Tonga's former captain Viliami Vaki came off the bench to get the crucial score with ten minutes remaining.

Samoa meanwhile had begun with a disappointing 59-7 defeat by the Springboks. A game that the Samoans were well in for the first half-an-hour got away from them in a 15-minute period around half-time and they shipped several late tries.

Tonga also had the advantage that this match was played in Montpellier, at the same stadium where they had played their first match. But seemingly determined to get their RWC campaign back on track, Samoa came out firing and with a back division featuring such talented heavyweights as Alesana Tuilagi, Seilala Mapusua, Elvis Seveali'i and the magical Sailosi Tagicakibau. Tagicakibau, born of a Fijian father and Samoan mother (hence why he can play for Samoa while his brother, Michael, plays for Fiji), has played much of his club career in the English Premiership, primarily with London Irish. He has thrilled fans all over the world with his pace and his ability to score noteworthy tries – his 37 tries in 111 matches for the Irish is all the more impressive when you take into account that for much of his career the team has been in the lower reaches of the Premiership and quite frequently involved in battles to avoid relegation.

After an early penalty from Tongan fly half Pierre Hola with just three minutes played – for not rolling away – Samoa played some good rugby, resulting in regular penalties for Gavin Williams to slot home and take his side into a 12-3 lead. Samoa nearly scored a brilliant breakaway try, taking a quick line-out and running almost the full length of the pitch, but TV match official Kiwi Lyndon Bray couldn't see the ball being clearly grounded so the decision was a five-metre scrum which Samoa lost, turning over the ball. But Samoa did win another penalty when Maka was penalised for pulling down a maul, only for Williams to fail to curl the ball in, instead pushing it past the far post.

Williams's second successful penalty came when Tonga illegally killed a Samoan move following a swift break from scrum half Steve So'oialo. It could have been a yellow card offence but referee Jonathan Kaplan decided to let it go at a warning. From the restart, touch judge Alan Lewis flagged for a Tongan offence and a huge clearance put Samoa back on the attack. Alesana Tuilagi came crashing through the midfield and Tonga were once more penalised for slowing the ball down; yet again the Tongans got away with a warning but at least Williams slotted the kick to put Samoa 9-3 up.

A fourth penalty followed six minutes later, and this time centre Epi Taione was yellow-carded, so as well as Williams putting Samoa 12-3 ahead, Tonga were down to ten men for most of the rest of the first half. Impressively, they didn't concede a point during that time – if anything they started to run the ball more than they had with 15 players – and they even managed to hit back just before the half-time whistle when Hola notched his second penalty to keep Tonga in touch at 12-6 down, after Ulia Ulia was penalised for 'lazy running', i.e. not making strenuous enough attempts to get out of the way. Hola did the job. Hola even had one final chance, but his long-range attempt just missed, so Tonga came out for the second half still trailing by six points.

They were the first to score, however, when Kane Thompson was penalised for coming over the top and Hola made it 12-9 seven minutes into the second half. There followed a flat ten-minute period in which Samoa tried to do something with the ball but Tonga defended well and effected several turnovers whenever danger was threatening, and that prevented Samoa ever really getting into a rhythm.

Tonga's try on the hour was one of the few good moments in the match – a driving maul resulted in a penalty and they opted for a kick to the corner which they then drove over for a try to Taione, at the centre of the rolling maul, and Hola gave his side a four-point lead at 16-12.

Seven minutes later, the gap widened to seven when Tonga won a penalty for offside and Hola kicked another simple one. But five minutes after that, disaster struck for Tonga when blindside flanker Hale T. Pole was sent off for striking replacement Samoan lock Leo Lafaiali'i with a forearm at a ruck. Pole had already been warned twice, for an innocuous-looking elbow on the floor and then an awful neck tackle which should have resulted in a yellow card and did result in Williams kicking his fifth penalty to bring the score back to 19-15. Pole was the 13th man to be sent off in a RWC match, and the first in 2007.

The red card meant Tonga would be playing the final nine minutes of the match with 14 men, and a yellow card for their replacement prop Toma Toke on 75 minutes – for the latest in a series of high tackles – reduced them to 13. Samoa kicked to touch on the Tongan 22 but didn't really make much of the chance. A lacklustre Samoa were unable to make their numerical advantage count and Tonga wound down the clock for a famous victory.

Their win over Samoa seemed to inspire Tonga and they pushed South Africa all the way in their next outing. Late tries from Sukanaivalu Hufanga and Viliami Vaki in the last ten minutes of the game brought Tonga back to as close as 30-25, but they just ran out of time to pull it back any further. Looking at the faces of the two teams in the immediate aftermath it appears that South Africa were relieved and Tonga were thinking, 'Just a little more time...'

In theory, their final match, against England, gave Tonga a chance to snatch second place in the group. In practice, however, England were solid throughout, with Paul Sackey scoring two first-half tries and although Jonny Wilkinson missed both conversions, he kicked two penalties and a drop goal to give England a 19-10 lead. Mathew Tait and Andy Farrell made the game safe with second-half tries, both converted by Wilkinson, as England stretched away. Tonga did at least have the final word with Pole scoring a fine try, converted by Hola for a final score of 36-20 to England.

Samoa were also unable to make as much impression on England as many had thought, or even expected, after the champions' poor showing against the Springboks. Although scrum half Junior Polu wriggled over for a good try early in the second half, by that time England had scored two through Martin Corry and Sackey, both converted, and the same players each scored their second in the second half for an ultimately convincing 44-22 win. Loki Crichton, who converted Polu's try and kicked five penalties from five attempts, was a worthy winner of the man of the match award but it was scant reward for the end of another World Cup campaign.

All that remained for a rather disappointed, and disappointing, Samoa team was for them to beat the United States, which they did thanks largely to first-half tries from winger Lome Fa'atau, Tuilagi and Thompson. The US hit back in the second half with tries of their own from Takudzwa Ngwenya and Stanfil but Samoa held on to win 25-21 to at least record a World Cup victory.

38

29 September 2007
Venue: Stade de la Beaujoire, Nantes
Attendance: 37,000

Fiji 38 Wales 34

Fiji	Wales
Kameli Ratuvou	Gareth Thomas (capt)
Vilimoni Delasau	Mark Jones
Seru Rabeni	Tom Shanklin
Seremaia Bai	James Hook
Isoa Neivua	Shane Williams
Nicky Little	Stephen Jones
Moses Rauluni (capt)	Dwayne Peel
Graham Dewes	Gethin Jenkins
Sunia Koto Vuli	Matthew Rees
Jone Railomo Taginayaviusa	Chris Horsman
Kele Leawere	Alun Wyn Jones
Ifereimi Rawaqa	Ian Evans
Semisi Naevo	Colin Charvis
Akapusi Qera	Martyn Williams
Sisa Koyamaibole	Alix Popham

With Samoa and Tonga knocking lumps out of each other but neither ultimately progressing to the next stage of the competition, it was left to those hardy perennials of Fiji to provide the biggest upset of the group stages, and once again it was Wales who, having lost twice previously to Samoa in World Cups, felt the full force of the Pacific Islanders' brilliance.

Pool B had progressed largely as predicted, with 2003 runners-up Australia coasting through their matches to take first place. Wales had had an early scare from Canada in their opening match, trailing 17-9 shortly after half-time to three Canadian tries, but then exploded into action to score 33 unanswered points for an ultimately comfortable 42-17 victory. Wales had looked much more at ease against Japan, winning 72-18 after running in 11 tries, seven of which they converted, to two.

Fiji had had a tougher time, beating Japan just 35-31, four tries to three, thanks largely to a double either side of half-time from Akapusi Qera. It was a similar story against Canada where, despite being ahead for almost the entire game, Fiji were unable to put their opponents away and James Pritchard's 74th-minute penalty meant the Canadians trailed by just six points with a few minutes left to go searching for the try which would turn the game around. Instead Kameli Ratuvou got the last-minute try, converted by Nicky Little, which gave the final 29-16 scoreline a look of comfort which was never present in the match.

So to their winner-takes-all clash and a full-strength Fiji side probably had the edge in the backs, for pace and skill, but it was a question of whether their forwards could win enough ball against an experienced Welsh pack. Stuart Dickinson was in charge, and as he blew his whistle to start the match Wales were straight on the attack with Stephen Jones breaking the gain line and then putting Tom Shanklin away. A great tackle by Vilimoni Delasau prevented the score but when play was switched left to right it appeared that Wales had an overlap only for Shane Williams to be tackled into touch just short of the line. As a statement of intent, it was an impressive opening from Wales but Fiji won their line-out and cleared well. Continuing Welsh pressure ended in a penalty which Jones kicked to open the scoring after four minutes. A raking kick into the right-hand corner again saw Fiji under huge pressure and the resulting penalty had an air of inevitability about it, but this time Jones hit the post.

At this stage Fiji were under pressure in all the set pieces and had hardly had their hands on the ball at all, but from a Wales free kick on their own ten-metre line the Fijians turned the ball over and quick movement of both ball and players saw Akapusi Qera blast over from a few metres out. Somehow, despite playing poorly, the Fijians found themselves 7-3 in front.

As is often the case with Fiji, a score sparked them into life and less than three minutes later, following a Fiji scrum just outside their own 22, Delasau found himself away down the right. As the cover came across he chipped ahead and a kind bounce enabled him to re-gather ahead of two covering defenders in Mark Jones and Gareth Thomas and get the score.

If he was fortunate with the bounce, it was still a spectacular solo try, the kind which the flying winger was famous for. Although Nicky Little missed the conversion, it was 12-3 to Fiji, and Alix Popham was pinged for not releasing when he had the Fijian tacklers all over him and Little made it 15-3 as the first quarter drew to a close.

Fijian tails were up and suddenly Wales were rattled and struggling to contain the Islanders. Another straightforward penalty for Little for a ruck infringement made it 18-3, and it got worse for Wales when, from the restart, a break from Qera at the back of a ruck took play deep into the Wales half. He didn't have the pace to go all the way, but appearing again in the move enabled Fiji to recycle. Seremai Bai made a clean break to within a few metres of the Wales line and the big lock Kele Leawere peeled off and ploughed over despite the attentions of Martyn Williams. Little added the extras and after 26 minutes it was a scarcely believable 25-3.

An immediate penalty for offside against Qera saw Wales opt for a scrum but Little didn't buy James Hook's dummy and dumped the centre to the ground. However, Little was pinged for a high tackle on his opposite number. Wales turned down the virtually guaranteed three points and kicked to the corner but from the resulting play Jones knocked on and Fiji could clear. Constant pressure on the Wales line saw some tremendous defending – an aspect of the game for which Fiji are not normally renowned – and it took Wales almost ten minutes of play before they finally got over, through Popham, converted by Hook, as the Welsh pack rumbled over the line.

That made the half-time score 25-10 to Fiji, but significantly just on the stroke of half-time Qera was rightly penalised for lifting a knee at a maul to prevent Jones joining and was yellow-carded – on account of constant warnings – meaning Fiji would play out the first ten minutes of the second half with 14 men. Hook hooked the resulting kick horribly wide, though, to keep the gap at 15 points.

There was little immediate sign of Wales capitalising on the Fijian deficit as Seru Rabeni kept up his incredible form of the first half, making breaks and effecting turnovers with big hits, but when a loose ball found Shane Williams on the wide right with space in which to run it always looked like danger for Fiji despite it still being in the Wales 22. Sure enough, the speedy winger cut in past the first defender, opposition winger Isoa Neivua, and inside again past the last line of defence, full back Kameli Ratuvou for a splendid solo try under the posts. Jones converted for 25-17 and barely three minutes later Thomas cut the deficit still further – a Wales scrum move involving the back row sucked in the tacklers, and when Dwayne Peel spread the ball wide, a neat interchange of passes in midfield saw 'Alfie' go over in his 100th Test. Jones hit the post with his conversion attempt to keep the score at 25-22.

On virtually the very next play, a clever grubber from an inspired Thomas would have set Mark Jones away but for a brave challenge from captain Moses Rauluni who just got to the ball first and knocked it into touch, knowing that he was going to get a clattering from the fast-arriving Jones. Qera was back on for the resulting line-out, but could do little to prevent a third Wales try as a set move saw Alun Wyn Jones tap down for Peel to burst through the middle of the line-out. The ball was fed to Popham and the ball was moved swiftly through the hands from Gethin Jenkins, filling in as scrum half, to Jones, Hook and finally Jones, who had done well to get there having been on the other wing just seconds earlier. Jones had the wherewithal to run round behind the posts for an easy conversion and with half-an-hour left to play Wales had turned the game on its head to lead 29-25.

All credit to Fiji, though. Instead of panicking and trying to run impossible balls, they stayed calm and allowed Little to kick them back in front. His third successful penalty was in the 54th minute after Bai and Delasau had made ground down the right and when the ball came back into the middle, half of Wales were offside. It was only just on the Wales ten-metre line, but pretty much straight, and Little knocked it over. Two minutes later Little had another long-range pop, but just didn't have the distance and the ball fell under the posts. But then on the hour mark, with Fiji having rediscovered their ability to run the ball at the Welsh defence, with Ratuvou and, inevitably, Delasau doing the damage, they won another for Jones playing the ball while off his feet. It looked a harsh call, but that didn't matter to Little who slotted the penalty with the minimum of fuss to put Fiji back in front at 31-29.

It was nip and tuck for the next ten minutes, with Wales looking certain to score when they were on the Fijian line, but they were penalised for obstruction and Little cleared. Fiji then had their chance through a sensational run down the right wing by Bai; it looked a try initially but replays showed that he had just clipped the touchline an instant before getting the ball down. It was a great cover tackle from Gareth Thomas to get there.

Then, with Fiji attacking again, Martyn Williams capped a typically all-action game with a great intercept of a Little pass to give Wales a 34-29 lead with seven minutes to play. Worried about being hunted down, Williams didn't bother trying to make the conversion easier, and Jones consequently missed it, hitting a post for the third time in a match. Wales were ahead 34-29 and it appeared they had weathered the storm. Not so. Fiji re-gathered their kick-off and Bai and Ratuvou made ground deep into the Wales 22. Some good recycling saw Delasau brought down inches from the line and loosehead prop Graham Dewes was able to pick up and dive over. It took repeated viewings from the TMO, but the try was given and Little added the conversion.

Now we saw the implications of the Jones missed conversion – it meant Fiji led by four at 38-34 and Wales needed a try in the last three minutes rather than a penalty or a drop goal. Wales did have with the aid of another three-point kick some more possession, but they turned the ball over and Fiji ran it out of defence and played out the remaining seconds to clinch a quarter-final place.

'It was a hell of a game for sure and not the first half we had planned,' said Wales coach Gareth Jenkins. 'We got back into the lead but never had the chance to own and control the ball as we wanted.'

The last word should go to the Fijians, though, and their captain Rauluni, 'Years ago Fiji would have lost that game,' he said perceptively. 'I'm so proud of the boys. They stuck to it.' The only sour note was a serious knee injury to Little in virtually the last play of the game, but nothing could put a damper on Fiji's delight at reaching the knockout stages.

9 September 2007
Venue: Stade Geoffroy-Guichard, Saint Etienne
Attendance: 34,000

Portugal 10 Scotland 56

Portugal	Scotland
Padro Leal	Rory Lamont
David Mateus	Sean Lamont
Frederico Sousa	Marcus di Rollo
Diogo Mateus	Rob Dewey
Pedro Carvalho Cabral	Simon Webster
Duarte Pinto	Dan Parks
Jose Pinto Neves	Mike Blair
Rui Cordeiro	Allan Jacobsen
Joaquim Ferreira	Scott Lawson
Cristian Spachuk	Euan Murray
Goncalo Uva	Nathan Hines
David Penalva	Scott Murray
Juan Severino Somoza	Jason White (capt)
Joao Uva	Ally Hogg
Vasco Uva (capt)	Simon Taylor

Portugal were the only debutants at the 2007 RWC and as an amateur team they had done fantastically well to get all the way through an arduous qualification series. It had begun for them almost three years before the World Cup started, with their first match in the European Nations Cup First Division, which featured home and away games against Romania, Georgia, Russia, the Czech Republic and Ukraine.

Portugal had begun in stunning style, winning their first four matches – 36-16 against Ukraine in Odessa, beating Georgia 18-14, seeing off the Czech Republic 19-13 in Lisbon, and 18-16 against Russia in Krasnoyarsk. The final match of the 2004/05 season saw them lose to Romania in Bucharest, 14-10.

However, the second half of the competition, played in the 2005/06 season, didn't go so well for the Portuguese. They struggled to a 19-19 home draw with Russia and then got a 40-0 thumping by Georgia in Tbilisi. A week later, shattered by that defeat, they lost 27-3 to Romania in Lisbon. Fortunately, with easier games to come against Ukraine and the Czech Republic, they managed to recover sufficient poise to notch up a big 52-14 win over Ukraine in Lisbon and then snatch an 18-10 victory in Prague which meant that they finished in third place.

The next step along the way was a three-way contest with Italy and Russia. Italy were far too strong, beating Portugal 83-0 and Russia 67-7 to claim their place in the finals as 'Europe 1'. Portugal needed to repeat their European Nations Cup victory over Russia to progress to the final stage of qualification and they did, 26-23. In the other pool at Stage 5 Romania had qualified automatically (as 'Europe 2') by winning both games while Georgia had beaten Spain. That meant a home and away tie between Portugal and Georgia, and having lost 17-3 in Tbilisi the Portuguese felt they had a chance to turn the tie around in Lisbon. But Georgia battled hard to an 11-11 draw and took the slot as 'Europe 3', and condemn Portugal to the repechage.

The repechage proved an intense affair. First up were Morocco and having snatched a priceless away win, 10-5 in Casablanca, Portugal were just able to hang on in Lisbon, winning 16-15 for an aggregate score of 26-20. That put them into the final match against Uruguay for a place in the World Cup finals, and that final match was even closer than their win over Morocco.

The first leg in Lisbon ended in a 12-5 success for Portugal – yellow cards for Uruguay's centre Diego Aguirre and flanker Nicolas Brignoni costing them dear as Portugal won by two tries (from hooker Joao Correia and centre Diogo Gama, the latter converted by full back Pedro Leal) to one from Uruguay's captain and number eight Rodrigo Capo Ortega. After a scoreless first half, Portugal's opening try came from an interception by speedy winger Pedro Carvalho who raced almost the length of the field before passing to Gama to go in under the posts. The second try didn't come until inside the last ten minutes when Correia finally got over after a number of phases, but with Capo Ortega pulling five points back with three minutes to go, the tie was still finally balanced.

The second leg was in Montevideo a fortnight later and 12,000 fans gathered to see whether Los Teros could turn the tie around. However, an early red card for Uruguayan lock Juan Bado, issued by English referee Tony Spreadbury, made the South Americans' task much harder and although they won the game 18-12, scoring two tries to nil in the process, solid kicking from Portugal's fly half Duarte Pinto, who kicked four penalties, meant that Portugal edged through 24-23 on aggregate.

Uruguay had twice previously qualified for the World Cup, and on both occasions had managed to win a game. Could Portugal do the same?

Their first match was against Scotland and two early tries from full back Rory Lamont, both converted by Dan Parks, saw the Scots 14-0 in front inside 15 minutes. A quick tap penalty led to the first, and a simple line break, aided by some weak defensive tackling, to the second. When hooker Scott Lawson made it 21-0 after 23 minutes, benefiting from a pinpoint crossfield kick from Parks, Scotland had scored at almost a point a minute and one feared for Portugal. But then winger Pedro Carvalho scored his country's first World Cup try after 28 minutes. A series of close drives near the Scottish line and then quick ball from scrum half Jose Pinto Neves followed by a driving run from Pinto into the heart of the Scottish defence saw Carvalho burst through. The try was celebrated long and loud by the Portuguese fans as Pinto added the conversion.

Annoyingly for Portugal, Scotland scored their fourth try just moments later, when centre Rob Dewey gathered the restart and went all the way to the line. Pinto kicked a fine penalty in the 34th minute – awarded against Jason White for not binding at a scrum on his side's ten-metre line – to narrow the gap to 28-10, and that was the way it stayed until half-time.

The stats showed that Portugal had had to make more than three times as many tackles as Scotland, 73 to 21, and had had to make do with just 30 per cent of territory and possession. Clearly those figures were going to have an impact as the match wore on, but bravely the Portuguese held out without conceding any further score almost throughout the third quarter, despite having flanker Joao Uva in the sin bin: 57 minutes were on the clock before Parks scored his team's fifth try.

Some fine defending on their own line almost saw Portugal hold out, but eventually they just ran out of defenders and Parks was on hand to stroll over. In Parks's last contribution before being replaced by Chris Paterson, he converted his own try, and then three minutes later replacement centre Hugo Southwell added a sixth. Portugal were putting together a good-looking attack of their own when Carvalho lost the ball forward inside the Scottish 22, and a swift counter-attack resulted in a Scottish penalty on their own ten-metre line. Paterson took play up to midway between the Portuguese ten- and 22-metre lines, and quick ball off the top was followed by winger Simon Webster breaking the gain line, holding off two tacklers and flipping a simple pass to Southwell.

There was a possibility that the floodgates would open in the final quarter, but a game Portugal managed to hold the Scots to just two further scores. The seventh try went to replacement flanker Kelly Brown; Rory Lamont made the ground but despite being on a hat-trick he unselfishly popped the ball up for the supporting Brown who had an easy run in.

The final try went to replacement hooker Ross Ford, who'd only come on in the 68th minute. Portugal were right on the Scottish line, but were penalised for taking a man out at the ensuing ruck and a huge clearance from Southwell took play deep into Portugal territory. From the line-out a chip through bounced wickedly for the Portugal defence and up into the grateful arms of Ford.

Coupled with immaculate kicking from both Parks and Paterson, who between them converted all eight tries, the final scoreline was 56-10.

Portugal's second match was against New Zealand, and the pace and power simply overwhelmed them as they lost 108-13, shipping 16 tries in total, six in the final quarter. However, prop Rui Cordeiro scored a try for Portugal and Pinto hit a fine late drop goal to add to his conversion of Cordeiro's try. 'It was a very testing match,' said flanker Joao Uva with a degree of understatement. 'But it was a great honour to play against the All Blacks, a real privilege.'

Impressively, Portugal bounced back just four days after that crushing defeat to run Italy considerably closer than they had managed in the qualification stages. On that occasion, Italy had won 83-0, and we looked like we might be in for a repeat when centre Andrea Masi scooted over for a fourth-minute try, converted by David Bortolussi. Bortolussi added two penalties in the first half hour, and Italy even coped comfortably with the loss of captain Marco Bortolami to the sin bin. But in the 32nd minute Pinto ran at the heart of the Italian defence and when the ball was recycled Gama put lock David Penalva in at the corner. Bortolussi's third penalty stretched Italy's lead to 16-5 at the interval.

Portugal were unable to score again in a second half littered with errors on both sides, but equally they never let Italy get away from them. Two late tries – the first when Mauro Bergamasco scored at the back of a rolling maul, the other when Masi got his second of the game after latching on to a clever chip by fly half Roland de Marigny – put a gloss on the final scoreline of 31-5. But Portugal could be proud of their efforts, and they had at least scored a try of their own for the third match running.

And they kept that run going in their final match, against Romania. Portugal had lost home and away to Romania in the qualifying tournament but here they opened the scoring in the 18th minute through hooker Joaquim Ferreira, who was captain for the day. A terrible overthrow at a line-out put the Romanians on the back foot and they couldn't stop Ferreira ploughing over. Pinto converted, and that was the only score of the first half. A determined fightback from Romania in the second half brought them tries from replacement hooker Marius Tincu, from a powerful line-out drive, converted by Vali Calafeteanu and then flanker Florin Corodeanu from a series of rucks and mauls, converted by Dan Dumbrava. In between the Romania tries Portugal's replacement fly half Goncalo Malheiro kicked a 40-metre penalty to put his side back in front at 10-7, but after Corodeanu's 72nd-minute try, Portugal couldn't quite find the second try and lost 14-10.

It had been a great adventure for the amateurs, though, and it is also worth noting that in both the Italy and Romania games, Portuguese players received the man of the match awards – Jose Pinto against Italy and Diogo Coutinho against Romania. 'We'd struggled and worked so hard for years to reach the World Cup, it was a dream and in my opinion one of our great sporting moments,' said Joao Uva.

Scotland, meanwhile, progressed to the knockout stages. Despite failing to score a point in their 40-0 defeat by New Zealand, a 42-0 win over Romania meant that it all came down to the match with Italy in their final group game. Italy had scored a comfortable 37-17 victory at Murrayfield in that year's Six Nations Championship and clearly fancied their chances of a repeat dose, but despite scoring the only try of the game – through captain Alessandro Troncon – Italy couldn't prevent Paterson kicking six penalties. Bortolussi missed a penalty in the 76th minute, pushing his kick just wide when a successful three-pointer would have seen Italy regain the lead, and despite mounting some late pressure, Italy couldn't force another score. Scotland edged through to face unlikely quarter-final opponents in Argentina.

7 September 2007
Venue: Stade de France, Paris
Attendance: 80,000

France 12 Argentina 17

France	Argentina
Cedric Heymans	Ignacio Corleto
Aurelien Rougerie	Luca Borges
Yannick Jauzion	Manuel Contepomi
Damien Traille	Felipe Contepomi
Christophe Dominici	Horacio Agulla
David Skrela	Juan Martin Hernandez
Pierre Mignoni	Agustin Pichot (capt)
Olivier Milloud	Rodrigo Roncero
Raphael Ibanez (capt)	Mario Ledesma
Pieter de Villiers	Martin Scelzo
Fabien Pelous	Ignacio Fernandez Lobbe
Jerome Thion	Patricio Albacete
Serge Betsen	Juan Martin Fernandez Lobbe
Remy Martin	Lucas Ostiglia
Imanol Harinordoquy	Juan Manuel Leguizamon

When France got the 2007 Rugby World Cup under way in the magnificent Stade de France in front of almost 80,000 fans, one thing could be guaranteed: the supporters were not expecting to see their team get beaten. Drawn into Pool D alongside Ireland, Argentina, and the minnows of Georgia and Namibia, no French fan would have contemplated for a moment losing a match, particularly as they had beaten Ireland in Ireland (albeit it only 20-17) in that year's Six Nations Championship.

But that was to ignore Argentina's growing pedigree. Always dangerous outsiders, Argentina now had strength in every position and were agitating for inclusion in the Southern Hemisphere's Tri Nations competition (an eventuality which did not take place, bizarrely, until 2012). The Pumas had lost just 25-19 to New Zealand at Velez Sarsfield the previous summer, a match which had seen the All Blacks hanging on at the end to protect their lead. Then in the 2006 autumn internationals they had won at Twickenham for the first time, beating England 25-18. They followed this up with a 23-16 win over Italy in Rome and only lost 27-26 to France in the Stade de France in the final round of matches.

Clearly that demonstrated that the venue held no demons for the Argentines, and France might also have been wise to take note of the Pumas' wins over Ireland (22-20 and 16-0) and Italy (24-6) as they began their preparations for the World Cup.

English referee Tony Spreadbury got the game – and with it the 2007 RWC – under way and David Skrela kicked off only to see Juan Martin Hernandez return it with interest, to beyond the French ten-metre line. Argentina stole the throw, put Agustin Pichot through the gap and he chipped ahead. It went a little too far and was gathered by Cedric Heymans, but when he tried to run the ball out of defence he was tap-tackled by Pichot, following up determinedly. Although Heymans got the ball clear from way behind his own line, that set the pattern for the whole of the first half.

Argentina continued to take the game to France, and after a Felipe Contepomi drop goal attempt with his weaker left foot fell just wide and short, the French could clear only to the 22-metre line where they were penalised for holding on, and Contepomi kicked the opening score of the 2007 World Cup with a 45-metre penalty from wide on the right. It took France just two minutes to level the scores, however – Argentina could not collect the restart and the scrum went to France for a knock-on. Juan Martin Fernandez Lobbe was penalised for going off his feet and Skrela kicked a simple three points.

Imanol Harinordoquy was lucky not to be pinged for a knock-on from a superb up and under just a fraction outside his 22, but from the next play a beautiful behind-the-back flick pass from Contepomi found right wing Lucas Borges, and he was tackled from an offside position. Contepomi made it 6-3, and that became 9-3 in the 24th minute. A couple of minutes earlier Contepomi had hit a drop goal attempt narrowly wide – it looked a good strike when he hit it, but it skewed off to the right of the right-hand post. But he proved it hadn't rattled him when France were penalised for slowing the ball down at the breakdown and Contepomi calmly kicked the penalty.

The first 20 minutes showed Argentina with almost three-quarters of the territory, and that continued into the second quarter of the match, with the hammer blow coming in the 27th minute. France were on the attack after Damien Traille had broken powerfully through in midfield and found back-rower Remy Martin, showing a lot of bottle to get up in support. Disastrously for France, Martin's attempted pass over the top wasn't quite high enough and was intercepted by Horacio Agulla. He passed to full back Ignacio Corleto who showed an impressive turn of pace and an even more impressive understanding of angles as he took off on an arcing run which kept him out of the clutches of the French defence.

It did, however, take him a little wide and Contepomi's conversion attempt hit the post but stayed out.

Skrela did manage to pull three points back with his second penalty, awarded when Argentina didn't release at the breakdown, giving away another simple penalty in front of the posts. However, Argentina retained a measure of control and just a couple of minutes later Contepomi had the chance to extend the lead again; he landed a monster penalty from a few metres inside his own half to make the score 17-6. France did have the last word of the first half, in time added on, when Argentina ignored referee Spreadbury's instructions to leave the ball and tried to play it. Once again it was a straightforward kick for Skrela who made no mistake, so the half finished 17-9 in the Pumas' favour when really they should have been further ahead in terms of territory and possession.

The first half of the second half passed without any further score – though there was no lack of action or drama, clear-cut opportunities were few and far between. Perhaps the best came from a superb French driving maul which Argentina somehow stopped right on their own goal line, and when they tried to go wider, Christophe Dominici was isolated and penalised for holding on too long. Then Aurelien Rougerie made a splendid run deep into the Argentine half, but the French just couldn't keep the move going and although the resulting scrum turned into a penalty, Skrela missed with a simple kick. No real damage was done as Skrela was presented with another easy kick just moments later, after a driving maul was illegally stopped, and this time the French fly half made it 17-12.

On 60 minutes, France coach Bernard Laporte made a triple change in the forwards, replacing captain Ibanez, Pelous and Martin with Dimitri Szarzewski, Sebastien Chabal and Julien Bonnaire respectively, and all three gave France more power and go-forward: Chabal went on a great charge up the middle, but was stopped by, of all people, Contepomi. Next Rougerie got away down the right but just stepped into touch.

Nevertheless, it was the Pumas who had arguably the best chance of the second half when Corleto broke out of defence, hacked the ball upfield and re-gathered after a kind bounce – if his inside pass to Contepomi had gone to hand, Argentina would almost certainly have had their second try. Chabal effected a turnover at the resulting scrum, and now an Argentine seemed to be injured at nearly every stoppage in play. Genuine injuries they may have been, but they also had the effect of slowing the tempo down at precisely the time when France were building up some momentum and trying to play at pace.

Frederic Michalak was now on for Skrela, a completely different type of player who started teasing the Argentine defence with his variety of passes, runs and kicks. What he was not, however, was a reliable goal kicker and having created a chance with a superb chip through which resulted in a penalty for Corleto holding on, he sliced the penalty wide from about 25 metres. That would have brought France back to within two points with about nine minutes left to play, and it meant that instead they had to go looking for a try.

Contempomi attempted a drop goal which would have sealed the Argentine victory, but it was a poor effort, probably the only step he had put wrong all game, for which he was rightly awarded the man of the match award. He got much closer with a difficult penalty chance in the 77th minute, hooking it just past the post from about 40 metres out. But their tackling and defensive work was determined enough to keep France pinned in their own half and the Pumas had recorded a famous victory, their first over a Tier 1 nation at a World Cup.

'We are overcome with happiness,' said Argentine coach Marcelo Loffreda. 'But we shouldn't get above ourselves because it is only the first match. We have given ourselves a good start and we need to take advantage of it. We came with a plan to beat France and we knew that it would not be easy, but this is an important win for Argentina.'

Inspired by that win, Argentina went on to beat Georgia 33-3, scoring four tries in the process, and Namibia 63-3, scoring nine tries. In their final Pool D match they beat Ireland 30-15 and their discipline was so good as to allow Ronan O'Gara only one penalty shot at goal all match – which he got, inevitably. Each side scored two tries, but Contepomi's three penalties from four attempts and Hernandez's three drop goals made the difference. It was the first time Ireland had failed to reach the knockout stages of a World Cup, and a clear indication of the wider development or world rugby.

Thus Argentina progressed to the quarter-finals as group winners, meaning a tie against Scotland rather than the All Blacks. Argentina were back at Stade de France for that game, fielding a side showing just one change, Gonzalo Longo Elia getting the nod ahead of Leguizamon in the back row and rewarding his selection with a man-of-the-match performance. It was a nervy affair with lots of (often misplaced) kicking and the Pumas' only try coming from a Longo Elia charge-down which bounced kindly for him and cruelly for the covering Lamont brothers. Three penalties from Contepomi and another Hernandez drop goal eased Argentina out to 19-6, but a Chris Cusiter try, converted by Chris Paterson, gave Scotland a glimmer of a chance at 19-13 with about 15 minutes still to play. But as in the France match, the Argentines gathered themselves for a sterling defensive display which gave Scotland few opportunities.

The semi-final against South Africa looked to be a bridge too far for Argentina as the Springboks ruthlessly outplayed them, scoring three first-half tries. The Pumas rallied to narrow the gap to 24-13 early in the second half but could make no further headway and a converted try and two further Percy Montgomery penalties – in an immaculate kicking display – led to a final scoreline of 37-13.

Much to their credit, however, Argentina roused themselves for one final great performance in which they repeated their defeat of France in the third place play-off game. Although this is the game no one wants to play, it is noteworthy on this occasion as Argentina threw off the shackles of their traditional forward-oriented game to throw the ball about and have some fun.

In fact, France had the better of the first half but somehow found themselves 17-3 down following tries from Contepomi and prop Omar Hassan, though it might have been different had Jean-Baptiste Elissalde's 'try' not been harshly ruled out for a forward pass by Harinordoquy earlier in the move, and Yannick Nyanga not dropped the ball as he was attempting to ground it in time added on. That meant France had to press in the second half, and as they did so they twice got caught by sucker punches from turnover ball, first from Ferderico Martin Aramburu and then from Corleto who again showed impressive pace to beat the cover defence. Although Clement Poitrenaud pulled one back for the French, Contepomi fittingly had the final word with his country's fourth try, to make the final score 34-10 and cap off Argentina's best World Cup performance to date.

26 September 2007
Venue: Felix Bollaert, Lens
Attendance: 32,500

Georgia 30 Namibia 0

Georgia	Namibia
Malkhaz Urjukashvili	Heini Bock
Irakli Machkhaneli	Ryan Witbooi
Davit Kacharava	Piet van Zyl
Irakli Giorgadze	Corne Powell
Giorgi Shkinin	Bradley Langenhoven
Merab Kvirikashvili	Mot Schreuder
Irakli Abuseridze (capt)	Jurie van Tonder
Goderdzi Shvelidze	Kees Lessing (capt)
Akvsenti Giorgadze	Hugo Horn
David Zirakashvili	Marius Visser
Levan Datunashvili	Wacca Kazombaize
Mamuka Gorgodze	Heino Senekal
Grigol Labadze	Jacques Nieuwenhuis
Rati Urushadze	Jacques Burger
Girogi Chkhaidze	Tinus de Plessis

'I'd like to say a warm welcome, but it's 11 degrees and a horrible dank, wet evening here in Lens,' commentator Bob Symonds enthused when greeting TV viewers. 'We're used to it, I'm not quite sure these teams are – we're told it's 30 years since Namibia last played in the rain.'

It was the third Rugby World Cup running for which Namibia had qualified, but they had lost all seven of their previous games. In 1999 they had lost their Pool C matches to Fiji (67-18), France (47-13) and Canada (72-11), and in 2003 they had fared little better in Pool A, losing 67-14 to Argentina, 64-7 to Ireland, 142-0 to defending champions Australia and 37-7 to Romania.

In qualifying for the 2007 tournament, they had first topped a group including Tunisia and Kenya and with all three teams winning their two home games, Namibia's big 84-12 win over Kenya in Windhoek proved the decisive result in giving them the best points differential. Namibia were much more impressive in their final round of qualifying, beating Morocco at home (25-7) and away (27-8) for a comfortable 52-15 aggregate victory, sparing them the difficult task of the repechage round and putting them through as the second African team alongside the 1995 champions, South Africa.

Georgia for their part had qualified for the first time at the previous RWC, in 2003, and had also gone home winless on that occasion. They lost 84-6 to England, 46-9 to Samoa, 46-19 to South Africa and, most disappointingly, 24-12 to Uruguay, which would have been the match they had been focusing on as their best chance of victory.

But the Lelos, as they are nicknamed – deriving from *lelo burti*, a traditional Georgian sport with many similarities to rugby, and the word 'lelo' has now been adopted as the word for 'try' – had determined to do better, and in 2007 they had come through a qualifying competition in which they had played a three-way group with Romania (losing 20-8) and Spain (winning 37-23). Their second place there took them through to a final European qualifying round against Portugal which they won 28-14 on aggregate to become 'Europe 3'.

In their opening matches, Namibia had given Ireland a real fright when from being 27-3 down they had scored two quick tries around the hour mark. Jacques Nieuwenhuis and Piet van Zyl had scored five-pointers and with Emile Wessels converting both, Namibia were back within ten points until a late Jerry Flannery score put Ireland out of sight at 32-17.

Georgia, meanwhile, were disappointed in their 33-3 defeat by Argentina, but had come back strongly to give Ireland an even bigger scare than Namibia had. A try by winger Giorgi Shkinin, intercepting an attempted long pass by Ireland fly half Peter Stringer, was converted by Merab Kvirikashvili – who also added a penalty – which gave Georgia a 10-7 lead five minutes into the second half and although Girvan Dempsey's 55th-minute try, converted by O'Gara, had put Ireland back in front at 14-10, it was Georgia who were attacking fiercely in the final stages of the match, looking for what would have surely been the biggest upset in Rugby World Cup history.

For all their heroic performances against Ireland, though, both Georgia and Namibia knew that the most, if not only, realistic prospect of winning a match at the 2007 RWC was when they faced each other. They had met just once before, in the Nations Cup in Bucharest that June, a clash which Georgia won 26-18.

At the 2007 World Cup, Namibia had lost their other two matches, 87-10 against France and 63-3 to Argentina. 'The team will be stronger against Georgia,' promised coach Hakkies Husselman after the defeat by the Pumas. 'It is difficult to play three big games in a row and the last one just four days later but the Georgia game is the one we have been targeting for our first win. The odds are against us, but if we stick to our gameplan and do what we practised, then we can beat them. But at this level if you make a mistake you concede a try.'

Georgia had still to face France, but weren't expecting much change out of their hosts, rightly so as it turned out – they lost 64-7. Consequently not too many risks were taken in the opening stages of the game, and the first half-hour passed without incident, apart from the occasional handbags and a simple penalty from Merab Kvirikashvili after a clean break from centre Irakli Giorgadze.

Malkhaz Urjukashvili tried an optimistic long-range drop goal after 15 minutes, and Kvirikashvili missed a fairly routine chance after 23 minutes, awarded for the Namibian front row popping up at a scrum, curling the ball too much and past the right-hand post. Two minutes after that he had an even easier kick to make it 6-0, after the Namibians had dived in at the breakdown, and this time made no mistake.

Some hope was given to the Africans when they won a penalty on their first visit to the Georgian 22; they opted to kick for goal but Mot Schreuder's attempt, which looked bang on target, was blown off it at the last minute by the strong winds.

It wasn't until shortly before half-time that the first try was scored, when good line-out ball on the Namibian 22 led to a rolling maul. Grigol Labadze made ground on the left-hand touchline, then the ball was brought back inside for more mauling until eventually they got over through Akvsenti Giorgadze. Kvirikashvili added the extras to make it 13-0 after 37 minutes.

The second half started in similarly attritional fashion, but Kvirikashvili missed another penalty chance six minutes in after Namibia were penalised for hands in the ruck, and then another from his own half which fell well short of the target. Namibia did eventually get into the Georgian 22 again, but Jacques Nieuwenhuis gave away the penalty for a line-out tackle which was clumsy at best (Nieuwenhuis had received only the tournament's second red card in the match against France for a 'clothesline' tackle on Sebastian Chabal), allowing Georgia to clear. In the next play Namibia won a penalty and kicked to touch midway inside the Georgian 22, but it was slow ball which came to nothing against solid Georgian tackling.

Five minutes later Georgia put the game to bed. In the 69th minute, Kvirikashvili kicked his third penalty of the match after the Namibians had gone offside to put his team 16-0 ahead, a significant difference in that it meant they were more than two scores to the good. And then a minute later came the killer blow.

As is often the case with the minor nations, the effort and tackling couldn't be faulted, but there wasn't quite the precision or the cutting edge in attack. With 70 per cent territory and possession, Georgia were well on top, but their inability to score the points which their domination deserved meant that Namibia were still in a game in which they had been comprehensively outplayed. And as is equally often the case, the try, when it did come, came from a piece of individual magic – Machkhaneli put in a massive hit on Heini Bock, which knocked the ball free and he gathered himself and sprinted in under the posts. Kvirikashvili converted and it was 23-0.

Namibia to their credit did not give up and threw everything at Georgia in the last ten minutes, even though the game was lost. They had a pretty good chance to at least get on the scoreboard when they won a penalty advantage on the wide right, but they got carried away and knocked on the penalty in their haste and although Jacques Burger charged down the clearance kick, the ball went dead to give the Georgians a 22 drop-out.

As the clock went red, the Namibians launched one final attack which almost had the same result as the previous one as Machkhaneli came in for a huge hit from the blindside. The Namibians did exceptionally well to retain possession, but when the ball came out it was slow and in trying to force a pass they merely gave an interception to Davit Kacharava who had the speed and the composure to run in from the Namibian ten-metre line and under the posts to give Kvirikashvili his third conversion of the match with the final kick of the game. It was a sad end for the Africans, but there's no doubt that Georgia deserved their first World Cup win.

'Our goal was to win a match and the players gave it everything they had,' said Georgia coach Malkhaz Cheishvili, while flanker Rati Urushadze added, 'This is the best day yet for Georgian rugby, and for all of Georgia. We don't even know what to expect of our celebrations. It's our first victory, we're amateurs at winning.'

That may still be true of the Georgian team internationally, but increasingly their players are becoming better known on the European club scene. Their star name remains Mamuka Gorgodze who played 168 times for Montpellier before switching to Toulon on a three-year deal at the start of the 2014/15 season. However, of this 2007 Georgian squad, Shvelidze has also played in France – at Brive, Montauban and Montpellier – as have Akvsenti Giorgadze (at Castres and Toulouse), David Zirakashvili (Clermont), Labadze (Toulon) and Giorgi Chkhaidze (also Montpellier).

'They made Georgia proud and showed that Georgian rugby has a future,' said coach Cheishvili after the win over Namibia. It certainly did. Georgia are a growing power in world rugby; going into the 2015 RWC they had a world ranking of 14, and will be favourites to repeat their 2007 win over Namibia in the pool stages. They might even have a shot at beating 13th-ranked Tonga, who can be inconsistent, and will hope to run eighth-ranked Argentina closer than they did in 2011 when they led 7-5 before going down to a second-half blitz and losing 25-7. Given more money and resources – not to mention more regular competition against the Tier 1 nations over the next few years – it is certainly by no means inconceivable that Georgia could become a major rugby-playing nation.

6 October 2007
Venue: Millennium Stadium, Cardiff
Attendance: 71,660

New Zealand 18 France 20

New Zealand	France
Leon MacDonald	Damien Traille
Joe Rokocoko	Vincent Clerc
Mils Muliaina	David Marty
Luke McAlister	Yannick Jauzion
Sitiveni Sivivatu	Cedric Heymans
Dan Carter	Lionel Beauxis
Byron Kelleher	Jean-Baptiste Elissalde
Tony Woodcock	Olivier Milloud
Anton Oliver	Raphael Ibanez (capt)
Carl Hayman	Pieter de Villiers
Keith Robinson	Fabien Pelous
Ali Williams	Jerome Thion
Jerry Collins	Serge Betsen
Richie McCaw (capt)	Thierry Dusautoir
Rodney So'oialo	Julien Bonnaire

D efeat in Paris by Argentina in the opening match of the 2007 RWC had left the host nation facing the quarter-final which nobody wants, against perennial favourites New Zealand. To make matters worse, they had even lost home advantage. Three of the four quarter-finals were slated to be played in France, two at the Stade Velodrome in Marseilles, the other at the Stade de France. Of course everyone expected France, as the winners of Pool D, to be in the last of these, to be taking on – and comfortably disposing of, presumably – Scotland. Indeed a winning campaign would have seen France remaining in Saint-Denis throughout, but being condemned to a runners-up spot against the winners of Pool C meant they faced not only the might of the All Blacks, but a trip to the Millennium Stadium.

What followed was a World Cup quarter-final which has passed into legend.

France made a statement of intent when they lined up on the halfway line to face the Haka, arms linked to show they were not going to be intimidated, and then England's Wayne Barnes got the game under way.

The first two scrums looked pretty solid, with France not caving in to the New Zealand pressure as they had done in the past, and the first chance the All Blacks had to run the ball, they turned it over and Damien Traille cleared. Serge Betsen took a heavy blow while trying to stop a Joe Rokocoko charge and after lengthy treatment on the pitch by medical staff he had to leave the field after just five minutes, to be replaced by Imanol Harinordoquy.

A minute later, Traille was nicely sat back in the pocket for a shot at a drop goal and he hit it sweetly but it veered past the left-hand post, and there followed a period of kicking for field position. But on the French ten-metre line Richie McCaw was penalised for not rolling away and France cleared the danger. The first score of the game came after 14 minutes when France were penalised for not rolling away, and Dan Carter had a nice, simple kick from inside the 22 and almost in front of the posts.

Two minutes later and alarm bells were ringing for a French side which had been set up to defend and kick when they fell 10-0 behind. Luke McAlister took line-out ball in the middle of the park, stepped off his right foot back inside and was away; the ball was recycled and Ali Williams went over in the left-hand corner but Vincent Clerc just managed to get to him and replays showed a clear foot in touch. However, the clearing kick was run straight back at France and a beautiful little pop pass from Carter saw McAlister burst through again on the angle. Support came in from Jerry Collins and back to McAlister, who wriggled over.

Lionel Beauxis did have a chance to pull three points back in the 24th minute with a penalty from wide on the right after the All Blacks were again pinged for not rolling away at the breakdown, but his kick faded across the posts. Instead it was New Zealand who scored next when France were penalised for offside in their urgency to stop the All Blacks runners. This one was from some way out, about 43 metres, but fairly straight and Carter slotted it, no problem. New Zealand led 13-0 and France desperately needed something in the final ten minutes of the half.

Jean-Baptiste Elissalde did have the chance to do just that in the 35th minute, but his kick, aimed at the far post, did not curl in enough to get the French on the board. France were at least getting some of the play now, however, which they hadn't in the first half, and getting some confidence in their handling. With the clock turning red, they had one final chance after the All Blacks were again penalised at the breakdown and a great strike from Beauxis made it 13-3 to New Zealand at half-time.

The half-time stats showed New Zealand ahead 60-40 on possession but with territory split absolutely evenly at 50-50. The French had, however, made 57 tackles compared with New Zealand's 19 which accurately reflected the pattern of play and seemed to point to an ultimate All Blacks victory. The fireworks were reserved for the second half, however.

'All Blacks dominating much of the first half, but just the one try. Referee Wayne Barnes has been very hard on the All Blacks at the breakdown,' said the commentators on TV3, New Zealand's national TV channel.

The All Blacks started the second half on the attack, taking yet another line-out against the throw, their fourth, but the French defence remained strong and their tackling on the gain line very solid. Carter was still pulling the strings, increasingly bringing Sitiveni Sivivatu into the play and working the blindside which New Zealand do so well, but a loose ball was hacked through and out of nowhere the French were on the attack. From a line-out they tried to get a rolling maul going and caught the All Blacks offside, gaining a penalty advantage. Matters went from bad to worse for the Kiwis as while still playing the advantage McAlister was guilty of taking out a supporting player. The commentators felt it was harsh, but referee Barnes could clearly be heard describing it as 'cynical'. On the replays it looked like Yannick Jauzion had made the most of it, but equally McAlister did definitely drop his shoulder into Jauzion to make sure he couldn't get through – a harsh call but not a terrible one. More saliently, it was completely unnecessary as New Zealand had plenty of defenders covering the chip kick so McAlister really didn't need to do anything stupid. Beauxis kicked the simple penalty to make it 13-6.

Being a man down didn't seem to have an immediately detrimental effect on the All Blacks as they went straight back on the attack, running the ball down their left-hand side, then keeping the ball tight with a series of pick-and-gos to prevent the French taking advantage of their extra man in the backs. Eventually they fired the ball out, but the pass was hardly sympathetic and Tony Woodcock knocked it on; the resulting scrum saw France awarded a free kick and they cleared almost up to halfway. The All Blacks had used up more than half of McAlister's time in the sin bin when Carter had an ill-advised attempt at a drop goal – it went well wide and the French moved the ball quickly from the 22, David Marty taking play almost up to the halfway line and then providing the link man when the ball was moved back to the right where Harinordoquy and Traille combined and almost got in in the right-hand corner. The All Blacks hung on well but eventually just ran out of defenders and Thierry Dusautoir beat one tackle to go over close to the posts. Beauxis almost missed a simple conversion, dragging the ball left but it bounced in off the left-hand post to tie the scores.

Before the All Blacks could kick off again, Carter had to be replaced – by Nick Evans – on account of a calf muscle injury while Brendon Leonard took over at scrum half from Byron Kelleher. McAlister returned to the field after his ten-minute rest and the game got going again through Evans. The All Blacks went back on the attack, but Leon MacDonald knocked on, only for their pack to turn the scrum over and get the put-in. Leonard made a half-break, as did Evans, but once more the French managed to slow things up and Sebastien Chabal got his hands on the ball. A French scrum turned into a French penalty when Collins – who was having a great game – was penalised for breaking off too early but then Ali Williams stole the line-out on their own ten-metre line and Collins and Rodney So'oialo combined to almost put Sivivatu away down the left-hand touchline.

A good pick-up and drive from replacement hooker Andrew Hore took New Zealand to within a couple of feet and then the impressive So'oialo burrowed his way to the try line. McAlister took over the kicking duties but pushed a tough kick past the right-hand post so the All Blacks' lead remained at five, at 18-13.

Then Cedric Heymans dropped a high one midway between the French ten- and 22-metre lines and from the All Blacks' scrum, Evans made a clean break through the middle but tried a tricky low pass and the ball was knocked forward. Beauxis cleared up to the halfway line, and that was his last piece of action as New Zealand threw a forward pass and before the scrum was set, Frederic Michalak came on to replace him.

Possession was now up to two-thirds to one-third in favour of the All Blacks, but the French remained dangerous as they proved when, from that scrum, Traille did exactly what Evans had done and burst the gain line with a clean break. His pass to Michalak could have been forward, but play was allowed to go on and Michalak found Jauzion inside him to send the big centre over. That tied the score and Elissalde put France ahead for the first time at 20-18. That pass, which became a cause celebre after the game, wasn't dwelt on much by the commentary team at the time, and undoubtedly rugby fans all over the world will see the irony of the All Blacks moaning about a possible forward pass.

There were still ten minutes to play at that point, but instead of going through the phases and carrying on doing what they had been doing, an air of panic crept into the All Blacks' play. They had plenty of the ball, but couldn't quite work out what to do with it – the pick-and-gos were still working well, but French tackling around the fringes was strong and determined. Harinordoquy could possibly have been penalised at one ruck near the French line, but Barnes ruled that he was on his feet and stole the ball legally. The All Blacks never looked for a drop goal option until almost the final whistle and by then they were too far away.

It was a stunning upset, the only time in World Cup history that New Zealand have failed to reach at least the semi-finals, and was such a shock that there was talk in the air about incompetent refereeing at best, conspiracy at worst. Although the match stats on the day showed the All Blacks with 72 per cent possession and 62 per cent territory, they also showed that France had made fewer handling errors and won more turnovers. Some years later Graham Henry hinted in his autobiography that there might even have been some match-fixing involved, a disgraceful slur for which he should have been roundly carpeted.

In the immediate aftermath, Henry had offered a more measured response. 'The French played particularly well defensively, were pretty astute in their gameplan and took their opportunities,' he said. 'We understand the better side won on the day and a lot of credit goes to them.' Perhaps he just had a book to sell.

As for the French, their captain Raphael Ibanez said, 'Every time you play New Zealand you have to play out of your skin, and that's what happened this evening. In the World Cup, courage and team spirit can make a big difference. The players really gave everything right until the end.'

43

20 October 2007
Venue: Stade de France, Paris
Attendance: 80,400

England 6 South Africa 15

England	South Africa
Jason Robinson	Percy Montgomery
Paul Sackey	JP Pietersen
Mathew Tait	Jaque Fourie
Mike Catt	Francois Steyn
Mark Cueto	Bryan Habana
Jonny Wilkinson	Butch James
Andy Gomarsall	Fourie du Preez
Andrew Sheridan	Os du Randt
Mark Regan	John Smit (capt)
Phil Vickery (capt)	CJ van der Linde
Simon Shaw	Bakkies Botha
Ben Kay	Victor Matfield
Martin Corry	Schalk Burger
Lewis Moody	Juan Smith
Nick Easter	Danie Rossouw

A ustralia had looked a good bet to reach the World Cup Final, if only they could overcome New Zealand in the semi-final. In the event, neither of the two Southern Hemisphere giants were able to take their appointed places in that semi-final – New Zealand, as we have seen, were beaten by France in their quarter-final while Australia, just as incredibly, were beaten by England for the second World Cup in a row.

The Wallabies had opened their 2007 campaign in fine style by crushing Japan 91-3. Blindside flanker Rocky Elsom scored a hat-trick while Chris Latham and replacements Berrick Barnes and Drew Mitchell each weighed in with a double. Adam Ashley-Cooper, George Smith, Nathan Sharpe and substitute hooker Adam Freier also got their names on the scoresheet. A sharp, determined-looking Australian outfit had then comfortably held off Wales 32-20, beating them for the third time in a row having won both games during Wales's tour of Australia earlier that summer.

Australia had gone on to record victories against Fiji (55-12, with Mitchell getting a hat-trick) and Canada (37-6, with Mitchell scoring two more). It had made for a successful group stage for Australia, and put them in the position of strong favourites against a slightly dishevelled England. An early penalty from Stirling Mortlock plus a 33rd-minute try from Lote Tuqiri (converted by Mortlock) did little to disturb that assessment, though Jonny Wilkinson kept England in touch through penalties in the 23rd and 26th minutes, restricting Australia's half-time lead to 10-6.

But in the second half, England's forward dominance prevented Australia from getting into any sort of rhythm and meant that their dangerous back division only got the ball when they were going backwards. Jason Robinson and Paul Sackey made good bursts and kept Australia under the cosh, and the Wallaby scrum could not cope with Andrew Sheridan in particular as his massive power won penalties at both set scrum and breakdown, allowing Wilkinson to pull England within one point after 52 minutes. And on the hour they were in front, their scrum driving Australia back over their own line and gaining an inevitable penalty.

Remarkably that was the end of the scoring in the match, though it certainly wasn't the end of the efforts of both sides to do so. England's best chances came from a Wilkinson attempt at a drop goal which slid past the post and a long-range penalty which also missed. Australia almost scored but for Sackey's excellently timed man-and-ball tackle on a charging Latham and a late penalty chance for Mortlock from the left-hand touchline which went wide.

So it was another France v England semi-final instead of a Southern Hemisphere one, and England set the cat among the Stade de France pigeons early on when an Andy Gomarsall chip kick from the base of a ruck appeared to be covered by Damien Traille but bounced up and was seized by Josh Lewsey, who managed to get the ball down in the corner. France had the better of the first half, with 65 per cent of the territory, and edged 6-5 ahead with two penalties from Lionel Beauxis. A third from the French fly half four minutes into the second half, after England were penalised for offside, was swiftly cancelled out by Jonny Wilkinson's first. A superb interception from Moody, taken on by replacement Dan Hipkiss, who almost put Tait in for a try, resulted in a penalty when the French killed the ball illegally.

Despite chances for both teams – Wilkinson's right-footed drop goal which hit the post was probably England's best opportunity, while the French countered with a driving maul which went well into the English 22 and a run from Vincent Clerc which was stopped only by a desperate ankle tap – there were no further scores for almost half an hour. Then in the 75th minute Wilkinson got the chance for his second kick at goal after Dimitri Szarzewski was penalised for a high tackle on Robinson, and he nudged England ahead 11-9. Then that famous left boot knocked over a long-range drop goal in the 78th minute and England – against all the odds and certainly against expectation given their form earlier in the competition – were into their second consecutive World Cup Final. But there they were to face the team which had humiliated them just under a month earlier: South Africa.

It was a very different-looking England from that pool match which took the field for the final. Lewsey had been injured in the semi-final, pulling his hamstring, so into his place on the wing came Mark Cueto. Mike Catt moved into the centres (in place of Andy Farrell) to provide that reassuring presence which had helped Wilkinson so much in extra time of the final four years earlier, and his partner there was Mathew Tait. Gomarsall started at scrum half while in the pack captain Paul Vickery returned in place of Matt Stevens and Lewis 'Mad Dog' Moody got the nod in the back row. South Africa, by contrast, fielded not only the same starting line-up but five of the same seven bench replacements.

All the odds seemed to be in South Africa's favour – a settled team; four consecutive wins over England, including that 36-0 thrashing at the pool stages; an easier passage to the final; and a brilliant coach in Jake White.

Under the watchful eye of Alain Rolland, Wilkinson got the 2007 Rugby World Cup under way and Butch James returned it almost to the ten-metre line. South Africa stole the line-out only to knock on the ball in midfield and hand the scrum to England; the first scrum saw England rumble forward a bit but ultimately turn the ball over. England lost their second line-out too, although having it stolen by Victor Matfield is no disgrace, as he is arguably the greatest line-out exponent of all time. Matfield is a giant of a man, but it isn't his size so much as his technique which makes him an all-time great of the line-out. Winner of more than 120 caps for his country, Matfield has won the Tri Nations with the Springboks and Super Rugby and the Currie Cup with the Bulls and is certain to be part of South Africa's 2015 RWC squad, which will mark his fourth World Cup appearance.

The first penalty opportunity came when Tait thought he saw a chance to run the ball from inside his own 22, but a slip forced him to go to ground and he held on too long, gifting Percy Montgomery an easy three points. England kept playing a surprising amount of rugby when they had possession, but Paul Sackey couldn't get away from Bryan Habana down the right-hand wing, although England did ultimately win a penalty from that phase of play.

There was only one man who had managed to get away from Habana at the 2007 RWC: step forward America's Takudzwa Ngwenya. The Springboks were dealing comfortably enough with the Eagles, and the score was already 24-3 in their favour as they mounted another attack near half-time. But at the breakdown deep inside the USA's 22, Fourie de Preez tried a floated pass which was picked off by Eagles openside Todd Clever. Clever made a power run upfield, linked up with the supporting Alec Parker and the second row found his captain, Mike Hercus, who immediately launshed a long pass to Ngwenya. Although the winger had space, he was still in his own half and opposite number Habana looked to be lining him up to guide him towards the right-hand touchline and force him out. Ngwenya shimmied as if to cut back inside, then hit the afterburners and went round the outside of Habana, leaving one of the greatest wingers the world has ever seen for dead, clutching at vapour fumes. It was one of those glorious moments in sport which, even if they have no bearing on the destination of the prizes, was nevertheless destined to pass into legend.

Back to the final itself, and Wilkinson tied the game up at 3-3 with a magnificent kick from the right-hand touchline. Parity only lasted three minutes, however, as Lewis Moody stupidly had a sly trip of James when he was chasing his own high kick, resulting in a penalty where the ball landed, which in this instance was comfortably within his range and he made it 6-3. England had the next chance as Wilkinson took a snap shot at a drop goal but it drifted just wide of the posts.

Vickery then fell off his feet at a ruck on the halfway line and Francois Steyn had a pot at goal, but in getting the distance he just fell off the accuracy and missed to the left. But 14 minutes later, Steyn started the move which ultimately led to the Springboks' third penalty. Breaking in midfield he got through a couple of tackles and as play moved first right and then left hooker John Smit almost got over but for some desperate English defence. The scrum initially went to England, but after a couple of re-sets South Africa wheeled it sufficiently to get the put-in and England were penalised for hands in the ruck. Montgomery made it 9-3 at half-time.

England came out with renewed passion for the second half, and a superb clean break by Tait took him to within metres of the South African try line, and when the ball was recycled Cueto almost got over in the left-hand corner but just clipped the touchline in the act of scoring. From the reactions it looked like both sets of players thought Cueto had scored, but Rolland referred it to the TMO, Australian Stuart Dickinson, who decided he had touched the line. Cueto, who retired at the end of England's domestic season in May 2015, told *The Telegraph*'s excellent rugby correspondent Mick Cleary on the eve of his last professional game, 'In my mind, it was a try. It was the early days of the TMO and I've seen far less obvious tries given. In any other game I'm convinced it would have been given.'

The call was a tight one, and England did at least come away with points as Rolland brought play back for an earlier penalty for Schalk Burger going offside, and Wilkinson landed a simple kick to make it 9-6.

Matfield then put in a neat little kick into the England 22 and while South Africa were setting up their scrum, Robinson had to go off, to be replaced by Dan Hipkiss. Steyn again made good ground and Martin Corry was penalised for not moving away after a tackle and Montgomery restored South Africa's six-point advantage. Before the restart Catt also had to go off with injury, replaced by Toby Flood, so within five minutes England had lost two of their more experienced backs. Flood might have been more heavily penalised for pushing Montgomery when chasing a kick over the top which ran away from him, but in general England's kicking was just a little too heavy, then Ben Kay was penalised for obstruction – a tough call, and it looked a less obvious offence than Habana's a little earlier, and possibly J.P. Pietersen's a little later, but Steyn kicked a monstrous 49-metre penalty to put South Africa 15-6 ahead, and give them that crucial two-score margin.

England attacked for the rest of the game but just could not find a way through, Wilkinson kicked a penalty into the South African 22 following a block on Cueto, only for England to lose their line-out ball. Wilkinson tried a long-range drop goal which didn't get anywhere near, and they had another line-out inside the 22 but again knocked on and lost the ball. The precision and the creativity were just not quite good enough to find a way through.

The end-of-play stats actually showed England ahead on territory (57-43) and possession (55-45), but they made more errors and conceded more penalties, and the injuries they suffered forced them to empty their bench and they finished with the reserve scrum half Peter Richards playing on the flank after Moody and bench replacement Joe Worsley were both forced off. Most neutrals, while praising England's efforts, felt that the Springboks were worthy winners of the 2007 RWC.

'Everyone in the squad made a contribution, from number one to number 30,' said Habana. 'Every player who's represented the country in the last four years made a contribution.'

44

1 October 2011
Venue: Westpac Stadium, Wellington
Attendance: 32,700

France 14 Tonga 19

France	Tonga
Maxime Medard	Vungakoto Lilo
Vincent Clerc	Viliame Iongi
Aurelien Rougerie	Siale Piatau
Maxime Mermoz	Andrew Ma'ilei
Alexis Palisson	Sukanaivalu Hufanga
Morgan Parra	Kurt Morath
Dimitri Yachvili	Taniela Moa
Jean-Baptiste Poux	Soane Tonga'uiha
William Servat	Aleki Lutui
Luc Dulcacon	Kisi Pulu
Pascal Pape	Tukulua Lokotui
Lionel Nallet	Paino Hehea
Thierry Dusautoir (capt)	Sione Kalamafoni
Julien Bonnaire	Finau Maka (capt)
Raphael Lakafia	Viliami Ma'afu

The top 20 ranked nations all qualified for the 2011 Rugby World Cup in New Zealand, which meant that Russia made their first appearance, in place of the game Portugal side which had graced the 2007 tournament. Russia had actually been invited to take part in the inaugural RWC but declined as a protest against South Africa being allowed to be members of the IRB (now World Rugby) despite the existence of apartheid at the time. Having narrowly failed to qualify in the intervening years, Russia took its place in 2011 courtesy of finishing in runners-up spot in the 2008 to 2010 European Nations Cup, thereby becoming the 25th country to take part in a Rugby World Cup.

Russia proved to be a welcome addition to the party, and acquitted themselves well, scoring tries in their defeats by Italy (53-17), Ireland (62-12) and Australia (68-22).

Only in the 13-6 defeat by the United States were they disappointed with their performance, and much of the 2011 tournament was a tale of the so-called 'minnows' of world rugby narrowing the gap on more illustrious opponents. For all the closing of some gaps, however, the first real major upset of the tournament didn't come until the final round of group matches.

Pool A had progressed as many had predicted it would, with hosts New Zealand pretty much coasting through their games, beating Tonga 41-10, Japan 83-7, France 37-17 and Canada 79-15.

Despite that 20-point defeat by the All Blacks, France knew, going into their final pool match, that they were all but guaranteed the runners-up spot, having beaten Japan 47-21 and Canada 46-19. Tonga had too big a points differential – they would have had to beat France by 28 points to close the gap – while Canada could only overtake them in the unlikely scenario of France losing and

Canada beating the All Blacks the following day, and scoring five tries in the process.

So it was possibly a mildly complacent France that took the field at the Westpac Stadium in Wellington, and not helped by the obvious dissension in the French ranks, with several of the players criticising coach Marc Lievremont and unhappy about being played out of position or taken off. An early offside against Kisi Pulu gave Dimitri Yachvili a simple penalty from 36 metres out and straight in front of the posts, which he duly kicked, but France found themselves under some pressure for the next few minutes with Finau Maka (who played in France for Toulouse) running hard and straight, and on one occasion straight into Morgan Parra, playing out of position at fly half.

The dynamism of their play inevitably brought Tonga a penalty and fly half Kurt Morath tied the scores up at 3-3.

France did try to mix and match an all-court game, combining chips and grubbers with running from deep, but never appeared particularly threatening except when Aurelien Rougerie and then Maxime Medard broke the gain line but weren't able to find a colleague with their offloads. Then chunky Tongan scrum half Tanieli Moa broke out from loose line-out ball and relieved the pressure by taking play into the French half and winning his team a second penalty. On this occasion Morath, who'd had a successful tournament with the boot, curled his right to left kick too much and it went past the left-hand post.

The next penalty also went Tonga's way, but this time too far away for them to go for goal so Morath sent the ball deep into the French half instead. A chip in behind looked a good option but winger Sukanaivalu Hufanga got a little over-excited and was a couple of metres offside, giving the French the chance to clear. Then it was France's turn to attack and some good offloading saw Mermoz and Raphael Lakafia take the ball to within a few metres of the line. It ended with another offside decision, a general warning from referee Steve Walsh, and another three points from Yachvili.

A Tongan move which looked like going nowhere was rescued by Moa who ran hard and straight and when the ball was recycled Morath picked a great crossfield kick to give Hufanga a one-on-one with Julian Bonnaire and the Tongan wing showed his strength to get over the line for a try which put his country 8-6 ahead. Morath added a wonderful conversion from out wide on the right to make it 10-6.

In response, Alexis Palisson and Rougerie got away down the left, and Maka was penalised for offside but somehow escaped further punishment. Parra punted it into the corner and from the line-out the French drove to within a couple of metres but couldn't get the ball down. William Servat thought he had scored, but Walsh ruled it a double movement and gave the penalty to Tonga. A multi-phase attack from Tonga, involving forwards and backs, resulted in several French players being caught offside and Morath made it 13-6 to Tonga.

France's play was a little directionless but as they spread the ball wide right to Vincent Clerc, Hufanga put in a huge hit, driving the French winger up and back. Unfortunately for Hufanga he didn't bring Clerc back down to the ground safely enough for the referee's liking, and it cost him ten minutes in the sin bin. Interestingly, touch judge Carlo Damasco and Walsh seemed to think a penalty was sufficient but after a chat and a review Walsh went to his pocket. Only two of those sin bin minutes were left in the first half and despite some frantic French attacking in those 90 seconds or so, the whistle went with Tonga still leading 13-6.

Morath started the second half and immediately the disjointed French knocked forward to hand Tonga the advantage which became a penalty against Parra. But Morath pulled his kick. It also seemed as if Tonga hadn't realised that it wasn't just about winning, they also had to score four tries if they were to pip France for the runners-up spot.

France continued to give them opportunities to do just that, however, turning the ball over in their own half and almost encouraging the Tongans to run at them – an invitation they were happy to take up. Siale Piatau made a half-break, but his offload was too ambitious and from the scrum they won a penalty, with which they missed touch and full back Vungakoto Lilo took play back into the French half.

Suddenly the French put a running move together as Medard charged forward and moved the ball on to Parra, but his pass to Yachvili was batted down, and Walsh went back for a penalty awarded for a shoulder charge on Parra after the ball had gone. Yachvili kicked the three points to make it 13-9 with half an hour to play, but from the restart Tonga gained possession and got to within five metres of the French line and gained an obvious penalty for offside. They kicked for touch and won the line-out but then France managed to turn it over and clear.

France rang the changes, with Parra and Rougerie replaced by Francois Trinh-Duc and Fabrice Estebanez, but the pattern of the game did not change, except that now Tonga were getting a little nervy themselves and not taking their chances – Morath pushing yet another kick left of the uprights, then desperate scramble defence from the French just keeping the Tongans out after a clean break by Piatau, but at the cost of losing Estabanez for ten minutes for a tip tackle. Morath kicked the resulting penalty to increase Tonga's lead to 16-9.

And before Estabanez came back, Morath had kicked his fourth penalty to make it 19-9, when the French again went offside. At that point, France were without a bonus point, although Tonga still hadn't scored enough tries to snatch the second place from their opponents. With seven minutes left, Tonga should have had their second try when Viliami Ma'afu broke clean through the French defence and with supporting runners on either side there were several options; he passed to Samiu Vahafolau but he turned back into traffic instead of arcing his run away from it and towards the posts, and the chance went begging.

France did finally raise the siege and get some territory of their own, and with the clock showing red they were awarded a penalty under the posts. The obvious decision would have been to take the simple three points on offer and ensure a losing bonus point, but bizarrely they went for a scrum and rather fortuitously they put Clerc over in the right-hand corner. It made the final score 19-14 and while that wasn't enough for Tonga to go through, it was still a major upset.

'I don't think we can be happy with this qualification,' said Lievremont, 'but we have qualified. We're still part of this adventure.'

Tongan coach Isitolo Maka was proud of his team's performance, 'For us to beat France is very special. It's good for Tongan rugby and for our people who have supported us since we've been in New Zealand. People are going crazy in Tonga right now.'

Of course, a factor was that several of the Tongan players – full back Vunga Lilo, winger Hufanga, prop Kisi Pulu, and back-rowers Maka and Ma'afu among them – played their club rugby in France and were familiar with both the players and the style of play the French preferred. Captain Maka, who has won both the Heineken Cup and the Top 14 title with Toulouse, and whose distinctive afro hairstyle makes him instantly recognisable, is probably the best known of the French contingent and could actually have opted to play for France so long has he lived in the country. Instead he swore his allegiance to Tonga, to whom he brought an extra dimension in enabling his country to compete in the forwards, at the set pieces and the breakdown.

Probably the best-known Tongan is Soane Tonga'uiha who played over 200 times for Northampton Saints in the English Premiership during seven years at the club. Tonga'uiha had been at Auckland but his failure to gain a Super Rugby contract led to him seeking work in England where he first played for Bedford. Scoring a try for Bedford against Northampton brought him to the latter's attention and he moved there at the start of the 2006/07 season. He became a firm favourite with both crowd and fellow players at Northampton, where the 6ft 3in, 20st prop was known as 'Tiny'.

The added professionalism brought to the Tongan team by the players who are playing professionally in France and England, and elsewhere such as in Italy or in Super Rugby, makes them a genuine threat to the Tier 1 nations. The 2011 RWC proved that they are now able to mix play up and be competitive in the forwards as well as devastating in their backs, and if they have a reliable goal-kicker too – which Morath was – they can pose danger for anyone.

The French looked disjointed and lacking in leadership, and it was hard to see where their World Cup campaign would go after this defeat.

45

25 September 2011
Venue: Westpac Stadium, Wellington
Attendance: 32,700

Argentina 13 Scotland 12

Argentina	Scotland
Martin Rodriguez	Chris Paterson
Gonzalo Camacho	Max Evans
Marcelo Bosch	Nick De Luca
Felipe Contepomi (capt)	Graeme Morrison
Horacio Agulla	Sean Lamont
Santiago Fernandez	Ruaridh Jackson
Nicolas Vergallo	Rory Lawson (capt)
Rodrigo Roncero	Allan Jacobsen
Mario Ledesma	Ross Ford
Juan Figallo	Geoff Cross
Manuel Carizza	Richie Gray
Patricio Albacete	Jim Hamilton
Julio Farias Cabello	Alistair Strokosch
Juan Manuel Leguizamon	John Barclay
Juan Martin Fernandez Lobbe	Kelly Brown

In terms of the world rankings, going into the 2011 Rugby World Cup, Scotland had nudged ahead of Argentina, at seven to nine, but in terms of recent World Cup performances and pedigree, the Argentines might actually have been slight favourites for the match – a quarter-final in 1999, a one-point miss from repeating that in 2003 (the 16-15 defeat by Ireland being all that stood between them and a second consecutive quarter-final), and then third place in 2007. Scotland always managed to get out of the group stages, but only on one occasion, in 1991, had they managed to go a stage further than that, and at the previous World Cup it was Argentina who had defeated them, 19-13.

However, since that 2007 game the teams had met five times and Scotland were ahead 3-2; furthermore that recent record included three victories in Argentina, never the easiest place for visiting teams to gain a result. Scotland's 2008 tour had seen the Test series split, with Argentina winning the first encounter 21-15 in Rosario, but Scotland hitting back a week later to claim the second Test 26-14. In the 2009 autumn international at Murrayfield, Argentina had won a tryless encounter 9-6 just a week after the Scots had beaten Australia at the same venue.

Then in June 2010, the Scots experienced an even better result on their summer tour of Argentina, winning 24-16 in Tucuman and a week later triumphing 13-9 in Mar del Plata. The first game saw Argentina score two tries to none, both in the first half-hour, but six penalties and two drop goals from the prolific boot of Dan Parks won Scotland the match. The following week the Scots crossed the Pumas' line within three minutes, thanks to Jim Hamilton, and in a low-scoring game the conversion and two penalties from Parks was just enough for Scotland to register their first Test series win in Argentina.

Despite Parks being the match-winner the previous summer, however, he was left on the bench for this crucial World Cup clash, with Scotland coach Andy Robinson believing that Ruaridh Jackson was a better bet in terms of giving the team the fast-moving running game he wanted to adopt. 'I believe Argentina are a better team now than the one we faced last year,' said Robinson in the build-up to the game.

Pool B had opened in slightly shaky style for Scotland, with an up-and-down win over a game Romania. Ahead 15-3 shortly after the end of the first quarter, Scotland were leading 18-11 at the break and seemingly in reasonable, if not total, control. But Romania's forward power began to tell and after loosehead prop Mihaita Lazar crashed over from a rolling maul for his side's first try, number eight Daniel Carpo broke off from the back of a scrum to score their second and put Romania briefly in front. Only two tries inside the final five minutes from Simon Danielli spared Scotland's blushes and gave them a slightly flattering 34-24 victory.

Parks was recalled for Scotland's second match, against Georgia, and it was just as well that he was as the battling Georgians came close to one of the RWC's biggest upsets before Parks's four penalties and drop goal secured a 15-6 win.

As for the Argentines, they had very narrowly lost to England in their opening match in a tale of missed kicks. Pumas full back Martin Rodriguez and Jonny Wilkinson had kicked just two from seven, but with Felipe Contepomi managing one of his two attempts, it was only a Ben Youngs try under the posts with 13 minutes remaining which saved England from defeat. The Pumas were disappointed by that defeat, but they bounced back to beat Romania comfortably, 43-8, scoring four first-half tries to one and adding two more late in the game to show that they had some firepower.

Argentina's pack was still one to be feared, of course, boasting a front five of Rodrigo Roncero, Mario Ledesma, Juan Figallo, Manuel Carizza and Patricio Albacete, all of whom had solid Top 14 experience in France. Juan Manuel Leguizamon and Juan Martin Fernandez Lobbe, two-thirds of their impressive back row, had both played in the Top 14 and in the English Premiership, but perhaps the biggest difference from Pumas teams of the past was in their increased cutting edge among their backs. Although the half back pairing was relatively young and untested, in the centres were Contepomi, who had moved to Toulon after a stellar club career at Leinster where he was the all-time top scorer, and Bosch, who was at Biarritz at the time and has since moved successfully to Saracens. Wingers Horacio Agulla and Gonzalo Camacho played at Leicester and Bath, and Harlequins and Exeter respectively. Big, quick men who knew their way to the try line. All they needed was more regular competition at the highest level of international rugby, and that was to come soon after the completion of this World Cup campaign.

With Georgia to face in their last group game, Argentina knew that a win over Scotland would all-but guarantee a place in the knockout phase yet again – although they had six points compared to Scotland's nine, a win over the Scots would lift them to ten points. That would leave England and Scotland to face each other for one spot and Argentina would go into their final game, against Georgia, knowing exactly what was needed. England were on 14 points at that point but with Scotland still to play, that wasn't as comfortable a lead as it sounded should Argentina win. A Scottish win would have put both the Northern Hemisphere teams through and the match between them would then have been only to decide who was first and who second.

Interestingly, Wayne Barnes was refereeing when it could have been argued that an Englishman wasn't entirely neutral in this matter, but of course the Scots were familiar with his style of refereeing and coach Andy Robinson seemed happy with the appointment.

The experts called it as a very evenly matched, probably low-scoring game, and they were spot on, with a lot of early kicking, particularly up-and-unders of more or less precision. The normally metronomic Chris Paterson had the first penalty opportunity but from a difficult spot out on the wide left, he narrowly failed to get enough curl on his attempt after about seven minutes. The Scots had plenty of possession, but too much of it was one man making a break and getting isolated, and the Argentine defence was solid, creating a number of turnovers (a staggering 12 in the first half alone) whenever Scotland threatened.

When the Pumas did finally get some territory they drove deep into the Scottish 22 and Rodriguez had a simple drop goal attempt but didn't set himself properly and pushed it horribly wide. A simple Contepomi penalty for offside – after he had earlier hit the post – was the only score of the first quarter, but a double strike by Scotland in the last five minutes of the half nudged them ahead 6-3 at the break. The first of these came after Scotland had started to commit more men to the breakdown and win quicker, cleaner ball and play at a pace with which the Argentines were uncomfortable and they disrupted an Argentine scrum on the left sufficiently to get the penalty against prop Rodrigo Roncero. While Paterson kicked the goal to tie the scores, Roncero was forced off (to be replaced by Martin Scelzo), joining Juan Martin Fernandez Lobbe on the sidelines.

Three minutes later Jackson took over the kicking duties when the Scots were awarded another penalty as they made good ground from a rolling maul which the Argentines dragged down illegally. It was only just inside the Argentine half and deemed outside Paterson's range, but with just a minute left, Jackson thought he might as well have a pot, and he nailed it.

Remarkably there was no further scoring from either side in the third quarter, as the rain continued to beat down in Wellington, although as commentator Nick Mullins rightly pointed out, it showed that a match doesn't need spectacular tries to be engaging, or even gripping.

Paterson had a good attempt at a snap drop goal after 57 minutes, changing direction and making room for himself cleverly but just pulled the kick past the left-hand post. A couple of minutes later, Allan Jacobsen was penalised for offside but from the ten-metre line, wide on the right, it was a tricky kick in the conditions and Contepomi's effort was always curling away to the left.

An easier chance came after 64 minutes, Contepomi knocking over his second penalty following an infringement by Geoff Cross at a scrum and Argentina tied the scores up at 6-6. Barely a minute later, though, Jackson restored Scotland's three-point advantage when slow ruck ball ended with a fine strike from Jackson from about 30 metres out. The opportunities for both sides were coming thick and fast and after 66 minutes Contepomi had a chance from a similar range as his last successful kick but this time he hooked it just wide.

With ten minutes remaining Dan Parks came on to replace Jackson at fly half and almost immediately took a leaf out of the youngster's book by dropping a goal of his own. Parks kicked a great penalty from the Scottish ten-metre line to within five metres of Argentina's line and after a couple of plays, the Scots won a penalty so Parks had a free shot at a drop, and calmly slotted it over.

But straight from the restart, Argentina reclaimed the ball and won a penalty. A quick pass from Contepomi saw Marcelo Bosch break one tackle in midfield and pass out right to Lucas Gonzalez Amorosino. With virtually no room to play with on the right-hand touchline, the replacement full back beat Paterson's attempts to force him out, then stepped in off his right foot and went over.

'Magical by Amorosino,' said Scott Hastings admiringly on the commentary. 'Individual brilliance and skill, the ability to beat the man on the outside and then step back inside.'

Contepomi converted to make it 13-12 with seven minutes remaining. It still only required a penalty or drop goal for Scotland to snatch back the lead, but would they get the chance? They did, as a penalty from Parks was dropped into touch by Amorosino giving the Scots ruck ball right in front of the Pumas' posts. Parks dropped back into the pocket for a drop goal, but a charge from Contepomi – probably offside but not spotted by Barnes – forced Parks to switch feet and he never got it right.

'We got to 12-6 and I felt we were in control of the game,' said Robinson. 'You've got to take your hat off to Argentina, to find a way of being able to win a game when in that second half I thought they were outplayed, but their never-say-die attitude got them through.'

A week later Argentina trailed 7-5 at half-time to Georgia, but 20 unanswered points in the second half, including tries from Contepomi and replacement centre Agustin Gosio, gave the Pumas the four points and a place in the quarter-finals.

46

17 September 2011
Venue: Eden Park, Auckland
Attendance: 58,600

Australia 6 Ireland 15

Australia	Ireland
Kurtley Beale	Rob Kearney
James O'Connor	Tommy Bowe
Anthony Fainga'a	Brian O'Driscoll (capt)
Pat McCabe	Gordon D'Arcy
Adam Ashley-Cooper	Keith Earls
Quade Cooper	Jonathan Sexton
Will Genia	Eoin Reddan
Sekope Kepu	Cian Healey
Tatafu Polota-Nau	Rory Best
Ben Alexander	Mike Ross
Dan Vickerman	Donncha O'Callaghan
James Horwill (capt)	Paul O'Connell
Rocky Elsom	Stephen Ferris
Ben McCalman	Sean O'Brien
Radike Samo	Jamie Heaslip

E den Park was a blaze of green and gold as Australia and Ireland came out for their crunch game in Pool C of the 2011 Rugby World Cup. Both had started their campaigns with victories, albeit in contrasting styles. Australia had started slowly against Italy, drawing 6-6 at half-time after two penalties apiece, but they had exploded into life in the second half, scoring tries through Ben Alexander, Adam Ashley-Cooper, James O'Connor and Digby Ioane, all but the first converted by O'Connor, for an ultimately easy 32-6 win.

Ireland had been much more scratchy against the USA, and although never in real danger of losing, they never really threatened to break loose either. A Tommy Bowe try on the stroke of half-time gave them a 10-0 lead at the interval, but it was only the quickfire double strike from hooker Rory Best and Bowe's second around the hour-mark which gave them a measure of control. Centre Paul Emerick's injury-time try, converted by replacement fly half Nese Malifa, was no more than the Eagles deserved and the final score was 22-10.

That meant that Australia were one point ahead of Ireland going into the second round of matches, courtesy of managing four tries in their opening game, but both sides knew that this was likely to be the crunch match, and accordingly named their strongest available line-ups.

The first penalty chance went to O'Connor after six minutes following a high tackle from Rob Kearney, but he drifted it just wide of the left-hand post. From the very next play, the Wallabies went back on the attack and got within a couple of metres of the line; they got the put-in at the resulting scrum, but it ended in another penalty and O'Connor took the safe option of chipping it over for 3-0.

Hardly a minute later, the Aussies tried to run the ball out of defence only to be met by a crunching Paul O'Connell tackle which brought a penalty for holding on. Like O'Connor before him, Jonathan Sexton hit a sighter which didn't curl in at all but stayed just right of the posts. Ireland kept the pressure on, however, and like O'Connor, Sexton's second chance was much easier and he kicked it over for 3-3.

A great series of attacks by Ireland resulted in another penalty, and Sexton hit a snap drop goal knowing that a reasonably simple penalty chance was coming should he miss. He didn't and Ireland had their reward for a sustained passage of play.

And that was the position at the end of the first quarter, with Australia dominating territory but Ireland being ruthlessly efficient when they were in the red zone with the chance of points.

But with 23 minutes gone, Australia won another penalty, Gordon D'Arcy making no semblance of an attempt to get out of the way at the breakdown – he was so offside that he was lucky not to be punished more heavily, but O'Connor made no mistake from around 35 metres out. A minute later, Jamie Heaslip was pinged for playing the ball at a ruck and from the ten-metre line, and wider out, O'Connor pushed it past the far post to leave the scores tied at 6-6.

The next penalty went Ireland's way when Australian props Ben Alexander and Sekope Kepu were both penalised for getting their heads and shoulders below the height of their hips. From an almost identical position to O'Connor's miss, Sexton did the same, however, and left it wide of the posts. Both sides were winning their own set pieces, and occasionally getting some go-forward in the scrums, but neither were making much headway on opposition ball. From one Australian scrum, though, with about a minute left in the first half, Will Genia was driven some way backwards and the Wallabies were lucky to avoid giving away a penalty.

And that's how the first half finished, with the teams still unable to be separated. Quade Cooper and Kurtley Beale combined well to make ground up their left at the start of the second half, but the supporting Ashley-Cooper's pass didn't go to hand when, if it had, the Wallabies could have been in. It seemed to indicate that Australia planned to stretch Ireland and play a wider game than they had in the first half, using their superior handling skills.

Just a few minutes into the second half D'Arcy picked up a hamstring injury which was to force him off the pitch by the 50th minute, breaking up his world record partnership with O'Driscoll, but by then Sexton had put Ireland ahead. After the Irish back row made ground, James Horwill went offside at the breakdown, giving the Irish fly half a fairly straightforward kick to put Ireland ahead 9-6 nine minutes into the second half.

Ireland took the interesting decision to bring Ronan O'Gara on as D'Arcy's replacement rather than Andrew Trimble who was the more obvious cover for centre and wing. Declan Kidney, Ireland's coach from 2008 to 2013, clearly thought a solid kicking game allied to the increasing influence of his back row and Paul O'Connell was the way to go, and stop Australia building momentum.

Within a minute of O'Gara's introduction, Ireland won yet another scrum penalty for breaking the bind and Sexton hit the post. For a moment it looked like Ireland might re-gather the loose ball, but Australia just managed to scramble it away and won a penalty when Sean O'Brien came in from the side at the ensuing ruck. That put the Wallabies back in possession and they moved the ball deep into the Ireland 22 but again the final, killer, pass just didn't go to hand and with it going forward the scrum went to Ireland. They ambitiously run it out from there, working Tommy Bowe into a little bit of space down the right wing and he took play up to the halfway line.

In the absence of the injured David Pocock, their brilliant openside, Australia's back row was slightly unbalanced and the Irish trio of Ferris, O'Brien and Heaslip began to take charge and they were quickly on to Cooper when he tried to run the ball out of his own half on the hour and forced a turnover. From the scrum, Australia's front row was penalised for collapsing the scrum and with O'Gara taking over the kicking he slotted it easily from around 35 metres, putting Ireland 12-6 up.

Cooper took the restart immediately and swiftly pinned Ireland back just outside their own 22, but Heaslip made the catch and O'Brien took the play up a fair way, but now it was Australia's ball and one off the top saw Ashley-Cooper make ground but when Genia picked the ball up at the back of the ruck some inadvertent blocking gave Ireland the relieving penalty. Even though there were still 14 minutes to play, Ireland were happy to play possession and territory and keep the game tight through a series of close drives and pick-and-gos, and eventually replacement prop James Slipper was penalised for collapsing. O'Gara knocked it over from right in front of the posts, just 15 metres out, to make it 15-6.

The wet conditions were also making it hard for Australia to play the running game they wanted, and it was all a bit too stop-start for their liking. Beale and Cooper continued to try things, but they never quite came off and Ireland's tackling was strong and determined, and that was epitomised by O'Brien's stunning last-ditch tackle on Genia as Australia threw everything at Ireland in the dying minutes. Cooper almost created something with an outrageous behind-the-back pass, but Bowe spotted and intercepted. Even with 80 metres to run, most people's money would have been on Bowe to go all the way but O'Connor brilliantly tracked him down and tackled him into touch just a few metres out.

It was in vain, however, as moments later the final whistle went, signalling Ireland's first World Cup victory over Australia after losing four times in succession, twice by the margin of just a single point. 'It's the fifth time we have played Australia in the Rugby World Cup, and you get a bit fed up with losing,' admitted coach Kidney. 'I was pleased with the way we went about our business, we managed to stifle a very good Australian side.'

'It's a performance we knew we had in us,' added Brian O'Driscoll. 'Our front row was immense and gave us the opportunity to play territory and get ourselves into situations where we could kick points. There were some phenomenal turnovers too.'

This fabulous win left the destiny of Pool C in Irish hands, but with two games still to go, it certainly wasn't all over, particularly as one was against Italy, who Ireland had struggled to subdue in that year's Six Nations Championship earlier in the year. First up was Russia, and Ireland scored nine tries in an easy 62-12 victory, with the bulk being spread evenly around the side (only Earls scored two). But with Italy beating the USA, they still had a chance of qualifying themselves – by picking up two bonus points, Italy had ensured that they were only three points behind Ireland, so a win, while denying Ireland a bonus point of their own, would have seem them overtake the Irish and all their hard work in overcoming Australia would have been undone.

In Rome, in the Six Nations, Luke McLean's 75th-minute try had put Italy within just a few minutes of recording a famous victory, their first over Ireland. But veteran Ronan O'Gara stepped up to slot home a drop goal, as he has done so many times in the past, and spare Ireland's blushes.

As it turned out, on this occasion Ireland had no such problems, although it did take them a while to subdue the stubborn Italians. At half-time the score was just 9-6, with three O'Gara penalties to two by Mirco Bergamasco, but Brian O'Driscoll's 47th-minute try gave the Irish more belief and they went on to score two more tries, both from Keith Earls. All three were converted to give Ireland an ultimately comfortable 36-6 victory and a place in the knockout stages as winners of Pool C.

Australia cruised through their other matches, picking up a try bonus in each of them, but there was nothing they could do to prevent Ireland winning the group. 'The Irish deserved their win,' said Wallabies captain Horwill. 'We didn't get enough clean ball to our backs and they did well to spoil our ball.'

That left Australia facing a quarter-final against the defending world champions South Africa, but they went into that game with no feelings of inferiority as they had beaten the Springboks home and away in the Tri Nations Series just a few months earlier. James Horwill's 11th-minute try settled any early nerves and although South Africa enjoyed the majority of the possession – and 76 per cent of the territory – with Pocock back the Wallabies ensured that it was never good possession. The Springboks nevertheless got their noses in front through two penalties and a drop goal from fly half Morne Steyn and it took a tricky 72nd-minute penalty from O'Connor, wide and from distance, to seal a narrow 11-9 victory and Australia were into their fifth semi-final in seven tournaments.

8 October 2011
Venue: Eden Park, Auckland
Attendance: 49,000

England 12 France 19

England	France
Ben Foden	Maxime Medard
Chris Ashton	Vincent Clerc
Manu Tuilagi	Aurelien Rougerie
Toby Flood	Maxime Mermoz
Mark Cueto	Alexis Palisson
Jonny Wilkinson	Morgan Parra
Ben Youngs	Dimitri Yachvili
Matt Stevens	Jean-Baptiste Poux
Steve Thompson	William Servat
Dan Cole	Nicolas Mas
Louis Deacon	Pascal Pape
Tom Palmer	Lionel Nallet
Tom Croft	Thierry Dusautoir (capt)
Lewis Moody (capt)	Julien Bonnaire
Nick Easter	Imanol Harinordoquy

After unexpectedly reaching the final of the 2007 Rugby World Cup, England might have expected a successful 2008, but it didn't turn out that way and when they lost Six Nations matches to Wales and Scotland, coach Brian Ashton lost his job to Martin Johnson. The great former England captain and 2003 World Cup winner didn't have immediate success either, England losing heavily in the 2008 autumn internationals to each of the Southern Hemisphere giants at Twickenham. In the 2009 Six Nations England finished second and a year later, third, so in 2011 Johnson decided to change some of the personnel.

There were recalls to the starting line-up for veterans Jonny Wilkinson (Toby Flood, who had been playing fly half, was moved to inside centre) and Steve Thompson, back from what he had believed to be a career-ending neck injury. At the same time, other stalwarts were gradually eased out, with the likes of Mike Tindall and Simon Shaw no longer starting and sometimes not even in the matchday squad. Experiments with the New Zealand-born Riki Flutey and Shontayne Hape were abandoned and into the centres came powerhouse Manu Tuilagi.

Tuilagi was Samoan-born; indeed his brothers Alesana, Anitelea, Freddie and Henry have all represented Samoa at international level. But Manu was only a young boy when his family moved to the UK and said he felt English and that all his rugby education had been in England – he played for Hinckley RFC as a teenager and represented his school in the U15 *Daily Mail* Vase competition, which gave him an early taste of the Twickenham turf, albeit in a losing cause. Since his England debut Manu Tuilagi has been exceptionally unlucky with injuries, but he has amassed 25 caps, scoring 11 tries, and still only turned 24 in May 2015. Dropped from England's 2015 RWC squad in light of an assault charge, he still has time to recover his form and fitness.

Tom Croft, another Leicester Tigers player, and another whose career has been dogged by injury, also increasingly came into the reckoning. Croft made his debut after the 2008 Six Nations and played sufficiently well throughout 2009 to be shortlisted for the IRB Player of the Year award (won by Richie McCaw), but then missed the 2010 Six Nations with a knee injury. He was back later that year, however, playing in the autumn internationals against New Zealand and Australia and becoming an integral part of the back row.

England were scratchy throughout the 2011 RWC, though, just doing enough to pip Argentina 13-9 and Scotland 16-12 in the two crucial matches, either side of more convincing 41-10 and 67-3 wins over Georgia and Romania respectively. Johnson declared himself 'relieved' after replacement scrum half Ben Youngs had snatched victory from the jaws of defeat with a dart under the posts with 13 minutes remaining against Argentina, giving Wilkinson a simple conversion which left the South Americans needing more than a penalty or drop goal.

After subduing Georgia – final-quarter tries from Tuilagi and a double from wing Chris Ashton securing the bonus point – England went to town against Romania. Both wingers, Ashton and Mark Cueto, scored hat-tricks, with Youngs, Tuilagi, Croft and full back Ben Foden taking the tally up to ten. In the final Pool B match, Scotland needed to win by an eight-point margin to deprive England of a quarter-final place. Perhaps knowing that was what led to an erratic match by both teams, with even kickers of the quality of Wilkinson and Dan Parks missing their kicks with an unusual regularity. England gave away a hatful of penalties early on, but not many in kicking range so Scotland led 9-3 at the break; Wilkinson had reduced that deficit to 12-9 by the time Ashton went over for the decisive – and only – try of the game two minutes from the end. 'We got on top in the second half,' declared Johnson after the win, 'we kept hammering away. The game isn't always going to be beautiful, but we finished it off.'

The scrappy 16-12 victory gave England a largely unwarranted place at the top of Pool B, but Johnson was understating it to say it wasn't beautiful – England looked scrappy and out of sorts. And they looked scrappy and out of sorts off the pitch too.

They had already been enmeshed in one on-field scandal when against Romania they twice switched the balls with which a try had been scored so that Wilkinson could kick with one he preferred. Kicking coach Dave Alred and fitness specialist Paul Stridgeon were suspended from the Scotland game after they had switched the ball without asking the referee's permission. An RFU statement said, 'The RFU fully accepts that the actions of those team management members was incorrect and detrimental to the image of the tournament, the game and to English rugby.' England probably escaped more stringent punishment by taking swift measures themselves, and the organisers decided no further action was required.

But off the pitch also, there appeared to be some problems. Mike Tindall was in a bar after the Argentina match – not in itself usually a cause for comment among the rugby fraternity, but unfortunately for Tindall there was some sort of 'dwarf-tossing' going on at the time. That, coupled with slightly more alcohol than might have been wise during a World Cup tournament, led to some lurid headlines. To make matters worse, two other members of the squad were accused of sexual harassment by a female employee of one of the hotels they stayed in, in Dunedin. Although it sounded like a case of banter which went a bit too far rather than anything worse, the two players were both fined and given a warning as to their future conduct.

France had their own problems, however, with a cabal of senior players basically rebelling against their own coach. After criticism from Marc Lievremont following the defeat by Tonga, Imanol Harinordoquy said, 'I am not happy because all the media know what he said. He can say that to us, that is not a problem but I prefer that those kind of things stay in the room. I did not attach too much importance to what he said, when something goes wrong we are all in the same boat, there are no good guys and bad guys.' Lionel Nallet added, 'I did not appreciate [what he said] at all.'

So to a game between two unhappy teams, with one likely to be even unhappier at its conclusion.

In the Six Nations meeting between the two teams in February, Toby Flood's three penalties were matched by the three from Dimitri Yachvili, and full back Ben Foden's 42nd-minute try was the difference between them, England winning 17-9. On this occasion England made a positive start, running the ball from their very first piece of possession, with Tuilagi making ground down the left, then switching right for Ashton but France stole the England line-out on their five-metre line.

England kept up the pressure, with Tuilagi flattening Morgan Parra in midfield, but the first penalty opportunity went to France when England were penalised by referee Steve Walsh for slowing the ball down at the breakdown, and Yachvili kicked the three points. Then Wilkinson kicked the ball out on the full from the kick-off, handing possession back to France, and they almost made the most of it when Vincent Clerc twice got within a few metres of the line down their right. Another penalty came when Matt Stevens was pinged for collapsing the scrum and Yachvili easily kicked the penalty from just past the England ten-metre line to make it 6-0.

And it only took France a further six minutes to put their first try on the board. A very quick follow-up to a chip kick into space saw France win the scrum put-in and although England did well to spoil it, they could never really quite get the ball clear and when the French ran it back a couple of missed tackles allowed Clerc to cut infield, spin though a tackle from Foden, and get over for 11-0 to France.

And before the half was up, France had another. England had had several minutes of possession and had made ground, again through Tuilagi, but their passing was not accurate enough, or went to someone who wasn't expecting it, and when Louis Deacon was pinged for not retreating quickly enough, France punted it deep into the England 22. A long pass to Alexis Palisson drew all the cover, and the winger was clever enough to take the tackle and flip the ball inside to the supporting Maxime Medard. Yachvili again missed the kick, but at 16-0 it was already a long way back for England with half an hour gone.

The momentum was with France and England would have been relieved not to concede any more in the final nine minutes of the first half.

Croft took a heavy blow to the head in the early seconds of the second half, which forced him off after six minutes, another harsh blow for a player who has been injured so often. The 22-year-old Courtney Lawes replaced him. England huffed and puffed, but couldn't get the ball into the hands of the dangerous Ashton enough until Youngs took a quick tap penalty after a line-out infringement, Simon Shaw set back equally quick ball and Foden dummied Clerc and stepped back inside Harinordoquy and over. Wilkinson converted for 16-7 with 25 minutes still to play.

Lievremont had brought on Francois Trinh-Duc in place of Yachvili, moving Parra from fly half to his more accustomed position of scrum half, an odd decision given how well Yachvili had been playing. However, after 72 minutes, and with England looking like they could get back into the game, Trinh-Duc proved his worth by dropping a goal which increased the margin to 19-7. With just under seven minutes left to play it was too big a gap for a still rather disjointed England. England did manage a second try, Mark Cueto sliding over. It came from a barnstorming run from replacement Matt Banahan and the ball being spread quickly wide, Cueto just getting the ball down despite a valiant attempt from Clerc to hold him up. Flood got the conversion all wrong, leaving England still 19-12 down with just under three minutes to play.

England never got the chance for another score, however, as France kept them pinned deep in their own half and eventually won a penalty. Parra rattled the posts with it, but it mattered not as he had carefully used up all the time available. France were through to the semi-final, and an England team which had been wholly unconvincing throughout the tournament went out.

Matt Dawson summed it up perfectly on BBC Radio 5 Live, 'England were blown away in the first half. They came out [after the break] with a little more pace and precision, but they made too many mistakes with knock-ons, penalties and turnovers. England weren't any different from their earlier matches, but whereas Argentina and Scotland couldn't last the distance and England won late on, France were a different outfit.'

Johnson commented, 'We created two or three real chances in the first half, made some breaks but couldn't finish them off. They scored their two tries, we should have had two but didn't have any. That was the difference.'

48

27 September 2011
Venue: McLean Park, Napier
Attendance: 14,350

Canada 23 Japan 23

Canada	Japan
James Pritchard	Shaun Webb
Matt Evans	Kosuke Endo
D.T.H. van der Merwe	Alisi Tupuailei
Ryan Smith	Ryan Nicholas
Phil MacKenzie	Hirotoki Onozawa
Ander Monro	James Arlidge
Ed Fairhurst	Fumiaki Tanaka
Hubert Buydens	Hisateru Hirashima
Pat Riordan (capt)	Shota Horie
Jason Marshall	Nozomu Fujita
Jebb Sinclair	Luke Thompson
Jamie Cudmore	Toshizumi Kitagawa
Adam Kleeberger	Sione Vatuvei
Chauncey O'Toole	Michael Leitch
Aaron Carpenter	Takashi Kikutani (capt)

In the entire history of all seven Rugby World Cup tournaments, there have only ever been three draws, and remarkably two of those have featured the same two teams. In 1987 France and Scotland famously played out a 20-20 draw in both those countries' first RWC match at Lancaster Park in Christchurch (though it's worth noting that if that match had been played under current scoring rules, France would have won 23-22). Both the other two draws have occurred between Canada and Japan.

In 2007, in a pool containing Australia, Wales and Fiji, both teams were already all but out of the running when they met at Stade Chaban-Delmas in Bordeaux. In a slightly dour struggle, Japan scored first and last – through wing Kosuke Endo after 12 minutes and replacement centre Koji Taira after 80 – while Canada scored their two tries in between, with hooker Pat Riordan going over on 48 minutes and wing D.T.H. van der Merwe on 65.

Going into the 2011 match, Japan fielded just two players who had been involved in the match four years earlier – try-scorer Endo (still holding on to his wing berth) and second-row Luke Thompson. Canada, however, had six; both the scorers from 2007 in van der Merwe and Riordan (the latter now captain of the side), plus backs James Pritchard and Ryan Smith and back-row players Aaron Carpenter and Adam Kleeberger. They had, however, lost some of their better-known names from that campaign in the likes of prop Rod Snow (who played much of his club rugby in Wales), lock Mike James (who had been at Perpignan and Stade Francais) and captain and scrum half Morgan Williams (who'd played successfully at Stade Francais and Saracens). All three players had represented their country over 50 times, so it was a lot of experience to lose.

Japan meanwhile was still trying to marry up the thorny task of fielding all homegrown players with the need to tap into the experience of some of those who were playing their club rugby in Japan. In 2007, fly half Bryce Robins and locks Luke Thompson and Philip O'Reilly were three New Zealand-born players who had qualified through residency and coach John Kirwan had no hesitation in bringing them into the squad once they became eligible. He also drafted in Tongan-born Christian Loamanu. By 2011 many were hoping that the Japanese team would be indigenous, but Kirwan remained practical – some would say realistic – in his selections and for the match against Japan he had, in his starting XV, New Zealand-born Shaun Webb at full back, James Arlidge at fly half, Michael Leitch in the back row and Luke Thompson was still there in the second row. In addition there were Samoan-born Alisi Tupuailei and Cook Island Maori Ryan Nicholas.

Interestingly, however, the past few years have also seen movement in the other direction, with Japanese players being deemed good enough to play in Australia and New Zealand. Kosuke Endo has been involved in the Air New Zealand Cup for Canterbury while scrum half Fumiaki Tanaka has played at Otago and in the Highlanders Super Rugby side, and hooker Shota Horie plays for the Melbourne Rebels.

Japan have played in every Rugby World Cup so far and are comfortably the best of the Asian nations – at the 2014 Asian Five Nations competition, which doubled as a 2015 World Cup qualifier, they won all four games by a large margin. They beat the Philippines 99-10, newly-promoted Sri Lanka 132-10, South Korea 62-5 and Hong Kong 49-8, claiming a try bonus point in each match and racking up a point differential of +309 (342 scored, 33 conceded). Now ranked 11th in the world, it will be interesting to see if they can record their first victory at the tournament – they should be favourites to beat 16th-ranked USA. And whether they can make any impression on either Samoa or Scotland, the two teams ranked immediately above them, and both in Pool B alongside them.

They are all too well aware that the eyes of the rugby world will be on them as they prepare to host the RWC for the first time in 2019.

Back to 2011, though, and the game which Japan and Canada will both have targeted as their most likely chance to win a match. Consequently it started off at breakneck pace, with two tries inside the first ten minutes. The first went to Canada and with van der Merwe being held up just short of the line it looked as if the chance might have gone, but from the very next play quick ball from a five-metre scrum gave him the ball again and he simply stepped inside the cover defence and jogged over. Pritchard, playing at full back, added the easy conversion to make it 7-0.

But within three minutes Japan were back on level terms. Canada rather ambitiously opted to try to run the restart out of their own 22 and a knock-on gave Japan the scrum. A strong run down the right from Arlidge took the ball to with a few metres of the Canadian line and from there hooker Shota Horie forced his way over the line. South African referee Jonathan Kaplan called on the TMO (Australian Matt Goddard) for confirmation, but it looked a good try both in real time and on replay. Arlidge added a tricky conversion from wide on the right-hand touchline to make it 7-7, and then kicked a penalty in the 24th minute to put Japan 10-7 ahead after a prolonged phase of possession and territory. It looked as if winger Hirotoki Onozawa might get away down the left-hand touchline, but he was just forced out by desperate Canadian cover defence – a combination of van der Merwe and second row Jebb Sinclair. From the line-out, replacement centre Bryce Robins – an early substitute for Tupuailai – made a clean break and almost put Ryan Nicholas over in the right-hand corner and quick recycling resulted in the almost inevitable penalty.

After Ander Monro had hit the left-hand upright with the simplest of penalties, that looked likely to be the half-time score. Then in the dying seconds of the first half Japan won a line-out deep inside the Canadian 22 and Arlidge and Nicholas worked a planned move in midfield to give Kosuke Endo the space to go in under the posts. It was Endo's second try in a World Cup match against Canada following his score four years earlier. Arlidge slotted a simple conversion from in front of the posts for a 17-7 lead to Japan at the interval.

Coming out for the second half, Canada knew that they couldn't afford to let Japan score next and stretch their lead any further. When a marginal forward pass was spotted by referee Kaplan, giving Canada the scrum put-in midway between the Japanese ten-metre line and 22, a simple flat pass saw wing Phil MacKenzie cut a great line through the defence. The tricky conversion was narrowly missed so the score was 17-12 to Japan.

And despite no lack of effort, there were no further scores for 20 minutes, during which much of the game was played out between the two ten-metre lines. After 63 minutes, and a period when Canada were going through the phases, gradually gaining ground, Japan were penalised for offside at a ruck and Monro kicked a simple penalty to make it 17-15. That lasted just 90 seconds, however, when an up and under was knocked on and picked up by a Canadian player standing in front of his colleague who tried to play the ball. Prop Jason Marshall compounded the error by refusing to give the Japanese the ball and Canada were marched back a further ten metres, which made it a comfortable kick for Arlidge to restore the five-point lead.

And that became eight points in the 73rd minute, when the massively experienced second row Jamie Cudmore (who has played over 200 matches for Clermont in the Top 14) was pinged for leaning on his elbow rather than supporting his bodyweight. From about 35 metres out, bang in front of the posts, Arlidge had no problems making it 23-15 and putting Japan two scores ahead.

This time it was Canada's chance to hit back instantly, though. A loose ball on the halfway line was secured by the forwards and moved from side to side until Ryan Smith made a break and it was taken on by his fellow centre, van der Merwe. Winger Matt Evans edged ever nearer, then the ball was switched to the left and Adam Kleeberger took it to within about three metres. When the ball came back quickly again Japan had finally run out of defenders and Monro just jogged over. That made it 23-20 with four minutes to go, but Monro then missed the relatively simple conversion.

Fortunately for Canada, and Monro, he was to get one last chance. In the 77th minute Canada were awarded a penalty after some great driving forward play had forced replacement prop Kensuke Hatakeyama to go off his feet. Canada opted for the kick at goal, to tie the scores, possibly thinking they might get one more play to try to snatch victory, or possibly thinking a draw would be sufficient to guarantee them third place in the group.

As it happened, neither of those things occurred. Japan gathered the restart but their attempt at a winning drop goal went a long way wide, and Tonga's shock defeat of France meant they finished ahead of Canada on nine points to Canada's six.

Like Japan, Canada have also played at every Rugby World Cup to date and, unlike Japan who have yet to register a first victory, the Canucks have never lost all their games at any tournament. They beat Tonga in 1987, Fiji and Romania in 1991 (which remains the only time to date that they have reached the knockout phase), Romania again in 1995, Namibia in 1999 and Tonga in 2003. In 2007, they could manage only a draw with Japan and finished bottom of their group on account of Japan winning a bonus point in their defeat by Fiji. It was a scenario they were desperately keen to avoid a recurrence of, and had already avoided by dint of their opening match victory over Tonga, 25-20 when late tries from Carpenter and MacKenzie had seen them come from behind to snatch a famous win. In their second game they had lost 46-19 to France, undone by a hat-trick – one scored very early and two more in the final couple of minutes – from Vincent Clerc after they had trailed by only three points with an hour gone.

This year Canada go into the RWC ranked only 17th, but will nevertheless expect to beat 18th-ranked Romania, and it will be interesting to see how they fare against 15th-ranked Italy, to whom they only lost 19-14 in 2003. And even whether they can leave their mark on France or Ireland.

Scheduling matches is always going to be an issue to a certain extent, as rugby is a sport where players do require sufficient rest and recuperation between high stakes matches – and increasingly so as the game gets more and more physical. Furthermore, all fans want to see the best players, playing at their best, or at least their fittest. But the Tier 1 nations already enjoy significant advantages over the smaller, semi-professional nations and a World Cup should be trying to even out those advantages rather than perpetuate them. It's an issue which, to its credit, World Rugby has tried hard to address and in the 2015 RWC Tier 1 nations have agreed to play midweek games in order to give the Tier 2 and 3 teams a fairer balance in terms of the gaps between matches, which should level the playing field somewhat.

49

15 October 2011
Venue: Eden Park, Auckland
Attendance: 58,600

Wales 8 France 9

Wales	France
Leigh Halfpenny	Maxime Medard
George North	Vincent Clerc
Jonathan Davies	Aurelien Rougerie
Jamie Roberts	Maxime Mermoz
Shane Williams	Alexis Palisson
James Hook	Morgan Parra
Mike Phillips	Dimitri Yachvili
Gethin Jenkins	Jean-Baptiste Poux
Huw Bennett	William Servat
Adam Jones	Nicolas Mas
Luke Charteris	Pascal Pape
Alun Wyn Jones	Lionel Nallet
Dan Lydiate	Thierry Dusautoir (capt)
Sam Warburton (capt)	Julien Bonnaire
Toby Faletau	Imanol Harinordoquy

The story of Wales's 2011 Rugby World Cup was one of inches, and tiny margins. Handed a tough Pool D alongside defending champions South Africa, and the Pacific Islands double jeopardy of Samoa and Fiji, Wales went into the World Cup without much form – fourth in that year's Six Nations with three wins and two defeats; splitting the warm-up matches with an equally lacklustre England (each team winning its home game), though they did manage to beat Argentina; and worst of all losing full back Morgan Stoddart to a badly broken leg in the match at Twickenham, an injury so severe that, sadly, it was to end Stoddart's career.

And yet when coach Warren Gatland named his team for the first match, it was immediately apparent that the core of his side showed strength in every position, a backline with the potential to score tries and reliable goal kickers in the shape of Rhys Priestland and Leigh Halfpenny. South Africa weren't on a great run of form either, having finished bottom of that year's Tri Nations, heavy defeats in both Australia and New Zealand being only partially redeemed by a victory over the All Blacks in Port Elizabeth (the first Tri Nations match to be held in the city), which handed the title to Australia. But a try count of only three for and 11 against in those four matches told its own story.

On thing that you can guarantee about a Springboks side, though, is that they won't give up without a fight, and they came out for their first Pool D match all guns blazing. The South Africa squad was not all that different from the one which had taken the field for the final four years earlier. Percy Montgomery and Os du Randt had retired, and Morne Steyn had got the nod ahead of Butch James at fly half, but the brilliant Fourie du Preez was still pulling the strings at scrum half, Bryan Habana and J.P. Pietersen were still providing the danger on the wings, Victor Matfield was still winning every line-out ball and the dynamic John Smit was still in charge.

The opening minutes of the game were ominous for Wales – James Hook knocked on an up-and-under, the Wales scrum were guilty of early engagement and conceded a free kick, Jaque Fourie took play up to the Welsh line and Francois Steyn forced his way over despite the attentions of Hook and Shane Williams. Morne Steyn converted from wide out for 7-0. The two sides exchanged penalties before the end of the first quarter, and the only score of the second quarter was a second Hook penalty which kept Wales in touch at 10-6 at half-time.

Wales, who had actually looked the better team for much of the first half after recovering well from the early try, started the second half much the stronger. Hook's third penalty brought them back to within a point, and four minutes later number eight Toby Faletau scored from close range. Hook added the conversion to make it 16-10 to Wales, and for a few minutes it took all South Africa's defensive skills to hang on without conceding another score. Inevitably having survived they hit back and after a period of pressure of their own, replacement Francois Hougaard, on for Habana, went in under the posts. Steyn slotted the easiest of conversions to put the Boks back in front, 17-16.

There were 13 minutes for Wales to score again, but Priestland missed a relatively straightforward drop goal and Hook missed a tough penalty chance from wide on the right, about 30 metres out. And thereafter South Africa used all their experience to keep the game tight and prevent Wales having another look.

A week later, Wales survived a scare – not to mention the prospect of a third World Cup defeat – against Samoa, sneaking home 17-10. After that, however, they went from strength to strength, despatching Namibia 81-7 in a 12-try rout with Williams scoring a hat-trick, and in their final group game scoring nine tries in a 66-0 win over Fiji. That took them into a quarter-final against Ireland, and although Ireland were on their uppers after their win over Australia, Wales could take confidence from their 19-13 Six Nations win earlier in the year. In traditional Six Nations weather, wet and windy, Wales took a leaf out of the Springboks' book and scored a very early try, Williams scooting in after impressive work from centres Jonathan Davies and Jamie Roberts. Priestland kicked the conversion and with Ronan O'Gara and Halfpenny exchanging second-quarter penalties, it was 10-3 to Wales at the break.

Keith Earls squared the match up in the 45th minute when his try was converted by O'Gara, but five minutes later scrum half Mike Phillips spotted half a gap round the short side and used his strength to squeeze over. Although Priestland missed that conversion, he made no mistake when Davies got over for their third try in the 64th minute – cutting through past Cian Healy – taking Wales's lead out to 22-10, and that's how it remained.

So Wales were into their first semi-final since the inaugural RWC in 1987, and their opponents were a stuttering France side who had already lost twice but somehow still found themselves in the last four. Pre-match predictions showed a pretty even split in opinion as to how the match would go. The rain was, if anything, even worse at Eden Park in Auckland than it had been in

Wellington the previous week, but it didn't stop both teams trying to play all-court rugby.

Hook got an early chance to settle the nerves – having had to move up to fly half in place of the injured Priestland – with an eighth-minute penalty which he struck beautifully from the touchline after France captain Thierry Dusautoir had strayed offside. But then things started to go wrong for Wales. First Adam Jones had to go off, to be replaced by Paul James; next Hook missed a reasonable penalty chance; and then, most disastrously, captain Sam Warburton got sent off. Warburton, the youngest ever World Cup captain, had been in impressive form – arguably he was the player of the tournament up to that point – but received a straight red card for a dangerous tip tackle on French winger Vincent Clerc. Was it harsh? Possibly a yellow would have sufficed, though it certainly wasn't 'an extraordinary decision' from referee Alain Rolland as TV commentator Nick Mullins opined.

Morgan Parra tied the scores with a penalty soon after, and added a further three-pointer in the 35th minute when Dan Lydiate was slightly unfortunate to be pinged for playing the ball on the ground. At half-time a shocked and stunned studio of Francois Pienaar, Lawrence Dallaglio and Martyn Williams declared that referee had 'killed the game' in sending off Wales's captain and best player. Dallaglio was spot on when he said he thought Wales would probably bring Stephen Jones on for his tactical kicking – it took coach Warren Gatland only six minutes of the second half before he made that change.

In the 51st minute Wales were again penalised and Parra notched his third penalty, but there was still hope for the men in red as even with 14 men they looked dangerous when they had the ball in their hands. Against all the odds, Phillips scored a try just before the hour. A good line-out take from Alun Wyn Jones on the French 22 was taken on by Welsh hands and as Phillips picked up at the back of a ruck he noticed a little space, and turned back inside the defence and went over for a dramatic score. Unfortunately, Jones missed an eminently kickable conversion, just glancing it wide of the left-hand post, so Wales remained a point behind at 9-8.

From the very next play, Faletau drove all the way to the French 22, but Jones never really got himself set for the drop goal attempt. Rolland called play back for a Wales scrum just inside the 22, but although it was clean ball, replacement back-rower Ryan Jones was forced into touch. Still Wales pressed, trying to re-gather possession at every opportunity and put pressure on the French, who now seemed to have settled for what they had and were content to let the Welsh batter away at them. It was a high-risk strategy given that Wales had already shown they had the skill to unpick the lock given half a chance, in particular the magician on the wing, Shane Williams.

Williams had said it would be his last international match – though he ultimately decided to play against Australia in December 2011 so he could finish his career with a home game. Although Wales lost 24-18, Williams scored a try with the last play of the match, his 58th. Including two for the British & Irish Lions, Williams is third on the all-time try-scoring list behind Australia's David Campese (64) and Japan's Daisuke Ohata (69), though it's worth qualifying Ohata's impressive record with the footnote that he never played against

England or any of the Southern Hemisphere's 'Big Three'. Only Bryan Habana and Japanese winger Hirotoki Onozawa, of players still active, have a chance of overtaking Williams any time soon.

But while Wales had plenty of possession, they didn't have as much territory as they would have liked and they could never work the ball to Williams in a threatening position. One of their best chances came from a line-out on the French 22, with Roberts then taking a crash ball in midfield, but Stephen Jones didn't look for the drop goal preferring to keep taking the ball up and after several phases he knocked on. He compounded the error by playing the ball on the ground and giving away the penalty. So Wales had to build again from deep, but they did get a penalty on the halfway line; it looked a tough decision against French prop Nicolas Mas as the ball appeared to be out of the ruck. It was beyond the range of Jones, so Halfpenny took on the responsibility and struck it straight and true – but just short.

Wales still had five minutes to mount another attack, and got the scrum put-in on the halfway line. They went through the phases and edged ever deeper into the French half, but just couldn't find a way through and the French were, for once, sufficiently disciplined not to give them a shot at goal. After 25 phases and nearly two minutes into injury time, the Welsh lost the ball and the game was over.

'When you have two quality team and someone goes down to 14 men, at this level the other team should win the game comfortably,' said Warren Gatland, rightly. 'I can't be more proud of the guys for what they achieved, they pushed France so close and gave themselves a chance to win the game. We just feel like the destiny of the result was taken out of our hands with the red card.'

Although there was plenty of emotion about, not least in the TV studio where there was much talk of 'ruining' the semi-final, referee Rolland later defended his decision, 'We can only officiate on the action itself, we don't officiate on intention. Unfortunately, what had happened gave me no option but to do what I did.'

Warburton has gone on to win over 50 Wales caps and captain his country on a record-breaking 35 occasions (plus two for the 2013 Lions side which won in Australia). A mark of the man is that he said at the time – even while everyone was raging about Rolland's decision – that he could see why his tackle might have been deemed a red card. 'There was no malicious intent,' he commented shortly after the incident, 'but the IRB said if you lift a player up and drop him it's a red card and that's exactly what I did.' Sam Warburton: a class act on and off the field.

50

23 October 2011
Venue: Eden Park, Auckland
Attendance: 61,000

New Zealand 8 France 7

New Zealand	France
Israel Dagg	Maxime Medard
Cory Jane	Vincent Clerc
Conrad Smith	Aurelien Rougerie
Ma'a Nonu	Maxime Mermoz
Richard Kahui	Alexis Palisson
Aaron Cruden	Morgan Parra
Piri Weepu	Dimitri Yachvili
Tony Woodcock	Jean-Baptiste Poux
Keven Mealamu	William Servat
Owen Franks	Nicolas Mas
Brad Thorn	Pascal Pape
Sam Whitlock	Lionel Nallet
Jerome Kaino	Thierry Dusautoir (capt)
Richie McCaw (capt)	Julien Bonnaire
Kieran Read	Imanol Harinordoquy

France coach Marc Lievremont was in bullish mood after the semi-final win over Wales. 'I don't care at all whether it was a good match or not, whether Wales deserve to be in the final, we won and that's all that counts for me,' he said. 'I think there are a lot of people annoyed that we have qualified, but we played with our hearts.'

It was certainly true at the time that rugby fans were a little equivocal about France's presence in the final – beaten twice at the group stage, a reasonable but by no means convincing victory over a shaky England and one-point victors over a Wales side who played the vast majority of the match with 14 men. There had been little evidence of the renowned French flair, or even of much attacking intent, in their semi-final win, and it was hard to see exactly where they could hurt New Zealand.

New Zealand had progressed steadily through the tournament and to the extent it was possible to conduct a low-key campaign in their home country when they were looking for a first World Cup in 24 years, then the All Blacks had managed it. It was the largest sporting event in New Zealand's history, and the number of visitors and the ticket sales vastly exceeded the pre-tournament estimates. The earthquake in February, which had killed almost 200 people, had devastated a number of buildings and the damage to the AMI Stadium meant it would no longer be able to host the World Cup matches which had been slated for it, but still the New Zealanders were hugely encouraging of the rugby fraternity to come to their country, and hugely welcoming when it did.

New Zealand had won all four of their Pool A matches, kicking off the tournament with a 41-10 win over Tonga and following that up with an 83-7 win over Japan, most notable for the fact that the 13 tries were scored by 13 different players. They then beat France easily, 37-17, and at one point in that game the French were looking at humiliation, trailing 29-3 with around an hour played. In their final group match, they scored a further 12 tries in routing Canada 79-15, with wing Zac Guildford scoring four, including a first-half hat-trick. However, the day before that game, New Zealand had lost the incredible Dan Carter to injury, tearing his adductor during kicking practice. Carter is one of just 35 players to have won over 100 Test caps for his country, currently lying in equal 28th, though he would have been a few places higher than that but for injuries. More significantly, he is the leading points scorer in history, his total of 1,457 being more than 200 ahead of second-placed Jonny Wilkinson and more than double that of anyone else still playing.

On 9 October, in their quarter-final win over Argentina, New Zealand also lost their back-up fly half Colin Slade. Slade started the game but was forced off after just 33 minutes, having also aggravated a groin injury so Cruden – originally no better than third choice – was now the man in possession of a key role. Although the All Blacks' 33-10 looks comfortable enough, they only led 12-10 five minutes into the second half, late tries from Kieran Read and Brad Thorn adding a certain gloss while Piri Weepu took over the kicking duties and performed them immaculately with seven penalties from seven shots at goal.

The semi-final was a match-up against the Old Enemy, and after New Zealand and Australia had split their Tri Nations meetings (each winning their home game), the stage looked set for another titanic battle. In the event, a storming first half which should have seen the All Blacks further ahead than just 14-6, allied to a solid defensive performance which kept the Wallabies scoreless in the second half, was more than enough to see the Kiwis through to their first World Cup Final since 1995.

And while New Zealand would start that final as almost unbackable favourites, they had suffered at the hands of the French more than once in a World Cup, and weren't going to take anything for granted.

After sterling renditions of the national anthems from New Zealand-born classical singers Will Martin ('La Marseillaise') and Hayley Westenra ('God Defend New Zealand') got things under way, Piri Weepu led a Haka on which the French advanced in a V formation, which made for great television. Then a blast from the whistle of South Africa's Andre Joubert began the match.

Cruden kicked off, the French knocked on and New Zealand re-gathered, but nothing came of it until Dimitri Yachvili kicked his clearance out of the full and the All Blacks had a line-out just beyond the French ten-metre line. However, an overthrow went into the grateful arms of Julien Bonnaire at the back and he took play back to the halfway line, where it remained for several scrappy minutes.

Already the officiating was causing comment, with several TV and radio commentators suggesting that the All Blacks were going offside at the breakdowns, and they were lucky to be awarded a penalty on the ten-metre line on the wide left with five minutes gone. Weepu took it and was well wide. From the drop-out, France regained possession and the French moved it into New Zealand's half but then knocked the ball on. Morgan Parra took a heavy knock in the course of trying to tackle Ma'a Nonu – a knee from Richie McCaw catching him on the side of the head – and went off for a 'blood' injury between the 12th and 18th minutes. He was replaced by Francois Trinh-Duc, who had been the first-choice fly half going into the World Cup.

Weepu and McCaw won a penalty for their side from an overthrown line-out and Weepu kicked the ball to within nine metres of the French line. The line-out was tapped down by Kaino for prop Tony Woodcock and he simply burst through the space to go over without a hand being laid on him. It was clearly a set play and it worked to perfection. Weepu missed the conversion from the right, not curling the kick in quite enough at the near post. Fifteen minutes gone, and had the French storm already blown itself out?

Parra did come on again, but only lasted a further five minutes before going off for good, a big blow for France. Meanwhile on the field, it was becoming a battle between the back rows, with McCaw and Thierry Dusautoir both playing captains' roles and vying for the title of the most influential player. The All Blacks were starting to dominate territory and possession, but the French defence for the most part coped well.

Weepu did have another penalty chance from about 30 metres out, but he sliced it well wide and although his kicking out of hand was good, his missed goal kicks were costing the All Blacks the chance to build a lead which their general play warranted. He again kicked deep into the French 22 but Lionel Nallet got up in front of Brad Thorn to steal the ball. The French did better on a line-out of their own just inside New Zealand's 22, but in the ensuing phase of play, hooker William Servat lost the ball forward.

By now Cruden was struggling with a knee after he appeared to hyper-extend it in a tackle with Trinh-Duc – it must have been bad as the New Zealand management team decided he couldn't get through the six minutes to half-time and replaced him with Stephen Donald, their fourth-choice fly half before the tournament started, who had never played in a World Cup match. Again, after the match there were comments that Joubert stopped the clock for Cruden's injury whereas he had forced the French to play on when Parra was hurt. It was France's replacement fly half who had the greater bearing on the play in the first instance, attempting a drop goal which drifted right and then spotting he was up against Jerome Kaino and cutting through the defensive line with a great run. It was Weepu, making up for his missed kicks, who got in the saving tap tackle.

The second half began with France on the attack, but Yachvili missed his team's first chance of points – incredibly the first one within range they had had in the match. It was wide out but not too far and Yachvili's kick looked good but just faded past the post. A moment later Trinh-Duc looked to be the victim of a high tackle, but Joubert let it go and then penalised France for illegally playing the ball on the floor. Donald stepped up and calmly kicked it over from about 30 metres out but bang in front.

It was 8-0 to the All Blacks, and France had also lost their main try-scorer Vincent Clerc, though at least they had a ready-made replacement on the bench in the shape of the experienced Damien Traille. From the restart, France went straight on to the attack, Trinh-Duc turning the New Zealand defence and getting in behind it. The All Blacks could never quite reorganise in time to re-set their defence and from quick ball on the left it was moved to Dusautoir who crashed over by the posts. A simple conversion from Trinh-Duc made it a one-point game at 8-7 to New Zealand. New Zealand responded by bringing on Andrew Hore at hooker and Ali Williams at second row in place of Mealamu and Whitelock. They also replaced the struggling Weepu with Andy Ellis, but they looked uncharacteristically jittery.

To calm their nerves, they decided to keep play tight for a little while and go through the phases without really going anywhere. When they did lose the ball, France enjoyed a spell of possession and got into the All Blacks' 22, but then they lost the ball and from the New Zealand scrum put-in they won a penalty and cleared to halfway. In the 64th minute, France were awarded a scrum penalty for Hore popping up, but at 48 metres it was right at the edge of Trinh-Duc's range; in going for the distance he got the angles wrong and it went well to the right of the posts.

Alexis Palisson made a good run down the left and who was there to tackle the speedster into touch but McCaw and although France carried on having more of the possession they just couldn't quite create another scoring chance.

'I'm so proud to be a New Zealander,' said coach Graham Henry in the wake of victory. 'Richie and the boys just hanging in there to win this thing is superb. This is something we've dreamed of for a while and now we can rest in peace.'

'It wasn't very pretty,' said an exhausted McCaw, 'but it came down to how much desire, how much courage the boys had. We probably didn't play our best, but we played good enough. I take my hat off to every single player who took to the field.'

There were comments during and after the game that referee Joubert had allowed the All Blacks to get away with a lot of offsides and playing the ball on the floor, and, to make matters worse, penalised French players for the same offences. It perhaps wasn't Joubert's finest hour, and if New Zealand didn't get the rub of the green in 2007 when they were beaten by France, they certainly did on this occasion.

That said, no one was in any doubt that New Zealand were the best team at the 2011 Rugby World Cup – they were the only unbeaten side at the tournament and worthy champions.